CW01514205

ABOUT THE

PAUL SPICKER holds the Grampian Chair of Public Policy at the Robert Gordon University, Aberdeen, and is Director of the Centre for Public Policy and Management. He has worked as a consultant for a range of agencies in social welfare provision. His research includes studies of poverty, need, disadvantage and service delivery, and he has published twelve books and over sixty academic papers in this field. His most recent title is *Policy Analysis for Practice* (Policy Press, 2006).

SONIA ALVAREZ LEGUIZAMÓN is Associate Professor of Urban Anthropology in the Faculty of Humanities, National University of Salta, Argentina. She specializes in social policies, segregation, exclusion and poverty, and the history of social policies in Argentina, and has published several articles on these issues.

DAVID GORDON is Director of the Townsend Centre for International Poverty Research, at the University of Bristol. He has researched and published in the fields of the scientific measurement of poverty, crime and poverty, childhood disability, area-based anti-poverty measures, and the causal effects of poverty on ill health, housing policy and rural poverty. He has published extensively in the field, and his latest title is *Poverty and Social Exclusion in Britain: The Millennium Survey* (Policy Press, 2006).

ELSE ØYEN is Professor of Social Policy at University of Bergen, Norway, Scientific Director of CROP, and past president of the International Social Science Council (ISSC). Her research interests include the theory of the welfare state, comparative studies of social policy programs in industrialized countries, analyses of poverty phenomena and most recently, processes of poverty production. She has published more than a dozen books and several dozen articles within these areas. Øyen has been a visiting professor at several universities outside of Norway and lectured widely internationally.

CROP INTERNATIONAL STUDIES IN POVERTY RESEARCH
PUBLISHED BY ZED BOOKS IN ASSOCIATION WITH CROP

David Gordon and Paul Spicker (eds), *The International Glossary on Poverty*, 1999.

Francis Wilson, Nazneen Kanji and Einar Braathen (eds), *Poverty Reduction: What Role for the State in Today's Globalized Economy?*, 2001.

Willem van Genugten and Camilo Perez-Bustillo (eds), *The Poverty of Rights: Human Rights and the Eradication of Poverty*, 2001.

Else Øyen et al. (eds), *Best Practices in Poverty Reduction*, 2002.

Lucy Williams, Asbjørn Kjønstad and Peter Robson (eds), *Law and Poverty: The Legal System and Poverty Reduction*, 2003.

Elisa P. Reis and Mick Moore (eds), *Elite Perceptions of Poverty and Inequality*, 2005.

Robyn Eversole, John-Andrew McNeish and Alberto Cimadamore (eds), *Indigenous Peoples and Poverty: An International Perspective*, 2005.

Lucy Williams (ed.), *International Poverty Law: An Emerging Discourse*, 2006.

Maria Petmesidou and Christos Papatheodorou (eds), *Poverty and Social Deprivation in the Mediterranean*, 2006.

Santosh Mehrotra and Enrique Delamonica, *Eliminating Human Poverty: Macroeconomic and Social Policies for Equitable Growth*, 2006.

Poverty

AN INTERNATIONAL GLOSSARY

SECOND EDITION

EDITED BY PAUL SPICKER
SONIA ALVAREZ LEGUIZAMÓN
& DAVID GORDON

International Studies in Poverty Research

International Social Science Council

Zed Books

LONDON & NEW YORK

Poverty: An International Glossary, Second Edition
was published in 2007 by Zed Books Ltd, 7 Cynthia Street, London N1 9JF, UK
and Room 400, 175 Fifth Avenue, New York, NY 10010, USA

www.zedbooks.co.uk

CROP International Studies in Poverty Research
CROP is a programme under the International Social Science Council,
which has also helped finance this publication

Editorial copyright © CROP 2007

The right of CROP to be identified as the author of this work has been
asserted by it in accordance with the Copyright, Designs and Patents Act, 1988

Designed and typeset in Monotype Janson
by illuminati, Grosmont, www.illuminatibooks.co.uk
Cover designed by Andrew Corbett

**Published in 2007 in India by Books for Change,
139, Richmond Road, Bangalore–560 025
www.booksforchange.net**

Printed and bound in India by National Printing Press, Bangalore

Distributed in the USA exclusively by Palgrave Macmillan, a division of
St Martin's Press, LLC, 175, Fifth Avenue, New York, NY 10010

All rights reserved

No part of this publication may be reproduced, stored in a retrieval system
or transmitted, in any form or by any means, electronic or otherwise, without
the prior permission of the publisher.

A catalogue record for this book is available from the British Library
Library of Congress Cataloging-in-Publication Data available
Library and Archives Canada Cataloguing in Publication Data available

ISBN 1 84277 822 6 Hb

ISBN 1 84277 823 4 Pb

ISBN 978 1 84277 822 7 Hb

ISBN 978 1 84277 823 4 Pb

ISBN 81 8291 035 8 Pb (Books for Change)

This edition is for sale in India only

Contents

EDITORIAL BOARD

Julio Boltvinik   *El Colegio de Mexico, Mexico*
Tim Forsyth   *London School of Economics and Political Science, UK*
Maliha Khan   *School for International Training, Brattleboro VT, USA*
Karima Korayem   *Al Azhar University, Egypt*
Rubén M. Lo Vuolo   *Interdisciplinary Center for the Study of Public Policies (CIEPP), Argentina*
Larissa Adler Lomnitz   *National Autonomous University of Mexico*
Santosh Mehrotra   *Planning Commission, Government of India, New Delhi*
Else Øyen   *Comparative Research Programme on Poverty*
Maria Petmesidou   *Democritus University of Thrace, Greece*
Asuncion Lera St. Clair   *University of Bergen, Norway*
Peter Saunders   *University of New South Wales, Australia*
Mohammad Shafi   *Aligarh Muslim University, India*
Carlos Barba Solano   *University of Guadalajara, Mexico*
Peter Townsend   *London School of Economics and Political Science, UK*
Francis Wilson   *University of Cape Town, South Africa*

CONTRIBUTORS

María Angela Aguilar   *National University of Salta, Argentina*
Daniel Dorling   *University of Bristol, UK*
Ray Forrest   *University of Bristol, UK*
Jose Burle de Figueiredo   *Institut International d'Études Sociales (ILO)*
Maryse Gaudier   *Institut International d'Études Sociales (ILO)*
Bjørn Halleröd   *University of Umeå, Sweden*
Ebrahim-Khalil Hassen   *National Labour and Economic Development Institute, Zambia*
Pauline Heslop   *University of Bristol, UK*
Marcelo Ibarra   *New School for Social Research, New York*
Martina Kampmann   *Deutsche Gesellschaft für Technische Zusammenarbeit, Germany*
Hans de Kruijk   *Erasmus University, the Netherlands*
Thomas Kuby   *Deutsche Gesellschaft für Technische Zusammenarbei (GTZ), Germany, and World Bank*
Caterina Ruggeri Laderchi   *University of Oxford, UK*
Stephan Leibfried   *Universität Bremen, Germany*
Ruth Levitas   *University of Bristol, UK*
Seosamh Mac Cárthaigh   *University College, Dublin, Ireland*
Maureen McDonald   *Australian Bureau of Statistics*
John MacNicol   *Royal Holloway, University of London, UK*
Neamat Mashhour   *Al Azhar University for Girls, Egypt*
Ben Oakley   *University of Bristol, UK*
Else Øyen   *University of Bergen, Norway*
Christina Pantazis   *University of Bristol, UK*
Robert Pinker   *London School of Economics and Social Sciences (LSE), UK*
Bayan Tabbara   *United Nations Economic and Social Commission for Western Asia (ESCWA)*
Peter Townsend   *University of Bristol, UK*
John Veit-Wilson   *University of Newcastle upon Tyne, UK*

ABOUT CROP

CROP, the Comparative Research Programme on Poverty, is a response from the academic community to the problem of poverty. The programme was initiated in 1992, and the CROP Secretariat was officially opened in June 1993 by the director-general of UNESCO, Dr Federico Mayor.

In recent years, poverty alleviation, poverty reduction and even the eradication and abolition of poverty have moved up the international agenda, and the CROP network is providing research-based information to policymakers and others responsible for poverty reduction. Researchers from more than a hundred countries have joined the CROP network, with more than half coming from so-called developing countries and countries in transition.

The major aim of CROP is to produce sound and reliable knowledge that can serve as a basis for poverty reduction. This is done by bringing together researchers for workshops, coordinating research projects and publications, and offering educational courses for the international community of policy-makers.

CROP is multidisciplinary and works as an independent non-profit organization.

For more information contact:

CROP Secretariat
Nygårdsgaten 5, N5020 Bergen, Norway
tel: +47 55589739 fax: +47 55589745
email: crop@uib.no
website: www.crop.org

Introducing the glossary

ELSE ØYEN

A glossary is 'a list of difficult terms with explanations'.¹ It is a scientific toolbox that provides a historical background for definitions linked to a certain field of research, the changes in contents they have undergone over time, and their current contents and use. Definitions are the stable element in an ever expanding theory formation – until they themselves are given a new content. Their present meaning is the result of a historical process of social change and dialogue in the scientific field.

Definitions are building blocks for theories. Although it may seem so, definitions are not neutral. In poverty research they are more value laden than in many other fields of research. The choice of one definition rather than another one may indicate not only academic preferences but at times also political, societal and moral preferences. The choice of one definition rather than another one may also provide quite different research results in a project.

Definitions are powerful tools for thought and action. The understanding of poverty is in the eye of the beholder. Different actors see different things, emphasize different aspects and develop different paradigms of poverty understanding according to their discipline, position or vested interests. There are many actors in the poverty landscape, and some try to establish ownership to poverty understanding through the use of certain poverty definitions. As a result a limited number of definitions have dominated academic and political discourse and poverty understanding during the last three or four decades.² The aim of the *Glossary* is to widen the choice of definitions available, thereby expanding the scientific field of poverty research so that it gets closer to the complex reality of poverty and the lives of poor people.

Many of the disciplines within the social sciences and several outside have incorporated poverty as a research topic, some of them fairly recently and some through a well-established tradition. As could be expected, the disciplinary approaches to poverty understanding are coloured by the discipline's theories, methodologies and established definitions. The understanding of poverty is fitted into the dominant paradigms of the discipline. Poverty is only one of many other topics being studied. To the extent that it is being studied it is not necessarily poverty as such that is being studied. Often it is the use of the different tools of the discipline that are being tested out.

The poverty phenomenon is complex and comprehensive and covers so many dimensions of human and social behaviour that almost any theory relating to human beings can add to a fragment of poverty understanding. As with all kinds of analysis of poverty, disciplinary or not, the picture is incomplete. Only fragments are presented. If a more complete picture is to emerge, some of the disciplinary bonding needs to be loosened, new links established and a wider array of definitions put to use, including outside their established context. That is a research challenge in itself. The *Glossary* can be used as a tool for those who want to move in that direction.

Poverty research has for a long time been closely linked to poverty reduction and has featured definitions that point to causes of poverty. Implicitly and explicitly those definitions point also to certain interventionist strategies and how resources are to be allocated. Bureaucrats, politicians, donors and voluntary organizations need definitions and benchmarks to carry through their programmes for poverty reduction and allocation of resources. The emphasis is to move towards well-defined and simple indicators that can be used also for evaluation of the programmes. The *Glossary* contains scores of definitions that at first glance do not fit this purpose. However, those definitions are closer to the reality of poor people, and if put to use are likely to offer better tools for efficient poverty reduction than simpler measures. People working with poverty reduction are invited to search the *Glossary* for new and better tools for their poverty-reducing interventions.

The *Glossary* is a thoroughly revised version of the first *Glossary*, which was published in 1999.[3] Not only has poverty research increased rapidly during the last few years. This in itself calls for an updating to catch the new and different poverty definitions that have arisen along with changing research foci. The first version was too Western in its presentation of poverty definitions. In particular, the Latin American perspectives were neglected due to language and the differences that arise when apparently similar terms take on dissimilar meanings. This is an inherent problem in all the social and human sciences. We have met the challenge by inviting a distinguished Latin American poverty researcher to join the two British editors and by creating an editorial board of international scholars who have provided inputs and corrections throughout the process of collecting and collating the *Glossary*. In addition, a call went out to all members of the CROP network inviting them to come forward with new or changed definitions and references. The result is a collective work in the sense that many of the entries are the product of several hands.

Constructing a glossary on poverty is an open-ended process. New definitions continue to trickle in, while definitions already established become altered as new or previously unknown literature emerges. At a certain stage the editors have to put a stop to this process; or, better, they have to decide that this *Glossary* is just another step in a process which may lead to a still more perfect glossary. The editors are the first to acknowledge that even this second *Glossary*, into which they have put so much effort, is not and cannot be the end product.

New entries have been added while old entries have been revised and updated. References have been extended and subjects further developed. Examples of national definitions of poverty and definitions of poverty lines have been added and the *Glossary* now comprises more than two hundred definitions. Each entry contains both definitions and explanations, with references to contemporary academic and professional literature. Altogether the new *Glossary* has been extended with about 16,000 words.

There is no universally agreed vocabulary for the analysis of poverty, and terms and concepts vary between the disciplines to such a degree that no scholar is familiar with the entire vocabulary. The editors have not always been in agreement when discussing an entry and the references needed to support it. Its meaning, roots and context have been argued, and its importance for poverty research has been questioned. Such disagreements are in the nature of a complex research field like poverty. Where disagreements have not been resolved through dialogue or external advice the three editors have used a simple majority vote to settle the dispute. Users of the *Glossary* will have similar experiences when entries are put to use in concrete research projects.

Paul Spicker, one of the volume's editors, provides a framework for the *Glossary* when in the last chapter he reviews and explains some of the many different and competing meanings associated with the word poverty.

Many are those who have given a helping hand in the construction of the *Glossary*. The Editorial Board and members of the CROP Scientific Committee have provided inputs and corrections, as have researchers from other parts of the CROP network. María Aguilar and Marcelo Ibarra have worked on the many new entries from Latin America. Inge Tesdal has taken care of the technicalities. While the International Social Science Council and GTZ (Deutsche Gesellschaft für Technische Zusammenarbeit) have helped finance the work. We are immensely grateful to all those who have taken part in developing this new tool for poverty research.

The work will continue.[4] Poverty research needs to develop its own toolbox if it is to advance further. A *Glossary* is a vital part of such a toolbox and it is our hope it will sensitize researchers, students and policymakers to the large variety of definitions available and the wide range of insights it offers to a broader understanding of poverty and the lives of poor people.

NOTES

1. Webster *New World Dictionary*.
2. Else Øyen (ed.), The Polyscopic Landscape of Poverty Research – 'State of the Art' in *International Poverty Research. An Overview and 6 in-depth studies*, Norwegian Research Council, 2005, www.forskningsradet.no/CSStorage/Flex_attachment/stateoftheart.pdf, and www.crop.org.
3. David Gordon and Paul Spicker (eds), *The International Glossary on Poverty*, CROP International Studies in Poverty Research, Zed Books, London, 1999.
4. Suggestions for new entries and references as well as changes to the present text are welcomed and will be considered for the next revised version of the Glossary. Send mail marked 'Glossary' to crop@uib.no.

Glossary

ABSOLUTE POVERTY

The concept of absolute poverty is a contested one. Absolute definitions of poverty vary considerably but they are often dominated by the individual's requirements for physiological efficiency. Poverty is defined without reference to social context or norms and is usually defined in terms of simple physical SUBSISTENCE needs but not social needs. Absolute definitions of poverty tend to be prescriptive definitions based on the 'assertions' of experts about people's minimum needs.

The Copenhagen Declaration of the World Summit for Social Development, which was signed by the governments of 117 countries, included a definition of absolute poverty, in these terms:

> Absolute poverty is a condition characterized by severe deprivation of basic human needs, including food, safe drinking water, sanitation facilities, health, shelter, education and information. It depends not only on income but also on access to social services.

A detailed debate on the merits of an absolute conception of poverty, occurred between Amartya Sen and Peter Townsend. Sen (1983) argued that 'There is ... an irreducible absolutist core in the idea of poverty. If there is starvation and hunger then, no matter what the relative picture looks like – there clearly is poverty.' Examples of this absolutist core are the need 'to meet nutritional requirements, to escape avoidable disease, to be sheltered, to be clothed, to be able to travel, to be educated ... to live without shame.'

Townsend (1985) has responded that this absolutist core is itself relative to society. Nutritional requirements are dependent on the work roles of people at different points of history and in different cultures. Avoidable disease is dependent upon the level of medical technology. The idea of shelter is relative not just to climate but also to what society uses shelter for. Shelter includes notions of privacy, space to cook, work and play, and highly cultured notions of warmth, humidity and segregation of particular members of the family as well as different functions of sleep, cooking, washing and excretion.

Much of the debate on absolute versus RELATIVE POVERTY revolves around semantic definitions. Sen (1985) argued that

> the characteristic feature of 'absoluteness' is neither constancy over time nor invariance between societies nor concentration on food and nutrition. It is an approach to judging a person's deprivation in absolute terms (in the case of a poverty study, in terms of certain specified minimum absolute levels), rather than in purely *relative* terms vis-à-vis the levels enjoyed by others in society.

This definition of absoluteness in non-constant terms is different from the notion of absolute poverty adopted by the OECD (1976: 69) as 'a level of minimum need, below which people are regarded as poor, for the purpose of social and government concern, and which does not change over time.'

If absolute poverty is defined in terms that are neither constant over time nor invariant between societies, then, Townsend and Gordon (1991) have argued, from an operational point of view the concepts of absolute and relative poverty become virtually indistinguishable – i.e. you could use the same methods and criteria in a social survey to measure absolute and relative poverty. Nevertheless, the distinction continues to exert an influence over the construction of measures of poverty, which are often based in a concept of subsistence, and on political debates, particularly in Latin America.

REFERENCES

OECD (1976) *Public Expenditure on Income Maintenance Programmes*, Paris: OECD.
Sen, A.K. (1983) 'Poor, Relatively Speaking', *Oxford Economic Papers* 35: 135–69.
Sen, A.K. (1985) 'A Sociological Approach to the Measurement of Poverty: A Reply to Professor Peter Townsend', *Oxford Economic Papers* 37: 669–76.
Townsend, P. (1985) 'A Sociological Approach to the Measurement of Poverty: A Rejoinder to Professor Amartya Sen', *Oxford Economic Papers* 37: 659–68.
Townsend, P., and Gordon, D. (1991) *What is Enough? New Evidence on Poverty Allowing the Definition of a Minimum Benefit*, in M. Adler, C. Bell, J. Clasen and A. Sinfield (eds), *The Sociology of Social Security*, Edinburgh: Edinburgh University Press, 35–69.
UN (1995) *The Copenhagen Declaration and Programme of Action: World Summit for Social Development 6–12 March 1995*, New York: United Nations.

ADMINISTRATIVE POVERTY

The welfare states have singled out certain groups such as the elderly, the disabled, the unemployed, single mothers, low-income groups, and large families as eligible for public assistance. Through a system of income transfers from the state or the municipality the groups are made visible and defined as needy, poor, disadvantaged, worthy, and so on. The labels vary, as do the criteria for transfer. Thus the WELFARE STATE *creates* categories of poverty. The poverty label disappears behind these categories and reappears when benefits are means-tested or reserved for selected groups. But those persons who receive some kind of social benefit are per se defined as poorer than the rest of the population, or at least poorer than some segment of the population with which it is considered just or legitimate to judge their degree of poverty.

REFERENCES

Øyen, E. (1992) 'Some Basic Issues in Comparative Poverty Research', *International Social Science Journal* 134: 615–26.

AMENITIES

Amenities are resources which offer basic facilities for daily living. In the context of HOUSING policy, the idea is commonly operationalised in terms of specific items that are available to residents (Hole 1972). Facilities for personal hygiene include water supply, hot water, fixed baths or showers, washbasins, water closets and facilities for the disposal of waste water. Facilities for warmth include heating or cooling systems. Facilities for the preparation of food include drinkable water, food storage and a sink. Other amenities may include a supply of electricity or gas. In developing countries, the focus on amenities tends to fall on the provision of basic services, like water supply or sewerage (Kundu 1993); in developed economies, the focus is liable to shift towards the amenities within the housing itself.

REFERENCES

Hole, V. (1972) 'Housing in Social Research', in E. Gittis (ed.), *Key Variables in Social Research*, London: Heinemann.
Kundu, A. (1993) *In the Name of the Urban Poor: Access to Basic Amenities*, New Delhi: Sage.

ARABIC (TRADITIONAL) DEFINITIONS OF POVERTY

The United Nations Economic and Social Commission for Western Asia (ESCWA) found that in the Arab world there were specific traditional definitions of poverty. In the literal sense, *Lisan al-Arab*, written by Ibn-Mandhur (d. *c.* 1311 CE) – the standard Arabic dictionary – defines poverty as the 'inability of an individual to satisfy his own basic needs and the needs of his dependants'. Another source, *Fiqh al-Lugha*, written by Tha'aliby (d. *c.* 1037 CE) identifies eight different levels of poverty, assigning to each a specific term:

- loss of savings;
- loss of assets or property due to drought or natural disaster (this type of poverty is temporary);
- an individual is forced to sell the decoration items on his sword (the equivalent in today's standards would be to sell non-essential material belongings);
- the individual/household can only afford to eat bread made of millet, which is cheaper than the usual wheat-flour bread;
- the individual/household has no food available;
- the individual/household has no belongings left which he/it can sell to purchase food;
- the individual/household has become humiliated or degraded due to poverty;
- the individual/household is reduced to ultimate poverty.

REFERENCES

Al Farqir fil Alam al' Arbi (1994) 'Poverty in the Arab World', background paper for the World Summit for Social Development, ESCWA Poverty Eradication Series [in Arabic].

AREA DEPRIVATION

Area deprivation has at least three different meanings (Macintyre 1997):

- A compositional meaning, whereby an area is considered to be deprived if it contains a large number of poor people. In this case the spatial effects are entirely due to the concentration of poor people in a given area; there are no independent area effects.

- A collective meaning, whereby an area is considered to be deprived because if it contains a lot of poor people a social 'miasma' may exist. That is, a concentration of poor people will exert a collective influence beyond their individual circumstances; for example, it may be difficult to find a job if you live in a deprived area because employers are prejudiced against people from poor areas.
- A public goods or environmental meaning, whereby an area is considered deprived because it lacks facilities (roads, hospitals, schools, libraries, etc.) or because it suffers from high pollution levels (Bramley 1997).

These three meanings of area deprivation are separate and distinct, but are often confused (Lee et al. 1995).

The belief that areas can be deprived or poor has been attacked as an example of the 'ecological fallacy', or an illegitimate attribution of characteristics to aggregate figures from the situation of individuals (Bulmer 1986). Against this proposition is the view that geographical areas have distinct characteristics and spatially organized patterns of behaviour, that the characteristics of an area affect all residents (not only those who are individually poor), and that by several definitions of poverty − including relational views and poverty in the sense of multiple deprivation − areas experience poverty.

REFERENCES

Bramley, G. (1997) 'Poverty and Local Public Services', in D. Gordon and C. Pantazis (eds), *Breadline Britain in the 1990s*, Aldershot: Avebury.

Bulmer, M. (1986) *Social Science and Social Policy*, London: Allen & Unwin.

Lee, P., Murie, A., and Gordon, D. (1995) *Area Measures of Deprivation: A Study of Current Methods and Best Practices in the Identification of Poor Areas in Great Britain*, Birmingham: University of Birmingham.

Macintyre, S. (1997) 'What Are Spatial Effects and How Can We Measure Them?', in A. Dale (ed.), *Exploiting National Survey And Census Data: The Role of Locality and Spatial Effects*, Manchester: Cathie Marsh Centre for Census and Survey Research.

ASSET VULNERABILITY FRAMEWORK

The asset vulnerability framework utilizes the link between assets and vulnerability to explain both the reasons why people move in or out of poverty and how they cope and adapt to the situations they find themselves in. Caroline Moser (1998) develops this concept 'to try to contribute to the debate on strategies to reduce poverty' at a local 'sustained [level] that reinforces the inventive solutions of the people themselves, rather than replace or block them'.

Moser characterises VULNERABILITY as insecurity in the well-being of individuals, households and communities faced by changing conditions in the environment, and implicit in this is their resilience and responsiveness to risk that they face during negative changes. Vulnerability in turn is related to the possession and control of assets. Assets are both tangible and intangible. Tangible assets include labour, and human capital, as well as housing and social and economic infrastructure. Intangible assets include household relations and SOCIAL CAPITAL. Access to and utilization of assets is central to whether people are able to take advantage of a set of circumstances, and to whether they would further slide into poverty. The more assets a person possesses, the less vulnerable they are; and the greater the erosion of the assets on the part of the people, the greater their insecurity.

Moser's research is based in four poor communities in cities whose countries were facing economic hardship in the 1980s: Lusaka (Zambia), Guayaquil (Ecuador), Metro Manila (the Philippines) and Budapest (Hungary). The results of the study identify household income-raising strategies, changes in household food consumption, and shows that the ability of homeowners to use their houses as assets depends on regulatory environment. Other strategies to reduce vulnerability include income diversification through renting and home-based enterprises, as well as children building houses on their parents' plots. In terms of social capital, community-led activity and informal credit networks are shown as important coping mechanisms.

Moser's research shows that the poor themselves are managing a portfolio of complex assets. This approach illustrates the way the management of assets affects vulnerability in the household. In operational terms, Moser's viewpoint adds to the development of tools to contribute to the interventions promoting opportunities and overcoming key obstacles. The asset vulnerability framework tries to help the poor in urban areas to use their portfolio of assets to optimize their position.

The framework has, however, had significant criticism. First, the framework sees SURVIVAL STRATEGIES as 'managing complex portfolios'. This may romanticize survivalist strategies. Moser, however, shows that some households were pushed beyond the point where they could sustain networks, and fell deeper into poverty. Second, the framework does not adequately capture questions of power relations and the structural nature of poverty.

The asset vulnerability framework has opened up new lines of argument and prompted other approaches to understanding household livelihood strategies. Bebbington (1999) develops a framework looking at assets that places questions of power and structure more central to the analytical framework, through focusing on social capital and the broader influences on policy. Rakodi (1999) brings in a time dimension to the analysis, by arguing that a household may be able to mitigate or cope in a given period, but that in subsequent periods they may not be able to manage, as assets may have degraded. He refers to this as a 'capital assets framework'.

REFERENCES

Bebbington, A. (1999) 'Capitals and Capabilities: A Framework for Analysing Peasant Viability, Rural Livelihoods and Poverty', *World Development* 27/12: 2021–44.

Moser, C. (1998) 'The Asset Vulnerability Framework; Reassessing Urban Poverty Reduction Strategies', *World Development* 26/1: 1–19.

Rakodi, C. (1999) 'A Capital Assets Framework for Analyzing Household Livelihood Strategies', *Development Policy Review* 3/17: 315–42.

AUSTRALIAN DEFINITIONS OF POVERTY

Virtually all studies on poverty in Australia over the past twenty years have used the broad framework and methodology developed by the Commission of the Inquiry into Poverty in 1975 (Saunders and Matherson 1992). The recommended methodology has since become known as the Henderson Poverty Line (HPL), after the Commission's chairman Roland Henderson. The HPL contains both relative and official elements in its definition of poverty and is based on a study of poverty in Melbourne undertaken by Henderson, Harcourt and Harper (1970):

> For our survey of income and needs ... we have accepted as a state of poverty the situation of a man with a wife (not working) and two children where total weekly income ...was less than the basic wage plus child endowment ... We chose this basic wage concept of the poverty line because of its relevance to Australian concepts of living

standards.... This poverty line also has international relevance since, in relation to average earnings, to average incomes and to basic social service rates, it is comparable to the poverty lines that have been adopted in some surveys carried out overseas.... We have deliberately confined ourselves to a study of poverty as determined by the relationship between the income of a family and its normal needs. ... We have not attempted to study the personal causes of poverty, its life cycle or its perpetuation, which would have taken us into the deep waters of the sociology of poverty.... Finally we consider poverty to be a relative standard, to be defined in relationship to the living standards typical of the community in which we live.

In their introduction, Henderson, Harcourt and Harper argued that they had used: 'a definition of poverty so austere as, we believe, to make it unchallengeable. No one can seriously argue that those we define as being poor are not so.'

The Poverty Commission (1975) used the poverty line from the Melbourne survey of 1966 and updated it using seasonally adjusted average weekly earnings. This procedure implies that 'Australian concepts of living standards' were reflected in basic wage and child endowment levels up until 1966, but in average weekly earnings movements thereafter (Saunders 1980). The Poverty Commission also needed to adjust the poverty line for household size, but no Australian household budget data were available at the time that could be used as the basis for EQUIVALENCE SCALES, so scales produced by the Budget Service Standard of New York in 1954 were used. These scales are clearly only appropriate if the expenditure patterns of New York families in 1954 and of Australian families in 1973 are similar, an unlikely situation. Subsequently, the work of the Poverty Commission equivalence scales based on Australian household budget data have become available.

REFERENCES

Commission of Inquiry into Poverty (1975) *Poverty in Australia*, Canberra: AGPS.

Henderson, R., Harcourt, A., and Harper, R.J.A. (1970) *People in Poverty: A Melbourne Survey*, Cheshire for the Institute of Applied Economic and Social Research, Melbourne.

Saunders, P. (ed.) (1980) 'The Poverty Line: Methodology and Measurement', *SWRC Reports and Proceedings* 2, University of New South Wales, Kensington.

Saunders, P., and Matherson, G. (1992) 'Perceptions of Poverty, Income Adequacy and Living Standards in Australia', *SPRC Reports and Proceedings* 99, University of New South Wales, Kensington.

AXIOM OF MONOTONICITY; AXIOM OF TRANSFERS

These are two tests of poverty measures, proposed by Sen.

Monotonicity requires that, given other things, a reduction in income of a person below the poverty line must increase the poverty measure. A measure with this property reflects changes that, despite leaving the number of the poor unchanged, cause a rise in the shortfall from the poverty line.

The axiom of transfers requires that, all things being equal, a pure transfer from a person below the poverty line to anyone who is richer must increase the poverty measure. This property makes a measure sensitive to the distribution of income between the poor.

An example of a measure that does not respect either axiom is the widely used HEAD-COUNT RATIO (the percentage of people below the poverty line). The POVERTY GAP ratio (the average shortfall from the poverty line of all the poor), while respecting monotonicity, may not always respect the axiom of transfers.

It should be noted that even if a measure respects these two axioms, it could still be criticized. Money transfers between the poor or the excluded do not necessarily alter their basic situation. Emphasis should be put on the complex nature of deprivation rather than on unidimensional, income-based, poverty measures.

REFERENCES

Sen, A. (1976) 'Poverty: An Ordinal Approach to Measurement', *Econometrica* 46: 437–46.

B

BASIC INCOME

Basic income schemes have been proposed as one method of relieving poverty in industrialized countries (Walter 1989). A basic income is a payment received by every person or household, which provides a minimum income and the amount is based only on age and family status, but is otherwise unconditional. The SPEENHAMLAND SYSTEM of 1795 was one of the earliest attempts at a workable guaranteed basic income, and since then many other basic income schemes have been proposed.

There are three main advantages claimed for Basic Income schemes (Brittan and Webb 1990):

1. They should plug the gaps and loopholes in social security and reduce the number of people living in poverty.
2. They should remove unemployment and the POVERTY TRAP that results from the high rates of benefit withdrawal when the unemployed obtain work, or people with low incomes move up the earnings ladder.
3. They are desirable because people should have a means of SUB-SISTENCE independent of needs and not dependent on complicated contribution records or intrusive scrutiny of personal means.

Other arguments in favour of a basic income have been:

- increased predictability for the receiver;
- increased legal protection of citizens in a complex welfare state;
- increased accountability and economic control (Øyen 1981).

Most existing social security benefits in industrialized countries are contingent. This means that they are related to misfortune or conditions such as age, sickness or unemployment. By contrast, a basic income depends only on very general characteristics such as the number of dependants. There are no questions or conditions relating to effort to find work, state of health, contribution records or capital holdings. Basic incomes could replace many existing specific social security benefits. There would always be people with special needs requiring extra sums on a conditional or discretionary basis but fewer cases than at present. Some advocates believe that basic income payments should take the form of a tax credit to be set off against tax but received as a positive payment from the state by those with insufficient tax liabilities.

Basic incomes are sometimes called minimum income guarantees, social dividends or negative (or reverse) income tax schemes (Parker 1988, 1989).

REFERENCES

Brittan, S., and Webb, S. (1990) *Beyond the Welfare State: An Examination of Basic Incomes in a Market Economy*, David Hume Institute, Aberdeen: Aberdeen University Press.
Øyen, E. (1981) *GMI. Garantert minsteinntekt i Norge*, Oslo: Universitetsforlaget.
Parker, H. (1988) 'Are Basic Incomes Feasible?', *Basic Income Research Group Bulletin* 7.
Parker, H. (1989) *Instead of the Dole*, London: Routledge.
Walter, T. (1989) *Basic Income: Freedom from Poverty, Freedom to Work*, London: Marion Boyars.

BASIC NEEDS

The idea of 'basic needs' was taken up in debates about development in the 1970s, although the idea has a longer history (see, for example, Drewnowski and Scott 1966; Drewnowski 1977). Basic needs were said to include two elements:

> Firstly, they include certain minimum requirements of a family for private consumption: adequate food, shelter and clothing, as well as certain household furniture and equipment. Second, they include essential services provided by and for the community at large, such as safe drinking water, sanitation, public transport and health, education and cultural facilities.... The concept of basic needs should be placed within a context of a nation's overall economic and social development. In no circumstances should it be taken to mean merely the minimum necessary for subsistence; it should be placed within a context of national independence, the dignity of individuals and peoples and their freedom to chart their destiny without hindrance. (ILO 1976: 243; see also ILO 1977)

Emphasis is placed on minimum facilities required by local communities as a whole and not only individual and family needs for physical survival and efficiency. The use of indicators on access to services is the basis of the UBN, or measurement of Unsatisfied Basic Needs. 'The UBN refers to those material manifestations that evidence the lack of access to certain types of services such as housing, drinking water, electricity, education and health, among others' (Golbert and Kessler 1996: 10–11). The Basic Needs Index of the INTERNATIONAL FUND FOR AGRICULTURAL DEVELOPMENT comprises an education index and a health index.

The concept of 'basic needs' has played a prominent part in a succession of national plans (see, for example, Ghai et al. 1977, 1979) and in international reports (see, for example, UNESCO 1978 and the Brandt Report 1980). In debates about development, the emphasis on basic needs was seen by its proponents as a way of expanding a narrow focus on economic development to include issues of human development. Its advocates emphasized the importance of efficient, labour-intensive production and the reduction of poverty through provision of public services – widespread education, health services, safe drinking water, and family planning. In practice, governments tended to focus primarily on the basic services. It became identified with top-down state planning and state action. At the same time, it provided the basis for later work on HUMAN DEVELOPMENT.

Conceptually, the idea of basic needs is an enlargement of the idea of SUBSISTENCE. Proponents of the concept have had great difficulty in producing acceptable criteria for the choice and definition of items included. The needs of populations cannot be defined adequately just by reference to the physical needs of individuals and the more obvious physical provisions and services required by local communities. The exposition of need depends on assumptions about the development and functioning of societies and, in particular, how the organization of markets can be reconciled with the organization of collective utilities and services.

In developed countries, the idea of subsistence has been used by liberal theorists to justify limiting state intervention, allowing poverty to be reconciled more easily with the individualism and free-market ethos underlying liberal pluralism.. The idea is seen as limited and limiting. While basic needs became particularly popular with international agencies, some developing countries regarded rich countries' support for basic needs as a ploy to divert attention from the need for changing international policies and for a 'new international economic order'.

REFERENCES

Brandt Report (1980) W. Brandt (Chairman), *North–South: A Programme for Survival*, London: Pan.
Drewnowski, J., and Scott, W. (1966) *The Level of Living Index*, United Nations Research Institute for Social Development Report 4, Geneva: UN.
Drewnowski, J. (1977) 'Poverty: Its Meaning and Measurement', *Development and Change* 8/2: 183–206.
Ghai, D.P., Khan, A.R., Lee, E.H., and Alfthan, T. (1977) *The Basic Needs Approach to Development: Some Issues Regarding Concepts and Methodology*, Geneva: ILO.
Ghai, D.P., Godfrey, M., and Lisk, F. (1979) *Planning for Basic Needs in Kenya*, Geneva: ILO.
Golbert, L., and Kessler, G. (1996) 'Latin America: Poverty as a Challenge for Government and Society', in E. Øyen, S.A. Samad and S.M. Miller (eds), *Poverty: A Global Review. Handbook on Poverty Research*, Oslo: Scandinavian University Press and UNESCO.
ILO (1976) *Employment Growth and Basic Needs: A One World Problem*, Geneva: International Labour Office.
ILO (1977) *Meeting Basic Needs: Strategies for Eradicating Mass Poverty and Unemployment*, Geneva: International Labour Office.
Townsend, P. (1993) *The International Analysis of Poverty*, Hemel Hempstead: Harvester Wheatsheaf.
UNESCO (1978) *Study in Depth on the Concept of Basic Human Needs in Relation to Various Ways of Life and Its Possible Implications for the Action of the Organization*, Paris: UNESCO.

BASIC SECURITY (SECURITY OF EXISTENCE)

Countries which formerly had a planned centralised economy based the organization of their societies on the principle of basic security. Ferge (1992) defines the concept as a combination of security of employment, security of income and security of accommodation. The right to employment was written into the constitution of these countries. Each citizen had a position or role in society, associated with a modest income and housing. Low wages were compensated for by various benefits and subsidies and free social services; the state redistributed a large part of the social product in the form of pensions, family benefits, food subsidies and transport. Businesses offered, for their part, a range of premiums and perquisites and services for health, education, holidays and culture and payments in kind. The funds for this came from the businesses themselves and trades unions.

REFERENCES

Ferge, Z. (1992) 'Marginalisation, pauvreté et institutions sociales', *Travail et société* 16/4: 447–69.

BEGGING

Begging is a request for alms or charity for oneself. The act of begging is understood differently in different cultures but it is strongly associated with both poverty and dependency and widely stigmatized. Although charity was a religious duty in Christian cultures, itinerant begging in Europe was associated with marauding and the spread of disease (Briod 1976) and concern with poor relief was a recurring issue in the Reformation (Salter 1926). Giving personal aid was discouraged under the Poor Laws in England in the belief that it was an encouragement to vice; 'scientific charity' selected the 'deserving poor'. In historical terms, long before capitalism, the Black Death forced people into itinerant lifestyles in their thousands. Begging was associated with danger, theft and the spread of disease. It was met with punitive sanctions including, whipping, branding and execution.

The association of begging with itinerant lifestyles could appear in any epoch. However, social control, in the sense of legal, institutional (mostly governmental) and social intervention for repression of begging, has been used as a fundamental strategy of the 'freed' social forces of capitalist society. The same is true of laws on begging and the repression of the unemployed, itinerant poor, in which work was promoted as a duty and control was exerted on the labour force (Donzelot 1997; Castel 1995).

In modern times, begging is generally viewed as a marginal or deviant activity (see, for example, Gmelch and Gmelch 1978) but there are still societies in which it plays a more institutionalized role as a means of social support (Bamisaiye 1974).

REFERENCES

Bamisaiye, A. (1974) 'Begging in Ibadan, Southern Nigeria', *Human Organization* 33/2: 197–202.

Briod, A. (1976) L'assistance des pauvres au moyen age dans le Pays de Vaud, Lausanne: Éditions d'en bas.

Castel, R. (1995) *Les Métamorphoses de la question sociale. Une chronique du salariat*, Paris: Fayard.

Donzelot, J. (1997) *The Policing of Families*, trans. Robert Hurley, Baltimore MD: Johns Hopkins University Press.

Gmelch, G., and Gmelch, S. (1978) 'Beggars in Dublin: The Strategies of a Marginal Urban Occupation', *Urban Life* 6/4: 439–54.

Salter, F.R. (1926) *Some Early Tracts on Poor Relief*, London: Methuen.

BEVERIDGE SCHEME

The Beveridge Report (Beveridge 1942) is widely considered to be the foundation of the British WELFARE STATE and has been influential in the development of a range of other social security systems. The details are concerned with National Insurance. Beveridge believed that his scheme would be 'comprehensive', providing a 'national minimum' in circumstances where people had to rely on INCOME MAINTENANCE benefits. The press referred to coverage 'from cradle to grave'.

The scheme was based on six 'principles' of insurance. First, there would be comprehensive coverage (which Beveridge referred to as 'universality'). Second, contributors would be identified in 'classes' of insurance; Beveridge arranged for classes of workers, self-employed, pensioners, married women and children, in an attempt to emphasize the comprehensive nature of the scheme. Third, there would be flat-rate benefits: every recipient would receive the same entitlement. Fourth, there would be flat-rate contributions: every contributor would pay on the same basis. Fifth, benefits would be 'adequate', by which Beveridge intended that they should offer basic subsistence. Finally, there should be a unified national administration. The scheme failed to provide universal coverage in practice, partly because any scheme which relies on contributions must leave gaps, partly because the UK government did not fully fund the scheme, and partly because Beveridge left certain contingencies outside the scope of the scheme, including housing costs and the situation of single parents.

The benefit levels proposed by the Beveridge Report claimed to be adequate for SUBSISTENCE. They were based on a version of Seebohm Rowntree's PRIMARY POVERTY measure of 1901, with an updated diet. But this measure was used solely to rationalise the proposed cash sums, which in reality were based on the requirement that they must not exceed the levels of pay for unskilled workers (LESS ELIGIBILITY). They were thus admitted to be inadequate for decent social life for the period when they were applied in 1942 (Veit Wilson 1992).

REFERENCES

Beveridge, W. (1942) Cmd 6404, Social Insurance and Allied Services, London: HMSO.
Veit Wilson, J. (1992) 'Muddle or Mendacity? The Beveridge Committee and the Poverty Line', *Journal of Social Policy* 21/3: 269–301.

BISMARCKIAN SOCIAL INSURANCE

Under Bismarck, Germany was the first nation to introduce a scheme of national insurance, covering sickness, industrial injuries and pensions. The operation of the scheme was based on previously existing mutual aid societies, and a 'Bismarckian' system is generally taken to include socio-professional social insurance, offering earnings-related benefits, in which the administration is delegated on a corporatist basis to independent insurance funds (Lenoir 1994).

REFERENCES

Lenoir, D. (1994) *L'Europe Sociale*, Paris: Découverte.

BRAZILIAN DEFINITIONS OF POVERTY

In the mid-1970s, Oscar Altimir (1982) wrote a study for the World Bank which estimated that 40 per cent of families in South America were living in poverty. Poverty was defined as not being able to acquire a minimum basket of goods to satisfy basic needs. Altimir also found that 20 per cent of all families were in a condition of misery – that is, could not afford to buy a subsistence diet. In Brazil, 49 per cent of families lived under this poverty line and 25 per cent of all families were to be found under the misery line, of which 42 per cent lived in rural areas and 15 per cent in cities.

However, a number of studies in Brazil in the 1970s produced different estimates of the amount of poverty. The differences were largely due to the discrepancies in the income estimates available from the three main data sources: the National Census, the National Accounts, and the National Survey of Homesteads. The large discrepancies in the data (over 40 per cent) were mainly due to the omission of non-monetary income, which made up a third of rural income in the 1970s (Rios 1984).

The most widely used definition of poverty in Brazil during the 1970s and 1980s was those families earning two minimum salaries or less. Using this POVERTY LINE the National Census showed that the number of poor people increased from 21 million to 26 million between 1970 and 1980 (Rios 1984).

In the 1980s, Family Budget Data became available from the National Study on Family Expenses (ENDEF) which were used to produce two 'poverty' lines (Singer 1997):

- The Indigence Line (In), the minimum monthly income to fulfil only the food needs of an individual.
- The Poverty Line (Po), the minimum monthly income to fulfil all the basic needs of an individual.

The Indigence Line is a similar concept to the misery line, and both the poverty and indigence lines are BUDGET STANDARDS which use a subsistence definition of poverty. They are similar in conceptualization to Rowntree's PRIMARY POVERTY idea.

REFERENCES

Altimir, O. (1982) *The Extent of Poverty in Latin America*, World Bank Staff Working Paper 522, Washington DC: World Bank.
Rios, J.A. (1984) 'The Invisible Economy of Poverty: The Case of Brazil', *Mondes en Développement* 12/45: 65–77.
Singer, P. (1997) *Social Exclusion in Brazil*, Discussion Paper 94, Geneva: ILO.

BUDGET STANDARDS

Budget standards are one of the oldest methods of exploring living standards and setting poverty lines. They were pioneered in

Britain by Rowntree (1901) in his famous study of poverty in York
(PRIMARY AND SECONDARY POVERTY), and in the USA by less well-
known analysts (e.g. Iowa Bureau of Labor Statistics 1891; Goodyear
1906) examining inadequate living standards in various cities and
states.

A budget standard is a specified basket of goods and services which
when priced can represent a particular standard of living. Budgets
can be devised to represent any living standard (Bradshaw 1993). They
can then be tailored to the circumstances of different households by
varying the quality and price of the items included in the basket
of goods and services. In practice, this process is less fraught with
problems when the standard being developed is one in which there
is little or no scope for satisfying other than basic survival needs. At
higher standards of living, the degree of choice which people have
over precisely how much they consume of each item makes the task
of drawing up a single budgetary representation more problematic
(Saunders 1996).

A budget standard estimates what families ought to spend rather
than what they actually do (or think they need to) spend. A characteristic of this approach is that the judgements of 'experts' are used
to create a basket of goods and services which represents the type of
commodities, quantities and quality of family consumption (Oldfield
and Yu 1993). However, in major budget standard studies in Britain
(Bradshaw 1993) and Australia (Saunders 1996), the 'experts' developing the budget standards took explicit steps to secure input from
representatives of the general population to help them determine
the contents of the budget standards; this input included feedback
from focus groups of consumers and findings from the 1990 Breadline
Britain survey (CONSENSUAL METHODS) of a nationally representative
sample of the population.

Although the standard of living depends upon the consumption
of goods and services, information is generally only available on the
price of commodities (or services). This means that, in deriving a
budget standard, it is necessary to impute a monetary value to the
consumption of each item in the budget. Bradshaw described the
requirements of a budget standard as follows:

> The task of those who draw up a budget is to decide what items
> are included in the budget, what quantity of items are included,

what quality the item should have, what price should be given to it, and where items are purchased intermittently or occasionally, what lifetime should be attributed to them. (Bradshaw 1993: 3)

Producing budget standards is therefore both expensive and extremely time-consuming since it requires a team of 'experts' to first decide on the contents of the budget (housing, transport, food, clothing, etc.) and for this budget to then be priced for different types of household in different circumstances.

Bradshaw et al. (1987) have argued that:

> It would be wrong to claim too much for budget standards methodology. There will be arguments about the components of a modern budget standard just as there were about Rowntree's standards. The quality of people's lives cannot be completely represented by the goods they consume. Budgets cannot represent fringe benefits, wealth and the consumption of unmarketed public and private services. Neither can a budget show how goods are consumed variously within households. However, budget standards are capable of incorporating elements concerned with social participation and can represent a measure of relative deprivation.

REFERENCES

Beveridge, W. (1942) Cmd 6404, Social Insurance and Allied Services, London: HMSO.

Bradshaw, J. (ed.) (1993) *Budget Standards for the United Kingdom*, Aldershot: Avebury.

Bradshaw, J., Mitchell, D., and Morgan, J. (1987) 'Evaluating Adequacy: The Potential of Budget Standards', *Journal of Social Policy* 16/2: 165–82.

Goodyear, C. (1906) 'The Minimum Practicable Cost of an Adequate Standard of Living in New York City', *Charities and the Commons* 17/7: 315–20.

Iowa Bureau of Labor Statistics (1891) *Fourth Biennial Report of the Bureau of Labor Statistics for the State of Iowa. 1890–91*, Des Moines: G.H. Ragsdale, State Printer.

Oldfield, N., and Yu, A. (1993) *The Cost of a Child: Living Standards for the 1990s*, Child Poverty Action Group.

Rowntree, B.S. (1901) *Poverty: A Study of Town Life*, London: Macmillan.

Saunders, P. (1996) *Development of Indicative Budget Standards for Australia: Project Outline and Research Methods*, BSU Working Paper 1, Sydney: University of New South Wales.

C

CALORIE-INCOME ELASTICITY (CIE)

The extent to which food intake varies with income (Lipton 1995: 140–41). As a general proposition, food intake represents a diminishing proportion of income as income increases: see ENGEL COEFFICIENT.

REFERENCES

Lipton, M. (1995) 'Growing Points in Poverty Research: Labour Issues', in G. Rodgers (ed.), *The Poverty Agenda and the ILO*, Geneva: ILO.

CAPABILITIES AND CHARACTERISTICS

These terms are developed by Amartya Sen. He distinguishes *capabilities* – the basic capacities which people need to have in order to function – from *commodities* and *characteristics*, which are the means through which these needs are interpreted or operationalized. A bicycle, for example, is a commodity. One of its principal characteristics is transportation. The capability which it offers is the ability to move about. 'The transportation characteristic of the bike gives the person the capability of moving in a certain way' (Sen 1983: 160). Sen argues that a standard of living is determined by capabilities rather than by characteristics or utility. Sen's conceptualization of poverty as capability deprivation focuses on the failure of some basic capabilities to function: for example, being adequately nourished, leading a long and healthy life, or being literate. Sen claims that a monetary measure of standard of living cannot capture the opportunities individuals have to lead minimally adequate lives as they do not take into account the individual specificities in transforming goods into functionings. Commodities and characteristics may be socially defined, but capability is absolute. If this argument is accepted then it provides a basis for sorting out the absolute–relative disputation in the conceptualization of poverty. At the risk of over-simplification, I would like to say that poverty is an absolute notion in the space of capabilities but very often it will take a relative form in the space of commodities or characteristics.

The material requirements needed to realise capabilities are determined not only by individual specificities; they may also be socially defined.

Capabilities are essential to the exercise of freedom, and poverty consequently limits personal freedom. The lack of capability implied by poverty is the product, Sen argues, of a lack of entitlement. Sen argues for social and economic development as the primary way of expanding entitlements, and so capabilities (Sen 1999). Atkinson (1993, 1995) has argued that poverty in terms of capabilities is itself dependent on, and relative to, the supply side of the economy – that is, in order to have the 'capability of moving', as discussed above, you have to be able first to obtain a bicycle. As the standard of living in a society increases, superior (and more expensive) products may displace those previously available (alloy mountain bicycles instead of simple three-gear bicycles) and firms may find it unprofitable to supply poor households. Therefore Atkinson (1993) argues 'that poverty cannot be seen independently of the working of the economy'.

REFERENCES

Atkinson, A.B. (1993) *Capabilities, Exclusion, and the Supply of Goods*, Welfare State Programme Discussion Paper WSP/97, London: LSE.

Atkinson, A.B. (1995) 'Capabilities, Exclusion, and the Supply of Goods', in K. Basu et al. (eds), *Choice, Welfare and Development: A Festschrift in Honour of Amartya Sen*, Oxford: Oxford University Press.

Sen, A. (1983) 'Poor, Relatively Speaking', *Oxford Economic Papers* 35/1.

Sen, A. (1999) *Development as Freedom*, Oxford: Clarendon Press.

CHARITY

Although many activities are taken to be 'charitable' in different social contexts, charity is often identified with voluntary, benevolent donations, or acts of benevolence towards the poor. A sense of moral obligation to the poor is a feature of many, if not most, known societies (Sahlins 1974). This obligation has been institutionalized in many cultures through formal systems of social organization. In many cases the process has been dependent on religious principles. In Judaism, the duties of benevolence were institutionalized in the principle of *zedakah*; in Christianity as charity; and in Islam as *zakat*. In medieval Christianity, the duties of charity included feeding and clothing the hungry, visiting the sick and relieving poverty. Charity recipients were indigent old people, orphans, blind people, widows with children, as well as all kinds of people with disabilities. The forms of charity that developed in medieval Europe were strongly linked to religious organizations (hospitals, homes for disabled people and abandoned children, orphanages and hospices for the deserving poor). The foundation of such organizations called for authorization and protection of religious leaders. As charity organizations they were also concerned not only with alms to the poor and their moralization but also with providing spiritual assistance and moral standards. During the Spanish Enlightenment, the hospice served the purpose of repressing vagrancy and moralization as a deterrent, forcing those said to lead a 'lazy' life to commit to some work, and at the same time the hospices provided discipline because those people were in seclusion (Trinidad Fernández 1985). With the development of Protestantism, similar arrangements were made by Lutheran communities through the development of 'community chests'. Over time, the patterns of charitable organization came increasingly to depend on individual, lay and secular patterns of organization.

The nature of charitable duties is such that the primary obligation is not necessarily held towards potential recipients. In religious charity, the primary duty is to God. In secular charities, the characteristic form of obligation is a trust, where the primary obligation is determined by the specified role of the organization or the wishes of the donor. In some countries, charities are granted special privileges over other forms of non-profit activity, including for example tax exemptions, special laws relating to charitable organizations and privileged access to public funds. Today, charity is sometimes identified with local PHILANTHROPY or NEO-PHILANTHROPY and INTERNATIONAL AID (Working Group of Charitable Sector Organization; 2005). Charity has become a type of social intervention on poverty, not necessarily linked to religious sentiments, but strongly motivated by the acceptance of moral responsibilities towards the poor.

REFERENCES

Sahlins, M. (1974) *Stone Age Economics*, London: Tavistock.
Trinidad Fernández, P. (1985) 'Asistencia y previsión social en el siglo XVIII', in *Seminario de Historia de la Acción social; en 4 Siglos de Acción Social de la beneficencia al bienestar social,* Seminario de Historia de la acción social, Madrid: Siglo XXI Editores.
Working Group of Charitable Sector Organization (2005) *Principles of International Charity,* Treasury Guidelines Working Group of Charitable Sector Organizations and Advisors, March, Washington DC: Council on Foundations.

CHARITY ORGANIZATION SOCIETY

Founded in Britain in 1869, the aim of the COS was to coordinate the diverse charities that existed in London and get them to administer relief on 'scientific' principles (Loch Mowat 1961). Basically, this involved strict means-testing of an applicant, who would only be granted relief if judged to be 'deserving'. The 'undeserving' in need were to be dealt with by a strictly administered POOR LAW, based upon the deterrent principles of 1834. The influence of the COS extended to many parts of Britain (significantly, these were mainly the big cities with large populations of casual labourers) and, until the 1890s, it was considered the leading exponent of classical economics as applied to welfare (particularly that indiscriminate relief payments were demoralizing) (Lewis 1995). In practical terms, however, the COS was a failure, in that it only gained control of a handful of Poor Law Boards of Guardians and was resented by other organizations that dealt with the poor (such as Barnardo's or the Salvation Army). It did, however, pioneer techniques of social casework and the training of social workers. By the eve of the First World War, the influence of the COS had waned considerably. Today, it still exists as the Family Welfare Association.

REFERENCES

Lewis, J. (1995) *The Voluntary Sector, the State and Social Work in Britain*, Aldershot: Avebury.
Loch Mowat, C. (1961) *The Charity Organization Society 1869–1913: Its Ideas and Work*, London: Methuen.

CHILD MALNUTRITION

In 1995, 174 million children under the age of 5 were estimated to be suffering from MALNUTRITION, defined as having a weight-for-age which is more than two standard deviations below median weight-for-age (using the World Health Organization's standards). The greatest incidence of child malnutrition is found in South Asia, where 86 million children under 5 are malnourished (Ramalingaswami et al. 1996). Half the world's malnourished children live in India, Pakistan and Bangladesh. Over a third of the world's malnourished children live in India, where the 1992–93 National Family Health Survey found that 53 per cent of all under-5s were affected. Only Bangladesh had a higher rate (67 per cent) of under-5 malnutrition than India.

In sub-Saharan Africa just over 30 per cent of children are malnourished, and India and Bangladesh have far greater child malnutrition rates than even the poorest countries in Africa. Poverty is no worse in South Asia than in Africa, yet child malnutrition rates are much higher; this puzzling phenomenon has been termed the 'Asian enigma' (Ramalingaswami et al. 1996).

Although poverty is the underlying cause of malnutrition, the distribution and extent of poverty cannot explain the differences between sub-Saharan Africa and South Asia. Nor can differences in food production, income inequality, government policy, diet or physiological factors explain the different malnutrition rates. The pervasive myth persists that lack of food is the only reason for malnutrition; however, the food requirements of young children are relatively small and there are many communities in the world where FOOD SHORTAGES are not a problem but child malnutrition is. In most of South Asia, children most commonly become malnourished between the ages of 6 months and 2 years rather than after the age of 2 when their food needs are greater.

Some researchers have suggested that the answer to the Asian enigma lies in the poorer hygiene and greater risk of disease that are a consequence of the greater overcrowding poverty in South Asia and in the low social status of South Asian women and girls. Ramalingaswami et al. (1996) consider that it is the difference in the quality of child care in poor families resulting from the relative lack of freedom of South Asian women that is a major cause of the very high rates of child malnutrition in South Asia.

Methods for the identification of child malnutrition are outlined in the entry on MALNUTRITION.

REFERENCES

Ramalingaswami, V., Jonsson, U., and Rohde, J. (1996) 'The Asian Enigma', in UNICEF, *The Progress of Nations*, New York: UNICEF.

CHILD MORTALITY

In 1994, there were approximately 2 billion children in the world, 87 per cent of whom lived in developing countries (UN 1995). Children in rich countries do not die from the common, preventable diseases of childhood. Children in poor countries do. Except in rare and isolated cases, measles, diarrhoea, malaria, pneumonia, and MALNUTRITION no longer claim the lives of children in the industrialized world. However, in poor countries, these five conditions kill more than 8 million children a year and account for two-thirds of all under-5 deaths (Sharma and Tulloch 1996). Although many statistical tables list the causes of child mortality by disease, it is usually the combination of malnutrition and disease that proves fatal, rather than disease in isolation. Well-off, strong, well-nourished children with access to good food and water rarely die even if they contract measles or diarrhoea.

The costs preventing mass childhood mortality are comparatively small and, over the past fifteen years, UNICEF and WHO have led a worldwide effort, working with governments and non-governmental organizations (NGOs) to begin reducing the death toll from the ordinary diseases of childhood. Immunization has been extended from about 25 per cent to almost 80 per cent of the developing world's children, preventing more than 3 million deaths a year from diphtheria, measles, whooping cough and tetanus. Similarly, polio cases have been cut from approximately 400,000 a year to fewer than 100,000.

Since 1980, the technique known as oral rehydration therapy (ORT) has been put at the disposal of most poor communities, averting approximately 1 million deaths a year from diarrhoeal dehydration. Since then, a sustained advance has also been made against specific nutrient malnutrition, particularly vitamin A and iodine deficiency, which renders common diseases more likely to be fatal and is associated with between 1 and 3 million child deaths each year. In sum, the progress made in less than one generation means that as many as 5 million fewer children each year are dying and that at least three quarters of a million fewer are being disabled. This must be ranked as one of the greatest achievements of the second half of the twentieth century (Sharma and Tulloch 1996).

REFERENCES

Sharma, M., and Tulloch, J., (1996) 'Unfinished Business', in UNICEF, *The Progress of Nations*, New York: UNICEF.
UN (1995) *Concise Report on the World Population Situation in 1995*, New York: United Nations Publications.

CHILD POVERTY

UNICEF defines child poverty as those children who

> experience deprivation of the material, spiritual and emotional resources needed to survive, develop and thrive, leaving them unable to enjoy their rights, achieve their full potential or participate as full and equal members of society. (UNICEF 2005)

Child poverty should be defined and measured independently from adult, family or household poverty, yet this is rarely achieved (Middleton et al. 1997). It differs from adult poverty in that the impact of even brief spells of severe poverty can cause children permanent damage physically and mentally, stunt and distort their development and destroy opportunities for fulfilment, including the roles they are expected to play successively as they get older in family, community and society (CHIP 2004; UNICEF–IRC 2005).

Child poverty is often understood in terms of family poverty, where the child suffers poverty as a consequence of sharing the circumstances of others within the household. The issue of family poverty depends on an understanding of the position of the child in the family. The presence of children can have a substantial impact on the lifestyle of the household, partly because children have needs which have to be met from limited resources, and partly because the process of childrearing makes it difficult for some parents, particularly mothers of young children, to participate in the labour market.

However, traditional monetary approaches to measuring child poverty in terms of low household or family incomes ignore the fact that children's needs are different from those of adults (Vandemoortele 2000). The standard, neoclassical anti-poverty solution of increasing individuals' income levels through paid work can result in intra-household deprivation. For example, when children work, their families' income may rise above the poverty line. These children are deprived, yet they would not be considered poor within the traditional income approach (Minujin et al. 2006).

Child poverty and its outcomes are arguably a violation of the UN Convention on the Rights of the Child (CIDA 2004), which has been signed by every member state of the United Nations (193 countries). It establishes that children have rights which are independent and coequal to those of adults. Therefore aspects of child poverty which violate children's rights, such as being denied a primary education, need to be measured independently from adult or family poverty. Furthermore, measures of child poverty need to be age-specific to reflect the fact that children's needs change as they grow and develop. There is a need to look beyond income and consumption expenditure poverty measures and at both the effects of low family income on children and the effects of inadequate service provision for children (Mehrotra et al., 2000; UNDP 2004).

Global estimates of severe deprivation of the basic human needs of children (Gordon et al. 2003) show that

- Almost a third of the world's children live in dwellings with more than five people per room or which have a mud floor.
- Over half a billion children (27 per cent) have no toilet facilities.
- Over 400 million children (19 per cent) are using unsafe (open) water sources or have more than a fifteen-minute walk to water.
- About one child in five aged 3 to 18 lacks access to radio, television, telephone or newspapers at home.
- A total of 16 percent of children under 5 years in the world are severely malnourished, almost half of whom are in South Asia.
- 275 million children (13 per cent) have not been immunized against any diseases or have had a recent illness causing diarrhoea and have not received any medical advice or treatment.
- One child in nine aged between 7 and 18 (over 140 million) are severely educationally deprived – they have never been to school.

REFERENCES

CIDA (2004) *The Challenges Facing Children*, Canada International Development Agency, Quebec, www.acdi-cida.gc.ca/cida_ind.nsf/f1b522f51afeefda8525697d005cce33/79ff 9190d6765b58.85256A69005ffe6f?OpenDocument#Children%20and%20poverty.

CHIP (2004) 'Children and Poverty – Some Questions Answered', CHIP Briefing 1: *Children and Poverty*, London: Childhood Poverty Research and Policy Centre, www.childhoodpoverty.org/index.php/action=documentfeed/doctype=pdf/id=46/.

Gordon, D., Nandy, S., Pantazis, C., Pemberton, S., and Townsend, P. (2003) *Child Poverty in the Developing World*, Bristol: Policy Press.

Mehrotra, S., Vandemoortele, J., and Delamonica, E. (2000) *Basic Services for All? Public Spending and the Social Dimensions of Poverty*, Florence: UNICEF Innocenti Research Centre, www.unicef-icdc.org/publications/pdf/basice.pdf.

Middleton, S., Ashworth, K., and Braithwaite, I. (1997) *Small Fortunes: Spending on Children, Childhood Poverty and Parental Sacrifice*, York: Joseph Rowntree Foundation.

Minujin, A., Delamonica, E., Davidziuk, A., and Gonzalez, E.D. (2006) 'The Definition of Child Poverty: A Discussion of Concepts and Measurements', *Environment & Urbanization* 18/2: 481–500.

Vandemoortele, J. (2000) *Absorbing Social Shocks, Protecting Children and Reducing Poverty*, New York: UNICEF, www.unicef.org/evaldatabase/files/Global_2000_Absorbing_Social_Shocks.pdf.

UNDP (2004) 'Dollar a Day, How Much Does It Say?', *Focus*, online bulletin of the UNDP International Poverty Centre, Brasilia, September.

UNICEF (2005) *The State of the World of the Children 2005 – Childhood under Threat*, New York: UNICEF, www.unicef.org/sowc05/english/sowc05.pdf.

UNICEF–IRC (2005) *Child Poverty in Rich Countries 2005*, UNICEF Innocenti Research Centre, Florence, www.unicef-icdc.org/publications/pdf/repcard6e.pdf.

CHINESE DEFINITIONS OF POVERTY

The People's Republic of China (PRC) contains over a fifth of the world's population, so any estimates of world poverty levels and trends are crucially dependent on the estimates for China. The Chinese 'official' poverty statistics differ significantly from those produced by international organizations such as the World Bank. The official poverty statistics show a dramatic reduction in poverty from 31 per cent of the rural population in 1978 to 3 per cent in 2000. However, the extent to which poverty has fallen in China is dependent on the method used to measure poverty (Park and Wang 2001).

The PRC uses a very austere per capita income poverty line of 676 yuan annual net income at 2002 rural prices. This is considerably below the $1 international dollar a day poverty line (equivalent to the purchasing power of 879 yuan in rural areas) used by the World Bank for the MILLENNIUM DEVELOPMENT GOALS targets (ADB 2004).

The PRC rural poverty estimates were first reported in the 1980s (Zhou 1990) and revised in 1994 (Tang 1994) based on the National Rural Sample Survey data for 1984. The poverty line was set at 200 yuan per person per day at 1984 rural prices (Yan and Wang 1996) by assuming a minimum necessary food intake of 2,400 kcal/day and costing an idealized food basket based on the actual consumption pattern of households consuming less than that. The cost of non-food items was assumed to be 40 per cent of the cost of the food basket, so the poverty line was the cost of the minimum food basket plus 40 per cent, and a person was poor if their income was below this level.

A new rural poverty line was set more recently based on 1998 national rural sample data. The minimum calorific food intake was reduced to 2,100 kcal/day and the cost of non-food items was reduced from 40 per cent to 17 per cent of the food basket costs based on a regression method proposed by the World Bank (Ravallion and Bidani 1994; Park and Wang 2001). A person living in a rural area is now defined as poor if their household income is below the poverty line and their household expenditure is also less than 1.5 times the poverty line *or* if expenditure is below the poverty line and income is less than 1.5 times the poverty line (Park and Wang 2001).

The PRC has no official urban poverty line. However the National Bureau of Statistics reported urban poverty rates in 2000 using a poverty line of 1,875 yuan annual net income per capita, which was three time the rural poverty line in that year (ADB 2004). Administrative poverty lines in urban areas below which people are entitled to Minimum Living Standard Scheme (MLSS) welfare benefits are set by the municipalities and vary across China from 3,360 yuan per capita per annum in Bejing to 2,028 yuan in Chongqing (ADB 2004).

REFERENCES

ADB (2004) *Poverty Profile of the People's Republic of China*, Manila: Asian Development Bank, www.adb.org/documents/reports/poverty_profile_prc/prc.pdf.
Park, A., and Wang, S. (2001) 'China's Poverty Statistics', *China Economic Review* 12: 384–98.
Ravallion, M., and Bidani, B. (1994) How Robust is a Poverty Profile?', *World Bank Economic Review* 8: 75–102.
Tang, P. (1994) 'Research on Poverty Criteria and the Poverty Situation in China', *Economic Research Reference Materials (jingji yanjiu cankao ziliao)* 52: 2–13.
Yan, R., and Wang, Y. (1996) 'China: Poverty in a Socialist Market Economy', in E. Øyen, S.A. Samad and S.M. Miller (eds), *Poverty: A Global Review. Handbook on Poverty Research*, Oslo and Paris: Scandinavian University Press and UNESCO.
Zhou, B. (1990) 'Review of the Poverty Alleviation Policies during the Seventh Five-year Plan Period', *Tribune of Economic Development (jingji kaifa luntan)* 12: 2–30.

CHRONIC POVERTY

This term has been favoured within the European Union by the organization Aide à Toute Détresse–Quart Monde, which has argued that

> chronic poverty results when the lack of basic security simultaneously affects several aspects of people's lives, when it is prolonged, and when it seriously compromises people's chances of regaining their rights and of resuming their responsibilities in the foreseeable future. (Wresinski Report of the Economic and Social Council of France 1987, cited in Duffy 1995: 36)

The World Bank uses the term in a different way; within countries the Bank uses income and consumption data to distinguish different groups such as the 'NEW POOR' (the direct victims of structural adjustment), the 'borderline poor' (those on the brink of the poverty line who are pushed under it by austerity measures), and the 'chronic poor' who were extremely poor before adjustment began (Wratten 1994).

REFERENCES

Duffy, K. (1995) *Social Exclusion and Human Dignity in Europe*, Council of Europe CDPS (95), 1 Rev.
Wratten, E. (1994) 'Conceptualising Urban Poverty', background paper commissioned for the United Nations Centre for Human Settlements (Habitat), *Global Report on Human Settlements 1996*, London: London School of Economics.
Wresinski, J. (1987) 'Grande pauvreté et précarité économique et sociale', *Journal officiel de la République française* 6 (February).

CLASS

A 'class' of people is defined in social science as a group identified by virtue of their economic position in society. In Marxian analyses, classes are defined in terms of their relationship to the means of production, and in developed countries poor people are primarily those who are marginalized in relation to the economic system. In the Weberian sense, classes refer to people in distinct economic categories: poverty constitutes a class either when it establishes distinct categories of social relationship (like exclusion or dependency), or when the situation of poor people is identifiably distinguishable from others. The idea of 'social class' identifies class with socio-economic status, a concept based on the linkage of class with social and occupational roles. The concept of class is used both as a means of conceptualizing the position of the poor in structural terms, and as the basis for empirical research on the distributive implications of policy (for example, relating to education or health care) (Edgell 1993).

REFERENCES

Edgell, S. (1993) *Class*, London: Routledge.

COMMAND OVER RESOURCES

'Command over resources' was the phrase used by Titmuss (1968) to refer to the ability to use resources over time. This is often referred to in terms of income and wealth, but income does not always entitle people to use resources and ownership is not always a guarantee of use. The ability to incur debts (i.e. to gain credit) may also be important as a means of commanding resources. Command over resources is related to Sen's concept of CAPABILITIES and to Drèze and Sen's use of the word 'ENTITLEMENT' (Drèze and Sen 1989).

REFERENCES

Drèze, J., and Sen, A. (1989) *Hunger and Public Action*, Oxford: Clarendon Press.
Titmuss, R.M. (1968) *Commitment to Welfare*, London, Allen & Unwin.

CONDITIONALITY

This term refers mainly to the conditions attached to the receipt of INCOME MAINTENANCE benefits as a means of regulation of behaviour. Some conditions are essential to the nature and function of specific benefits: unemployment benefits, for example, require a person to be unemployed, and disability benefits require recipients to be disabled. Some conditions, like MEANS-TESTING, are usually understood as defining criteria for distribution and modes of operation. But there may also be other conditions attached, such as residence, work record or criminality, which are not intrinsic to the benefit.

In this context, there are three main types of condition. The first relates to the administration of benefits. Requirements to treat forms as quasi-legal documents, to certify truthfulness or to signify awareness about rules relating to fraud are not necessarily effective for administration (Alabama Social Welfare 1965) but are generally used for that purpose. Second, conditions may be attached as a form of rationing or TARGETING: an example is differential treatment by age for claims relating to disability. Third, there are conditions imposed for moral or political reasons. Examples include penalties to avoid 'moral hazard' (e.g. restrictions on entitlement following voluntary unemployment or engagement in a trade dispute), and penalties for criminality. The distinction in the operation of the Poor Law between the 'deserving' and the 'undeserving' poor is the classic example.

Any of these conditions can be seen as a way of regulating the conduct or position of people who use social services. For Foucault, power is made up of 'a multiplicity of relationships of force which are inherent in the domain in which they are exercised, and which make up their organization' (Foucault 1976: 121–2). Conditionality is consequently identified with discipline or social control.

In international development, conditionality refers to those conditions, attached to a loan or to debt relief, typically imposed by the International Monetary Fund or the World Bank to the recipient country. Conditionality, since it includes highly controversial measures like privatization of key public services in the recipient country, is seen to undermine a country's authority and sovereignty to choose its own policy.

REFERENCES

Alabama Social Welfare (1965) 'A Simplified Method of Establishing Continuing Eligibility in the Adult Categories', *Alabama Social Welfare* 30 (January–February): 13–14.

Foucault, M. (1976) *Histoire de la sexualité: la volonté de savoir*, Paris: Gallimard.

IMF (2001) *Conditionality in Fund-Supported Programs – Overview*, prepared by the Policy Development and Review Department, International Monetary Fund, www.imf.org/external/np/pdr/cond/2001/eng/overview/.

CONSENSUAL METHODS

The consensual approach to the measurement of poverty was originally formulated by Mack and Lansley (1985). It is also known as the deprivation indicator approach, to distinguish it from the other empirical approach based on the public perception of poverty, which is the SUBJECTIVE POVERTY LINE or income proxy method. The deprivation indicator approach aims to discover if there are some people whose standard of living is below the minimum acceptable to society. It defines 'poverty' from the viewpoint of the public's perception of minimum necessities which no one should be without:

> This study tackles the question 'how poor is too poor?' by identifying the minimum acceptable way of life for Britain in the 1980s. Those who have no choice but to fall below this minimum level can be said to be 'in poverty'. This concept is developed in terms of those who have an enforced lack of *socially perceived* necessities. This means that the 'necessities' of life are identified by public opinion and not by, on the one hand, the views of experts or, on the other hand, the norms of behaviour *per se.* (Mack and Lansley 1985)

The approach is based on three steps: first, to identify what constitutes socially perceived necessities; second, to identify those who, because of lack of economic resources, are forced to do without these necessities; and third, to discover at what levels of income people run a greater risk of not being able to afford them. The first step is conducted with the help of a list containing examples of an extensive number of consumption items. Respondents are asked the following question:

> Please would you indicate ... the living standards you feel all adults should have in Britain today. For each item indicate which you think is necessary, and which all adults should be able to afford and which they should not have to do without.

The second step is based on answers about which items people had, or wanted but could not afford. Items defined as necessities by a specified majority of the population but which were lacked because of a shortage of money were then used to construct a deprivation index.

While Mack and Lansley found that households suffering one or two deprivations were widely distributed at all income levels, three or more deprivations were closely correlated with low income. The income levels of households suffering three or more deprivations was thus taken to be the poverty threshold in the UK at the time. It should be noted that questions such as what majority of the population must assent to an item being treated as a necessity, and how many deprivations constitute enforced poverty, are not laid down by the research method but are matters for further empirical enquiry and discovery.

Mack and Lansley's consensual approach has had a considerable impact on modern poverty research. The study was replicated in Britain in 1990 (Gordon and Pantazis 1996) and has been applied and developed by researchers in several countries (see, for example, Callan et al. 1993; Mayer and Jencks 1988; Muffels et al. 1992; Halleröd 1995).

The term consensual poverty line has also been used to describe another method, better known as the SUBJECTIVE POVERTY LINE; it is considered elsewhere under that title.

REFERENCES

Callan, T., Nolan, B., and Whelan, C.T. (1993) 'Resources, Deprivation and the Measurement of Poverty', *Journal of Social Policy* 22/2: 141–72.

Gordon, D., and Pantazis, C. (eds) (1996) *Breadline Britain in the 1990s*, Aldershot: Avebury.

Halleröd, B. (1995) 'The Truly Poor: Indirect and Direct Measurement of Consensual Poverty in Sweden', *Journal of European Social Policy* 5/2: 111–29.

Mack, J., and Lansley, S. (1985) *Poor Britain*, London: Allen & Unwin.

Mayer, S.E., and Jencks, C. (1988) 'Poverty and the Distribution of Material Hardship', *Journal of Human Resources* 24/1: 88–113.

Muffels, R., Berghman, J., and Dirven, H. (1992) 'A Multi-Method Approach to Monitor the Evolution of Poverty', *Journal of European Social Policy* 2/3: 193–213.

Veit-Wilson, J. (1987) 'Consensual Approaches to Poverty Lines and Social Security', *Journal of Social Policy* 16/2: 183–211.

CONSUMPTION

Much of the discussion on poverty and standards of living in the industrialized countries has focused, particularly in the 1980s and 1990's, on using income (amended in various ways) to measure living standards (Saunders 1996). However, Atkinson (1990) has argued that what determines people's STANDARD OF LIVING is what they consume rather than what they receive as income. Total consumption may appear to be a natural choice for a single index of economic resources since income may understate or overstate the level of living in a household (Atkinson 1991).

Consumption, like income, is a difficult concept to define. Consumption is the process of 'using up' goods and services. However, there are different types of goods and services and different definitions of 'using up'. The Australian Bureau of Statistics (ABS 1995) has proposed the following framework of concepts related to consumption:

> Goods may be non-durable consumer goods which are immediately used up in the process of satisfying needs and wants (e.g. food) or they may be consumer durables that are used up over a longer period during which time they provide a service to the household (e.g. car refrigerator).

Goods and services may be used up in a number of ways. From the household's point of view they may be consumed within the household or they may be transferred (in cash or in kind) to other households and private institutions who then undertake the actual consumption.

Consumption that takes place within the household is collectively termed actual final consumption. This consists of consumption of goods and services purchased in the market place, consumption of goods and services received as in-kind receipts and consumption of services provided from within the household. Consumption that is 'consumed' outside the household is termed current transfers outlaid (excluding direct taxes). These may be outlaid either in cash or in kind. Consumption is usually measured according to the market value of the goods and services consumed. For final consumption expenditure, the value recorded is that paid out by the household in return for the goods and services. It therefore includes the value of indirect taxes paid on purchased goods.

The Australian Bureau of Statistics is trying to get an international agreement on a broad definition of consumption (ABS 1995):

> The concept of consumption is based on the 'using up' of services and non-durable goods. In addition to final consumption expenditure, where households purchase non-durable goods and services, it also covers consumption of goods and services received in-kind from government, other households and private organizations. It also includes the using up of goods and services provided from within the household. This concept of consumption is therefore much broader then one which is based solely on the current consumption

expenditure of the household in the market place. Also included in the concept of consumption is the transfer of economic resources from one household to other households and private institutions such as charities. The transfers may be compulsory, such as some child support payments, or voluntary, such as gifts of money or goods.

Unfortunately many international comparative studies of consumption have tended to use a much narrower definition based on current expenditure of the household or individual (see, for example, Eurostat 1990; Hagenaars et al. 1994). The failure to take account of consumption of goods and services received in kind from government other households and private organizations makes it difficult to compare the results of such studies.

REFERENCES

ABS (1995) *A Provisional Framework for Household Income. Consumption, Saving and Wealth*, Australian Bureau of Statistics, Canberra: Australian Government Publishing Service.

Atkinson, A.B. (1990) 'Comparing Poverty Rates Internationally: Lessons from Recent Studies in OECD Countries', Suntory–Toyota International Centre for Economics and Related Disciplines, WSPI53, London School of Economics, London.

Atkinson, A.B. (1991) 'Comparing Poverty Rates Internationally: Lessons from Recent Studies in Developing Countries', *World Bank Economic Review* 5: 3–21.

Eurostat (1990) *Poverty in Figures: Europe in the Early 1980s*, Luxembourg: Eurostat.

Hagenaars, A.J.M., de Vos, K., and Zaidi, M.A. (1994) *Poverty Statistics in the Late 1980s: Research Based on Micro-data*, Luxembourg: Eurostat.

Saunders, P. (1996) *Development of Indicative Budget Standards for Australia: Project Outline and Research Methods*, BSU Working Paper Series No. 1, SPRC, University of New South Wales.

CONTEXTUAL POVERTY

Most poverty research is about the poor – that is, their numbers, their characteristics, their modes of life, their spending patterns, and so on. This kind of research and policy orientation casts the poor as set off from the rest of society, which, in important ways, they are. Hence, the notions of MARGINALITY, participation blockages and EXCLUSION are significant for thinking about poverty. Another way of understanding poverty is to analyse it in relation to a society's cultural, economic and political structures. In contextual poverty analysis the non-poor world and its institutions and their role in creating, sustaining and reducing poverty, are as important to understand as an insulated world of the poor. Within this perspective, the interaction between the poor and the non-poor is brought into focus, and poverty is seen as it is formed and treated by the non-poor world and its institutions. This important perspective has been largely neglected in research, thereby obscuring causes and processes involved in the production and continuance of poverty.

REFERENCES

CROP (1998) *Annual Report 1997*, Bergen: Comparative Research Programme on Poverty.

CONVERSION CAPACITY

This refers to the ability to transform income into the means of meeting requirements (e.g. calorific intake). Conversion efficiency refers to the relative cost per unit of conversion; because poor people pay more for similar goods than others, their conversion efficiency is lower (Lipton 1995) ENGEL COEFFICIENT.

REFERENCES

Lipton, M. (1995) 'Growing Points in Poverty Research: Labour Issues', in G. Rodgers (ed.), *The Poverty Agenda and the ILO*, Geneva: ILO.

CULTURE OF POVERTY

This theory was developed from the studies of Oscar Lewis in Mexico, Puerto Rico and New York (Lewis 1964, 1968). Lewis summarized some of the major characteristics as follows:

> On the family level, the major traits of the culture of poverty are the absence of childhood as a specially prolonged and protected stage in the life cycle, early initiation into sex, free unions or consensual marriages, a relatively high incidence of the abandonment of wives and children, a trend toward female- or mother-centred families ... a strong disposition to authoritarianism, lack of privacy, verbal emphasis on family solidarity which is only rarely achieved because of sibling rivalry, and competition for limited goods and maternal affection.

On the level of the individual, the major characteristics are a strong feeling of marginality, of helplessness, of dependence and inferiority. Other traits include a high incidence of maternal deprivation, or orality, or weak ego structure, confusion of sexual identification, a lack of impulse control, a strong present-time orientation with relatively little ability to defer gratification and to plan for the future, a sense of resignation and fatalism, a widespread belief in male superiority, and a high tolerance for psychological pathology of all sorts. (Lewis 1968: 53)

According to Lewis, the 'culture of poverty' represents the adaptation and the reaction of the poor to their 'marginal' status. This adaptation reflects problems of integration into modern society owing to migration from rural areas, and the adaptation of 'rural' and 'traditional' patterns of behaviour. This associates poverty with migrants and those who come from 'underdeveloped' cultures – which are believed both to 'lag behind' and to be a hindrance to 'development'. Lewis emphasized that his thesis referred to groups which did not possess a vigorous base of ethnic or class identity that could serve as support in the face of difficulties. Lewis argued that this culture was likely to trap poor people in their poverty, and could prove persistent even after the poverty which caused it had been alleviated. His emphasis on personal characteristics, however, has been attacked on the basis that it is not really about a 'culture' at all (Valentine 1968).

Lewis's conception of culture of poverty was taken to justify a view of poverty as attributable to the conduct and character of the poor rather than their economic circumstances (Alvarez Leguizamón 2002). It emphasises negative and devalued attributes of the poor, instead of explaining the causes of production and reproduction of poverty in structural terms.

REFERENCES

Alvarez Leguizamón, S. (2002) 'La pacificación de la multiculturalidad globalizada. Recomposición de campos del saber y nuevas formas de intervención social', in B. Lorente Molina and C.V. Zambrano (eds), *Estudios introductorios en relaciones interétnicas*, Sede Bogotá: Universidad Nacional de Colombia.
Lewis, O. (1964) *The Children of Sanchez*, Harmondsworth: Penguin.
Lewis, O. (1968) *La vida*, London: Panther.
Valentine, C. (1968) *Culture and Poverty*, Chicago: University of Chicago Press.

CYCLE OF DEPRIVATION

The circumstances in which poor parenting, it is held, generates a cycle of inadequate development, and further poor parenting. This term was coined by Keith Joseph, a former Secretary of State for Social Services in the UK, who argued that 'parents who were themselves deprived in one or more ways in childhood become in turn the parents of another generation of deprived children' (cited in Holman 1978: 117). The research subsequently sponsored by Joseph did not confirm the basic contention (Brown and Madge 1982).

REFERENCES

Brown, M., and Madge, N. (1982) *Despite the Welfare State*, London: Heinemann.
Holman, R. (1978) *Poverty: Explanations of Social Deprivation*, Oxford: Martin Robertson.

D

DEPENDENCY

The sociologist Georg Simmel argued that 'poverty', in sociological terms, referred not to all people on low incomes but to those who were dependent (Simmel 1908). In the literature relating to developed economies, the term 'dependency' is primarily used for people who receive social security benefits and transfer payments. The *dependency ratio* consists of the proportion of a population that is not economically active and that as a result consumes resources produced by others. *Structural dependency* consists of dependency that is required as a result of social or industrial organization: the dependency of pensioners is structural, rather than being based on individual capacity. The term 'dependency' has negative connotations: financial dependency is sometimes taken to imply psychological dependency. Titmuss argued that 'states of dependency' should be seen, by contrast, as a normal and accepted part of social existence (Titmuss 1968).

In development studies, dependency is related primarily to the relationship between rich and poor countries. DEPENDENCY THEORY represents a view that some countries are peripheral to the world economy and so in a relation of economic dependence (Samad 1996).

REFERENCES

Samad, S.A. (1996) 'The Present Situation in Poverty Research', in E. Øyen, S.A. Samad and S.M. Miller (eds), *Poverty: A Global Review. Handbook on Poverty Research*, Oslo and Paris: Scandinavian University Press and UNESCO.
Simmel, G. (1908) 'The Poor', reprinted in *Social Problems* 13 (1965) 118–39.
Titmuss, R. (1968) *Commitment to Welfare*, London: Allen & Unwin.

DEPENDENCY CULTURE

The term 'dependency culture' has been used to refer to the willingness of poor people to be financially dependent. Although it is commonly represented as a recent development, the idea is ancient: for example, Benjamin Franklin wrote of the situation in England in 1766 that

> there is no country in the world in which the poor are more idle, dissolute, drunken, and insolent. The day you passed that Act [the Poor Law], you took away from before their eyes the greatest of all inducements to industry, frugality, and sobriety, by giving them a dependence on somewhat else than a careful accumulation during youth and health, for support in age and sickness. (cited in Williams 1944)

The proposition that poor relief inculcates dependency has two main components. The first is that individuals respond directly to the INCENTIVES or disincentives of the benefits system in their decision to work. The second element is the belief that this behaviour is prolonged, with the effect that poverty becomes persistent. This view is not supported by the evidence: dependency tends to be episodic (Walker 1994), and the composition of the dependent population fluctuates (Buhr and Leibfried 1995).

REFERENCES

Buhr, P., and Leibfried, S. (1995) 'What a Difference a Day Makes: The Significance for Social Policy of the Duration of Social Assistance Receipt', in G. Room (ed.), *Beyond the Threshold*, Bristol: Policy Press.
Walker, R. (1994) *Poverty Dynamics*, Aldershot: Avebury.
Williams, H.W. (1944) 'Benjamin Franklin and the Poor Laws', *Social Service Review* 18/1: 77–91.

DEPENDENCY THEORY

Dependency theory emerged in Latin America in the 1960s and 1970s. It argues that

- underdevelopment is directly connected with the expansion of industrialized countries;
- DEVELOPMENT and underdevelopment are different aspects of the same process;

- underdevelopment is neither a stage in a gradual process towards development, nor a precondition, but a condition in itself;
- dependency is not limited to relations among countries, but also shapes structures within societies. (Blomstron and Hettne 1990)

Immanuel Wallerstein (1979) analyses capitalism as a system based on an economic, social, political and cultural relationship that came into view in the late Middle Ages and developed into a world system and a world economy. This approach, distinguishing a centre from a periphery and a semi-periphery, stresses the hegemonic role of central economies in organizing the capitalist system. There is an interconnected relationship of global poverty with social polarization and inequality between and within countries.

Andre Gunder Frank (1967, 1976) argued that relationships of dependency in the global market were reflected in relations of structured dependence within states and between communities. Although there are differences among dependency approaches, poverty is commonly explained as depending on the particular circumstances of the social structure, labour market, the condition of exploitation of the labour force, and the concentration of income.

Stages in the history of Latin America can be identified in terms of the dominant relationships of production in society (Sunkel and Paz 1975). For example, Cardoso and Faletto (1969) identify plantation and mining with semi-servitude or slavery, and the structure of land tenure explains the extended rural poverty that characterized some dependent countries in the nineteenth and twentieth centuries. Others, discussing industrial processes in Latin America, focus on poverty as a direct consequence of the process of exclusion from the urban labour market. For others, dependency is defined by the increasing importance of foreign capital along with the accumulation of capital in few hands, which drives people into mass impoverishment due to the concentration of income. Ruy Mauro Marini (1977) argues that dependency is characterized by the super-exploitation of labour.

REFERENCES

Cardoso, F.H., and Faletto, E. (1969) *Dependencia y Desarrollo en América Latina*, México: Siglo XXI.

Blomströn, M., and Ente, B. (1990) *La teoría del desarrollo en transición*, México: Fondo de Cultura Ecónomica.

Gunder Frank, A. (1967) *Capitalism and Underdevelopment in Latin America*, New York: Monthly Review Press.

Gunder Frank, A. (1976) *América Latina: Subdesarrollo o revolución*, México: Edición Era.

Marini, R. (1977) *Dialéctica de la dependencia*, México: Edición Era.

Sunkel, O., and Paz, P. (1975) *El subdesarrollo latinoamericano y la teoría del desarrollo*, México: Siglo XXI.

Wallerstein, I. (1979) *The Capitalist World Economy*, Cambridge: Cambridge University Press.

DEPRIVATION

Deprivation refers to a lack of welfare, often understood in terms of material goods and resources but equally applicable to psychological factors. Brown and Madge (1982) argue that

> Deprivations are loosely regarded as unsatisfactory and undesirable circumstances, whether material, emotional, physical or behavioural, as recognized by a fair degree of societal consensus. Deprivations involve a lack of something generally held to be desirable – an adequate income, good health, etc. – a lack which is associated to a greater or lesser extent with some degree of suffering.

Implicit in the statement that something is 'lacking' is some norm or standard which determines whether or not a person has sufficient. Townsend defines deprivation in comparative terms:

> Deprivation may be defined as a state of observable and demonstrable disadvantage relative to the local community or the wider society or nation to which an individual, family or group belongs. The idea has come to be applied to conditions (that is, physical, emotional or social states or circumstances) rather than resources and to specific and not only general circumstances, and therefore can be distinguished from the concept of poverty.

In order to measure poverty accurately, it is necessary to measure both resources and deprivation. Following Townsend (1979), poor people/households have increasingly been identified as those who both have a low 'standard of living' and low resources (e.g. Callan et al. 1993). Standard of living is generally measured using a deprivation index, and resources are usually estimated using disposable income or gross expenditure (MacGregor and Borooah 1992; Townsend 1993). A variety of statistical techniques can then be used to determine the level of the poverty threshold below which people are defined as 'poor'. Those who fall below this threshold suffer from multiple rather than single deprivations.

REFERENCES

Brown, M., and Madge, N. (1982) *Despite the Welfare State*, London: Heinemann.
Callan, T., Nolan, B., and Whelan, C.T. (1993) 'Resources, Deprivation and the Measurement of Poverty', *Journal of Social Policy* 22/2: 141–72.
MacGregor, P.P.L., and Borooah, V.K. (1992) 'Is Low Income or Low Expenditure a Better Indicator of Whether or Not a Household is Poor: Some Results from the 1985 Family Expenditure Survey', *Journal of Social Policy* 21/1: 53–70.
Townsend, P. (1979) *Poverty in the United Kingdom*, Harmondsworth: Penguin.
Townsend, P. (1987) 'Deprivation', *Journal of Social Policy* 16/2: 125–46.
Townsend, P. (1993) *The International Analysis of Poverty*, New York: Harvester Wheatsheaf.

DESERVING POOR

In many nineteenth-century analyses of poverty, particularly those by the CHARITY ORGANIZATION SOCIETY in Britain, a distinction was made between the deserving and the undeserving poor. The former were said to owe their condition to 'blameless misfortune' such as illness, disability, accident, death of a breadwinner, orphanhood, and so on. The latter were those judged to have fallen into poverty because they had failed to make proper provision for themselves during their life and were thus responsible for their misfortune. Voluntary or charitable committees, officials or caseworkers should decide the applicant's deservingness, and only the deserving poor should be offered relief or charity. Although such judgements were notionally based upon moral judgements, in practice they often re-flected labour market value: the deserving were groups such as the aged, disabled people, widows and orphans whose labour market value was marginal; the undeserving were generally the able-bodied males. Gradually this categorization fell into disuse, though arguably twenty-first-century attitudes to the poor retain such moral distinc-tions, albeit in a more subtle way. Nowadays the concept is more often used to refer to a particular form of social intervention, where the deserving poor are required to demonstrate their willingness to fulfil social responsibilities in order to receive assistance from the state: CONDITIONALITY.

DESTITUTION

Destitution refers to a total, or virtually complete, absence of resources. Although this is indicative of extreme poverty, it is not necessarily equivalent; a person may become destitute immediately through fire or natural disaster, while someone in chronic or extreme poverty may have experienced long-term malnutrition and disadvantage. The English POOR LAW (1601–1948) offered poor relief only to those who were destitute, rather than to those who were identified as poor; poverty outside the scope of the Poor Law was widespread (Webb and Webb 1927). Inventories were made of any goods remaining to paupers, and they renounced them as a condition of relief in the workhouse (King 1997).

REFERENCES

King, P. (1997) 'Pauper Inventories and the Material Lives of the Poor in the 18th and early 19th Centuries', in T. Hitchcock, P. King and P. Sharpe (eds), *Chronicling Poverty: The Voices and Strategies of the English Poor, 1640–1840*, London: Macmillan.
Webb, S., and Webb, B. (1927) *English Local Government: The Old Poor Law*, London: Frank Cass.

DEVELOPMENT

Development is conceived to be a continuing transformation of cultural, political, social, and economic conditions, patterns or situations of a region, society or country considered underdeveloped. Poverty is often linked to underdevelopment, and it should consequently be alleviated by development or developmental initiatives.

Early on, development was seen as a gradual economic change which would reflect the economic history of those countries branded as developed willing to improve people's standard of life, and remove any form of poverty (Rostow 1970). Some authors see development as a discourse imposing a particular way of life to the underdeveloped countries, where 'progress' is meant to be a unique, irreversible and ineluctable process. This discourse emerged at the onset of the post-war period with the establishment of the United Nations, as part of the growing influence of the USA over global geopolitics (Escobar 1995; Sachs 1999; Ferguson 1997).

In the 1950s, development and poverty alleviation were thought to be achieved by substantial investments in physical capital and infrastructure (World Bank 2000: 7). Increasing GDP per capita in a given country was held to be the benchmark for measuring progress. However, a growing body of evidence in the 1970s disputed the likelihood of ever alleviating poverty by growth alone; instead a 'redistribution with growth' was emphasized (BID–OVE 2002: 2). In addition, 'extra-economic factors' – the so-called social and cultural aspects – played a major role in promoting development by then (Ander-Egg 1981, 44–5). Development programmes, promoted by international agencies, were focused on clearing the hurdles linked to the mental, attitudinal and behavioural, aspects which had been as-signed to those individuals presumed to be underdeveloped, as a way to alleviate poverty. Individuals, cultures and societies characterized as underdeveloped, are said to be in an 'inferior' stage of evolution and values, and hence are required to promote changes so as to usher in 'modern' cultural values.

The development approaches to the 'social issue' that prevailed in Latin American societies from the 1950s to the 1970s believed that the industrial development model was a key central organizer of social processes. This encompassed a protective vision of 'universality' and equal care for all (even though the result tended in practice to be an incomplete welfare state) that inspired social policy and the crea-tion and operation of security systems that were later rejected and dismantled by neoliberal reforms (Brito Leal Ivo 2005: 85).

In the 1980s, the evidence suggested that economic growth was not necessarily connected with social development; hence the notion of development at minimal level was promoted by satisfying the minimum basic needs (Alvarez Leguizamón 2005; Sachs 1999: 9) of the poor through TARGETING. By the 1990s, 'the thought of develop-ment has focused on the capabilities and liberties as definitive goals' (BID–OVE 2002: 2) strongly swayed by the thinking of Amartya Sen, who asserts that poverty means not only the lack of resources but also a lack of capabilities. From this point onwards, the new stage of development is referred to as HUMAN DEVELOPMENT. Sen believes that 'the expansion of liberties is (i) *the main purpose* and (ii) *the main means* for development ... enrichment of human liberties is to include the removal of this person's deprivations. The various rights and opportunities add to the expansion of human liberty and to development' (Sen 2000: 36–7). This vision of a diminished poverty has been challenged since capabilities are promoted in an increasingly unequal world, with a growing reduction in opportunities, weak social rights and therefore limitation of liberties.

REFERENCES

Alvarez Leguizamón, S. (2005) 'Los discursos minimistas sobre las necesidades básicas y los umbrales de ciudadanía como reproductores de la pobreza', in S. Alvarez Leguizamón (ed.), *Trabajo y producción de la pobreza en Latinoamérica y el Caribe: estructuras, discursos y actores*, Buenos Aires: CLACSO/CROP.

Ander-Egg, E. (1981) *Metodología y práctica del desarrollo de la comunidad*, Buenos Aires: Editorial Humanitas.

BID–OVE (2002) RE-258, Reseña del trabajo del OVE relativo a la eficacia en función del desarrollo, Oficialmente distribuido al Directorio Ejecutivo el 9 de enero de 2002, Washington DC: Inter-American Development Bank.

Brito Leal Ivo, A. (2005) 'The Redefinition of the Social Issue and the Rhetoric on Poverty during the 1990s', in A. Cimadamore, H. Dean and J. Siqueira (eds), *The Poverty of the State*, Buenos Aires: CLACSO Books.

INDES, BID (2005) *El desarrollo: sus dimensiones y sus dinámicas*, Material del curso en línea de formación de profesores tutores del INDES sobre gerencia para resultados en el desarrollo, Módulo I, Washington DC: Inter-American Development Bank, Inter-American Institute for Social Development.

Escobar, A. (1995) *Encountering Development: The Making and Unmaking of the Third World*, Princeton NJ: Princeton University Press.

Ferguson, J. (1997) 'Antropology and its Evil Twin "Development" in the Constitution of a Discipline', in F. Cooper and R. Packard (eds), *International Development and the Social Sciences*, Berkeley: University of California Press.

Rostow, W. (1970) *Las etapas del crecimiento económico*, México: Fondo de Cultura Económica.

Sachs, W. (1999) *Planet Dialectics: Explorations in Environment and Development*, London: Zed Books.

Sen, A. (2000) *Development as Freedom*, New York: Anchor Books.

UN (1953) 'Desarrollo de la Comunidad y Desarrollo Económico', CN 5379, *Revista de las Naciones Unidas*, 29.

DIRECT AND INDIRECT MEASURES OF POVERTY

Ringen (1985, 1987, 1988) distinguishes between direct and indirect approaches to the conceptualization and measurement of poverty. He suggests that poverty studies frequently combine a direct definition of poverty with an indirect measure and that this 'causes there to be no logical line of deduction between definition and measurement and ... renders the statistics produced invalid' (1988: 351). For Ringen, the challenge facing poverty researchers is 'to re-establish the correspondence between definition and measurement by both defining and measuring poverty directly' (1988: 360). In a later paper, Ringen (1995) discusses direct and indirect approaches to the measurement of well-being. In apparent contrast to the position taken in his earlier work on poverty, he suggests that indirect measures of well-being are to be preferred over direct measures.

The distinction Ringen makes has gained considerable currency in the literature on poverty and has been widely adopted (see, e.g., Callan et al. 1993; Halleröd et al. 1997; McGregor and Borooah 1992; Nolan and Whelan 1996; Van den Bosch 1993). Writers have suggested that the main issue which divides poverty researchers is 'whether to study lack of welfare indirectly through incomes and/or other resources, or directly through living conditions or consumption' (Kangas and Ritakallio 1995: 1).

While the direct–indirect distinction has become part of the vocabulary of discourse on poverty, it is important to note that Ringen characterizes that distinction differently at different times. He suggests, for example, that:

1. To define poverty directly is to say that 'people are poor if they, in fact, have a way of life which is below [some] defined minimum standard, irrespective of what has determined this way of life', while to define poverty indirectly is 'to say that people are poor if they do not have the necessary resources, capabilities, or rights to achieve what is defined as a minimum standard in their way of life' (Ringen 1987: 145–6, 145).
2. Direct concepts 'define welfare in terms of intrinsic goods, such as consumption or quality of life' whereas indirect concepts define welfare in terms of resources which do not have intrinsic value but which we can use to produce or otherwise acquire things of intrinsic value (Ringen 1988: 355).
3. 'Poverty can be defined and measured either directly (in terms of consumption) or indirectly (in terms of income)' (Ringen 1988: 351).

4. Direct approaches to the measurement of well-being make use of information that describes the outcome of the choices people have made, 'whereas indirect approaches make use of information that describes the choices they can make' (Ringen 1995: 7).

5. The direct concept of welfare is 'not an alternative concept to income but a broader concept which includes income' (Ringen 1985: 104).

Ringen consistently suggests that the 'relative deprivation concept is a direct concept of poverty', and that the 'subsistence minimum concept is an indirect concept of poverty' (1987: 152).

Kohl (1996: 280 n5) questions whether Ringen is right in classifying relative deprivation definitions, such as the definition put forward by Townsend (1979), under 'direct concepts of poverty', since Townsend 'refers to (a lack of) resources as a determinant of the inability to participate in normal social activities'. A similar point can be made in respect of Ringen's classification of the 'subsistence minimum concept ... developed by Seebohm Rowntree as an indirect concept of poverty' (Ringen 1987: 146). Rowntree's (1901) definition of primary poverty refers both to 'the minimum necessaries for the maintenance of merely physical efficiency' and to the 'earnings' required to obtain those minimum necessaries.

Ringen (1988: 356) suggests that if poverty 'is defined directly it should be measured directly' and that if 'it is defined indirectly, it should be measured indirectly'. Confusingly he also argues that poverty should be measured using information both on resources and on way of life (or consumption) (Ringen 1987, 1988). The use of a combination of way of life (or consumption) and resource indicators is sometimes presented as 'a cautious step' in the direction of direct measurement, albeit one 'which fails short of direct measurement proper' (Ringen 1988: 361). However, it is also said to be consistent with an account of poverty which makes 'no choice' between direct and indirect understandings, but instead defines poverty 'as a combination of the two' (Ringen 1987: 146).

REFERENCES

Callan, T., Nolan, B., and Whelan, C.T. (1993) 'Resources, Deprivation and the Measurement of Poverty', *Journal of Social Policy* 22/2: 141–72.

Halleröd, B. (1995) 'The Truly Poor: Indirect and Direct Measurement of Consensual Poverty in Sweden', *Journal of European Social Policy* 5/2: 111–29.

Halleröd, B., Bradshaw, J., and Holmes, H. (1997) 'Adapting the Consensual Definition of Poverty, in D. Gordon and C. Pantazis (eds), *Breadline Britain in the 1990s*, Aldershot: Avebury.

Kangas, O., and Ritakailio, V.M. (1995) *Different Methods – Different Results? Approaches to Multidimensional Poverty*, Helsinki: National Research and Development Centre for Welfare and Health.

Kohl, J. (1996) 'The European Community: Diverse Images of Poverty', in E. Øyen S.A. Samad and S.M. Miller (eds), *Poverty: A Global Review. Handbook on Poverty Research*, Oslo and Paris: Scandinavian University Press and UNESCO.

McGregor, P.P.L., and Borooah, K. (1992) 'Is Low Income or Low Expenditure a Better Indicator of Whether or Not a Household is Poor: Some Results from the 1985 Family Expenditure Survey', *Journal of Social Policy* 21/1: 53–69.

Nolan, B., and Whelan, C.T. (1996) *Resources, Deprivation and Poverty*, Oxford: Clarendon Press.

Ringen, S. (1985) 'Toward a Third Stage in the Measurement of Poverty, *Acta Sociologica* 28/2: 99–113.

Ringen, S. (1987) *The Possibility of Politics*, Oxford: Clarendon Press.

Ringen, S. (1988) 'Direct and Indirect Measures of Poverty', *Journal of Social Policy* 17/3: 351–65.

Ringen, S. (1995) 'Well-being, Measurement and Preferences', *Acta Sociologica* 38: 3–15.

Rowntree, B.S. (1901) *Poverty: A Study of Town Life*, London: Macmillan.

Townsend, P. (1979) *Poverty in the United Kingdom*, Harmondsworth: Penguin.

Van den Bosch, K. (1993) 'Poverty Measures in Comparative Research', in J. Berghman and B. Cantillon (eds), *The European Face of Social Security*, Aldershot: Avebury.

DISABILITY AND POVERTY

Traditionally disability has been viewed as a state of being, a personal limitation understood primarily as a medical phenomenon. Based on the work of Wood (1981), the World Health Organization adopted a definition of disability which refers to a restriction or lack of ability to perform an activity in the manner or within the range considered normal for a human being, this restriction resulting from an impairment (an impairment being a loss or abnormality of anatomical, physiological or psychological structure or function). This view of disability is commonly referred to as the 'individual model of disability' or the 'medical model of disability'.

The interaction between disability (in this sense of the word) and poverty is twofold. First, poverty has been highlighted as one of the main causes of disability in the world (WHO 1995) (HEALTH AND POVERTY). A lack of resources at both community and individual levels results in unsatisfactory housing, an absence of clean water and effective sanitation, dietary deficiencies and hazardous work conditions, all of which make people susceptible to physical or psychological impairment or disability. Second, the occurrence of a disability may start or accelerate the collapse of a family's economic base, disability thus accounting for a 'substantial' proportion of poverty (Townsend 1979). There are two factors involved here: a fall in overall earning power, and additional financial costs which disabled people incur because of their disability – such as for special equipment, extra heating or clothing, individual transport, or for cleaning, cooking or personal care services. Attempts to gauge these extra costs are methodologically fraught with difficulties, and the results are dependent not just on the type, nature and severity of the disabilities but also on cultural factors and the availability and cost of social, educational and health services (Horn 1981; Chetwynd 1985; Graham 1987).

A second interpretation of the term 'disability' is provided by the 'economic model of disability'. This is grounded in the belief that it is not professional (medical) knowledge which adequately represents the reality of disability. Disability here refers to the economic disadvantages imposed by capitalist society on an individual with an impairment.

A third definition of disability is presented by disabled people and their own organizations and is known as the 'social model of disability' (sometimes referred to as the 'socio-political model of disability'). Rather than relating disability to a person's individual capacities, the social model of disability regards disability as a form of social exclusion which people with impairments experience as a result of the way that society is organized. Disability in this interpretation refers to the 'loss or limitation of opportunities to take part in the normal life of the community on an equal level with others due to physical and social barriers' (DPI 1982).

The DPI definition does not deny that some illnesses may have disabling consequences but the insistence is that disability itself is nothing to do with the body (Oliver 1996). Disability here is not a state of being; it is a social and political category, stemming from the failure of a structured social environment to adjust to the needs and aspirations of certain of its citizens, thus denying them their rights through processes of inequity and injustice. In particular, it is this politicization of disability which marks out the social model of disability from the medical or the economic model. The interaction between poverty and the social model of disability is similar to that with the economic model of disability: poverty is associated with people with impairments because of their exclusion from the ability to earn a living on a par with able-bodied peers due to the way societies are organized. Unlike the economic model of disability, however, which focuses on poverty-alleviating interventions at the level of the individual with an impairment, the social model of disability focuses on interventions at the level of society. What is required to combat the poverty of disabled people from a social model perspective is a social commitment to EQUALITY built upon a framework of civil rights. In order to eradicate the structural and attitudinal barriers that exist in society, financial and other forms of help would therefore be geared to the retention or achievement of integrated employment and arrangements which would include disabled people as an integral part of society.

Not all disability theorists are in agreement as to the exclusiveness of each of the conceptual schemes of disability and some accept that disability could be considered as an unstable relationship between a number of interrelated elements: those of the physical, psychological or sensory impairments of an individual and the social environment, artificial barriers and attitudes which prevent the individual from playing a full part in the life of the community.

REFERENCES

Chetwynd, J. (1985) 'Some Costs of Caring at Home for an Intellectually Handicapped Child', *Australian and New Zealand Journal of Developmental Disability* 2/1: 35–40.

DPI (1982), *Proceedings of the First World Congress Disabled People's International*, Singapore: Disabled People's International.

Finkelstein, V. (1981) 'Disability and the Helper/Helped Relationship: An Historical View', in A. Brechin, P. Liddiard and J. Swain (eds), *Handicap in a Social World*, London: Hodder & Stoughton/Open University Press.

Graham, S. (1987) 'The Extra Costs Borne by Families Who Have a Child with a Disability', *SWRC Reports and Proceedings* 68, University of New South Wales.

Horn, R. (1981) 'Extra Costs of Disablement Background for an Australian Study', *SWRC Reports and Proceedings* 13, University of New South Wales.

Oliver, M. (1996) 'Defining Impairment and Disability Issues at Stake', in C. Barnes and G. Mercer (eds), *Exploring the Divide: Illness and Disability*, Leeds: Disability Press.

Sutherland, G. (1984) *Ability Merit and Measurement: Mental Testing and English Education 1880–1940*, Oxford: Clarendon Press.

Townsend, P. (1979) *Poverty in the United Kingdom*, Harmondsworth: Penguin.

WHO (1995) *The World Health Report 1995: Bridging the Gaps*, Geneva: WHO.

Wood, P. (1981) *International Classification of Impairments, Disabilities and Handicaps*, Geneva: WHO.

DISADVANTAGE

A social relationship in which the position of one person is worse because the position of another person is relatively better. People may be disadvantaged in many contexts: in relation to poverty, the term most frequently refers to command over resources, the structure of opportunities and the distribution of power in a society. The term is directly equivalent to the concept of INEQUALITY in a social context (Spicker 1988).

REFERENCES

Spicker, P. (1988) *Principles of Social Welfare*, London: Routledge.

DISQUALIFICATION (*LA DISQUALIFICATION SOCIALE*)

Paugam describes social disqualification as

> a process which progressively brings together various fringes of the population in the sphere of professional inactivity and social assistance, while increasing for them the risk of an accumulation of difficulties or handicaps and the probability that they will increasingly experience a breakdown of social ties. (1993, 31–4)

Social disqualification has three elements:

- *Fragility* People within this category are subject to the experience of unemployment, problems in integration, and the abrupt loss of housing, which occurs because they live in depressed areas. They feel a sense of humiliation and failure, losing the hope to find a place, and fearful of falling further. They do not wish to be considered as recipients of welfare. They attempt to improve their social status.
- *Dependency* People within this category, after vain attempts and useless training courses, have no options but to accept the status of claimant. They depend on help provided by the collectivity for the poorest. Most have given up trying to find work. They justify their DEPENDENCY on assistance by citing their responsibilities to their children, health problems, and the difficulty in working.

They maintain social links with those responsible for their help and often seek to cooperate with them. However, their status as recipients remains socially unvalued and only permits them to avoid destitution.

- *Breakdown* This concerns a category of the population which has accumulated handicaps: lack of employment, poor health, bad housing, no stable income, broken family links. This is the final phase of social disqualification, produced by an accumulation of failures, which leads directly to marginalisation. Marginals have lost most of their social ties, including with those responsible for their welfare.

REFERENCES

Paugam, S. (1993) *La disqualification sociale: essai sur la nouvelle pauvreté*, Paris: PUF.

DISWELFARE

The view that society produces 'diswelfare' is a structural explanation of the causes of poverty. Titmuss (1968: ch. 11) argued that people in poverty were the casualties of a competitive society. If there is not enough work, or if work is available only on restrictive terms, then some people will be unemployed. If people have to be able-bodied in order to be eligible for work, then disabled people will be disadvantaged. Titmuss suggested that this could be seen as a form of 'diswelfare', the converse of a position in which others in society, and indeed society as a whole, produced material goods; there would be losers as well as gainers.

REFERENCES

Titmuss, R.M. (1968) *Commitment to Welfare*, London: Allen & Unwin.

E

ECONOMIC DEFINITIONS OF POVERTY

Literally dozens of economic poverty lines, poverty gaps and poverty orderings have been proposed (for discussion see Sen 1976; Atkinson 1987; Foster and Shorrocks 1988a, 1988b; Jenkins and Lambert 1993). In general these indices define poverty in terms of INCOME (or, more rarely, expenditure) distribution; the poor are defined as those people/households with an income below a certain threshold level irrespective of their standard of living. Thus economic poverty lines define the 'poor' as those with a low income even if they have a high standard of living. Most economic poverty indices are really measures of income inequality rather than poverty (Townsend 1979).

Many studies that make use of economic definitions of poverty provide information about income inequality; however, they are often of more limited use for understanding the distribution and dynamics of poverty. For this reason they are often termed 'income poverty' studies. They frequently exhibit the following problems:

1. They contain no measure of standard of living external to income.
2. They generally, due to limitations in the data, use only a narrow definition of disposable income which takes little account of non-monetary income and income transfers in kind from free or subsidized public services (free education, health services, etc.) (Evandrou et al. 1992; Bramley and Smart 1993).
3. They make use of an 'arbitrary' equivalization procedure to adjust income for different types and sizes of households (Bradbury 1989; Whiteford 1985).
4. They often fail to take full account of cost-of-living differences between areas and social groups (Borooah et al. 1994).

Nevertheless, most of our knowledge of poverty in many countries is primarily based on research that uses economic definitions of poverty.

REFERENCES

Atkinson, A.B. (1987) 'On the Measurement of Poverty', *Econometrica* 55: 749–64.

Borooah, V.B., et al. (1994) 'Cost-of-Living Differences between Regions of the United Kingdom', *Ulster Papers in Public Policy and Management* 34, University of Ulster.

Bradbury, B. (1989) 'Family Size Equivalence Scales and Survey Evaluations of Income and Well-Being', *Journal of Social Policy* 18/3: 383–408.

Bramley, G., and Smart, G. (1993) *Who Benefits from Local Services? Comparative Evidence from Different Local Authorities*, Welfare State Programme Discussion Paper WSP/91, London: LSE.

Evandrou, M., Falkingham, J., Hills, J., and Le Grand, J. (1992) *The Distribution of Welfare Benefits in Kind*, Welfare State Programme Discussion Paper WSP/68, London: LSE.

Foster, J.T., and Shorrocks, A.F. (1988a) 'Poverty Orderings and Welfare Dominance', *Social Choice and Welfare* 5, 179–98.

Foster, J.T., and Sharrocks, A.F. (1988b) 'Poverty Orderings', *Econometrica* 56: 173–8.

Jenkins, S.P., and Lambert, P.J. (1993) *Poverty Orderings, Poverty Gaps, and Poverty Lines*, Department of Economics Discussion Paper 93–07, University College of Swansea.

Sen, A. (1976) 'Poverty: An Ordinal Approach to Measurement', *Econometrica* 46: 437–46.

Townsend, P. (1979) *Poverty in the United Kingdom*, Harmondsworth: Penguin.

Whiteford, P. (1985) A *Family's Needs: Equivalence Scales*, Poverty and Social Security, Research Paper 27, Canberra: Australian Department of Social Security.

ECONOMIC DISTANCE

The term implies that poor people without a command over resources are significantly different from others in society. 'There is an inescapable connection between poverty and inequality: certain degrees or dimensions of INEQUALITY ... will lead to people being below the minimum standards acceptable in that society. It is this 'economic distance' aspect of inequality that is poverty' (O'Higgins and Jenkins 1990). The term was introduced in the Luxembourg Income Study to describe the situation of persons whose income is below 50 per cent of median income (Smeeding et al. 1990).

REFERENCES

O'Higgins, M., and Jenkins, S. (1990) 'Poverty in the European Community', in R. Teekens and B. van Praag (eds), 'Analysing Poverty in the European Community', *Eurostat News* Special Edition, Luxembourg: European Communities.

Smeeding, T., O'Higgins, M., and Rainwater, L. (eds) (1990) *Poverty, Inequality and Income Distribution in Comparative Perspective*, Hemel Hempstead: Harvester Wheatsheaf.

EMPOWERMENT

The idea of 'empowerment' means that people who are relatively powerless are able to gain more POWER. This may be achieved through some enhancement of the abilities and capacities of those who are lacking in power, or through the development of collective organization and decision-making. In the first sense, empowerment is often represented in individual terms, concerned with the capacity or CAPABILITIES of the poor person. Empowerment can be achieved by relieving poverty; action by the state to enhance the framework of RIGHTS can be viewed as a form of empowerment. It might also be achieved by facilitating social skills, improving communication or developing services more able to improve the quality of choices available to poor people (Pinderhughes 1983). In the second sense, empowerment is understood as both the product and the process of collective action. As a process, collective action puts people in a position where they are able to develop SOCIAL CAPITAL and to exercise power politically. In terms of outcomes, the ability to VOICE concerns and represent interests may have a substantial impact on the situation of poor people, while collective action (such as the development of collective infrastructure) makes it possible to expand the range of capabilities and commodities.

Empowerment of the poor has been strongly advocated by writers such as Freire (1972) and Max-Neef (1992), and has seen as a major strategy in DEVELOPMENT. Sen, conversely, argues that the effect of development is to empower people, by increasing their entitlements and capabilities (Sen 1999). Within the strategies for poverty reduction favoured by the World Bank, empowerment is understood as 'the expansion of assets and capabilities of poor people to participate in, negotiate with, influence, control, and hold accountable institutions that affect their lives' (World Bank 2002).

REFERENCES

Pinderhughes, E. (1983) 'Empowerment for Clients and for Ourselves', *Social Casework* 64/6: 331–8.

Freire, P. (1972) *Pedagogy of the Oppressed*, Harmondsworth: Penguin.

Max-Neef, M. (1992) *From the Outside Looking In*, London: Zed Books.

Sen, A. (1999) *Development as Freedom*, Oxford: Clarendon Press.

World Bank (2002) *Empowerment and Poverty Reduction: A Sourcebook*, http://siteresources. worldbank.org/intempowerment/Resources/486312–1095094954594/draft.pdf.

ENGEL COEFFICIENT

Ernst Engel, a nineteenth-century German economist, postulated that as expenditure increases, so the proportion devoted to food will decline (CALORIE–INCOME ELASTICITY). Because of the difficulty found in justifying any particular level of expenditure on fuel, clothing and rent as a SUBSISTENCE minimum on scientific grounds, Engel's observation was used to construct subsistence poverty lines on the basis that a subsistence diet could at least be prescribed and costed. The cost should then bear the same relationship to the household poverty line as food expenditure on average bears to total household expenditure, nationally. In other words, the subsistence diet cost could be multiplied by a set factor (for example 3.7) to yield a POVERTY LINE. A threshold distinguishing the poor from the non-poor can be framed in terms of either the proportion spent on food, or the income level at which this proportion is just spent. Provided that a country has reliable survey-based statistics of domestic expenditure patterns, the method can be used to prescribe a minimum income level, as indeed it has been in the USA for several decades: USA POVERTY LINE.

Callan and Nolan (1991) have argued that the food-ratio method for establishing a poverty line has the appeal of simplicity, in terms of its conceptual basis. Food-ratio poverty lines avoid the problems of defining what is 'necessary' for subsistence. However, the method involves prescriptive judgement about (a) the components and costs of a minimum dietary and (b) the proportion of total expenditure to devote to food. Judgements have to be made about what proportion of total expenditure on food is to be taken as the Engel coefficient.

The Engel approach has been widely applied (Rao 1981); it has also been used to make international comparisons of levels of living (Justice and Peace Commission 1978).

REFERENCES

Callan, T.. and Nolan, B. (1991) 'Concepts of Poverty and Poverty Lines', *Journal of Economic Surveys* 5/3: 243–61.

Justice and Peace Commission (1978) *Sao Paolo: Growth and Poverty*, São Paulo: Bowerdean Press.

Rao, V.V. (1981) 'Measurement of Deprivation and Poverty Based on the Proportion Spent on Food', *World Development* 9/4.

ENTITLEMENT

Entitlement refers to the complex ways in which individuals or households command resources (Sen 1981). In a narrower economic sense, it may be taken to refer to the distribution of purchasing power. Sen argues that it is the right to use resources, rather than the existence of the resources themselves, that is characteristic of extreme poverty. People are homeless because they are unable to use the homes or land that exists. The starvation suffered by millions in both the Irish famine of the mid-nineteenth century or the Bengal famine of the 1940s was caused not by lack of available food but by the failure to make it available to those who could not afford to buy or transport it. Drèze and Sen (1989: 46) make the case that FAMINE is not caused by shortages of food but by limitations in entitlements to food or food production:

> Famine is, by its very nature, a social phenomenon (it involves the inability of large groups of people to establish command over food in the society in which they live) ... it has to be recognized that even when the prime mover in a famine is a natural occurrence such as a flood or a drought, what its impact will be on the population will depend on how society is organized.

REFERENCES

Drèze, J., and Sen, A. (1989) *Hunger and Public Action*, Oxford: Clarendon Press.

Sen, A. (1981) *Poverty and Famines: An Essay on Entitlement and Deprivation*, Oxford: Clarendon Press.

EQUALITY

'Equality' refers to the removal of disadvantage. Although critics of the principle of 'equality' often identify equality with uniformity and the elimination of differences, this is not what equality means. Equality between men and women does not mean that men and women should be identical, and equality between 'races' does not mean that everyone should have the same ethnic background. People are advantaged or disadvantaged when their social relationships make them better or worse off. So, 'inequalities in health' does not mean simply that people have different needs; the extensive literature on inequalities in health is concerned with the relationship between ill health, material circumstances and social relationships, including poverty and social class (Townsend et al. 1988; Smith et al. 2000).

Poverty is sometimes seen as a form of inequality: the idea of ECONOMIC DISTANCE defines poverty in terms of inequality in command over resources. It is also often seen as the product of inequality. The most important inequalities are probably those of income and wealth, class, gender and race. These are not, however, the only kinds of inequality; part of the shift of perspective on the political left since the decline of Marxism has been an increasing emphasis on the importance of diversity and difference in the construction of disadvantage. People can be disadvantaged for many other reasons, like age, nationality, religion, disability and sexuality.

Policies for equality are of three main types:

1. *Equality of treatment* This does not mean that everyone is treated the same: equality before the law does not mean that everyone is put in prison, and equality in health care does not mean that everyone has a tracheotomy. People are treated equally when they are treated on an equal basis – that is, without disadvantage, bias, prejudice or oppression.

2. *Equality of opportunity* Rae distinguishes 'prospect-regarding' and 'means-regarding' senses (Rae 1971). Prospect-regarding equality of opportunity allows people equally to participate in competition to achieve their ends. This is associated with the idea of social mobility and the principle of 'the career open to the talents', which was argued for in the French Revolution. Beyond equal treatment it means that people are not prevented from changing their status or life-chances. Means-regarding equality of opportunity demands that people have the means, or BASIC SECURITY, to be able to participate in competition on equal terms.

3. *Equality of outcome* This is associated with a view that people share certain human rights, and that the establishment of fundamental conditions is necessary for them to function as humans. Vlastos argues for equal satisfaction of basic needs. Although there are essential needs that are equal and similar for everybody in a given society and time, 'it may be necessary to have a unequal distribution of resources in order to even up benefits in cases of unequal needs' (Vlastos, in Bobbio 1994: 778).

REFERENCES

Bobbio, N., et al. (1994) *Diccionario de Política*, México: Siglo XXI.
Rae, D. (1971) *Equalities*, New Haven CT: Harvard University Press.
Smith, G., Dorling, D., and Shaw, M. (eds) (2000) *Poverty, Inequality and Health in Britain 1800–2000*, Bristol: Policy Press.
Townsend, P., Davidson, N., and Whitehead, M. (1988) *Inequalities in Health*, Harmondsworth: Penguin.

EQUIVALENCE SCALES

Equivalence scales (or ratios) are measures of the relative income needed by different types of families to attain a similar standard of living. They are frequently used in economic studies of poverty. Equivalence scales are usually expressed as a set of numbers; some arbitrarily chosen family or household type is taken as the base and its value is set equal to 1.0. Other household types are then expressed as a proportion of this base. For example, if the benchmark is taken as a family of two adults, then if the figure for a single person household is 0.60 this implies that a single individual only needs 60 per cent of the income of a two-adult household to have the same standard of living (Whiteford 1985).

Equivalisation presents one of the major problems when measuring poverty. It is self evident that the larger the household or family the more income will be needed to maintain the same standard of living. It is also clear that economies of scale exist within a household – that is, it does not cost a family of four twice as much as a family of two to maintain the same standard of living. However, it is not self-evident how much extra larger households need to have the same standard of living as smaller households.

There is general agreement that 'standard of living', like 'poverty', is only measurable 'relative' to society. McClements (1978) states:

> living standards describe the material well-being of the household or family unit as perceived by it and society as a whole, rather than personal happiness per se.

Likewise, Jensen (1978) states:

> standard of living of a household is not an objectively defined function of its level of consumption, rather it is specified by the general consensus amongst members of the society about what the household's pattern of consumption is judged to represent in terms of material well-being.

Despite this agreement on the definition of standard of living in relation to the households and societies' perception and judgement of material well-being, in practice most equivalization scales are based on the assumption that equivalent standard of living can be measured from the types and quantities of goods and services households consume (Deaton and Muellbaur 1980).

There is currently no methodology that allows the objective determination of equivalence scales. Many equivalence scales are based on tautological reasoning. Equivalent income is determined from equivalent consumption patterns, but in order to know what equivalent consumption is, equivalent income must first be known.

Whiteford (1985) has argued that, while no objective equivalence scales have been derived, several proposed scales could be rejected on logical grounds. He states:

> equivalence scales should be plausible, generally rising with the size of the household but showing economies of scale. A priori, it is implausible that a single individual requires only 49% of the income of a couple, as suggested by Podder, or that an individual requires 94% of the income of a couple, as suggested by Lazear and Michael. Similarly, the detailed basic equivalence scales derived by SWPS and ABS, using the ELES method, are implausible when they imply that the costs of a sole parent with two children are less than the costs of a sole parent with one child. What is a plausible estimate of the costs of a child is more difficult to determine. It can be suggested, however, that Seneca and Taussig's estimate that a child adds only 1% to the cost of a couple is implausible as is Habib and Tawil's estimate that a child adds 47%. Similarly, the pattern of additional costs implied by

the detailed basic ELES equivalence scales is implausible – where the head works and the wife does not, the first child adds 11%, the second 6%, the third 16%, the fourth 3% and the fifth 17%. It is difficult to conceive of the reasons why this should be so. (Podder 1971; Lazear and Michael 1980a, 1980b; ABS 1981; Seneca and Taussig 1971; Habib and Tawil 1974; SWPS 1981)

However, even after many proposed equivalence scales have been rejected on grounds of implausibility, numerous plausible scales remain (for example, Whiteford (1985) lists 59 scales, of which over half are plausible). This is problematic because the results obtained from a poverty study are sensitive to the equivalence scale used (Bradbury 1989; Weir 1992). In poverty studies both the household composition of the 'poor' and the position of the poverty line can be influenced by equivalisation scale that is used. Equivalence scales have been used to study gender discrimination by showing how household expenditure reacts to the birth of a male versus a female child. For a review of the major issues involved and the reason for the disappointing performance of this methodology see Deaton (1997).

REFERENCES

ABS (1981) *Equivalence Scales: The Estimation of Equivalence Scales for Australia from the 1974/75 and 1975/76 Household Expenditure Surveys*, Canberra: Australian Bureau of Statistics.

Bradbury, B. (1989) 'Family Size Equivalence Scales and Survey Evaluations of Income and Well-Being', *Journal of Social Policy* 18/3: 383–408.

Deaton, A. (1997) *The Analysis of Household Surveys*, Baltimore MD: Johns Hopkins University Press.

Deaton, A., and Muellbauer, J. (1980) *Economics and Consumer Behaviour*, Cambridge: Cambridge University Press.

Habib, J., and Tawil, Y. (1974) *Equivalence Scales for Family Size: Findings from Israeli Data*, Jerusalem: National Insurance Institute, Bureau of Research and Planning.

Jensen, J. (1978) *Minimum Income Levels and Income Equivalence Scales*, Wellington: Department of Social Welfare.

Lazear, E.P., and Michael, R.T. (1980a) 'Family Size and the Distribution of Real Per Capita Income', *American Economic Review* 70/1: 91–107.

Lazear, E.P., and Michael, R.T. (1980b) 'Real Income Equivalence among One-earner and Two-earner Families', *American Economic Review* 70/2: 203–8.

McClements, L.D. (1978) *The Economics of Social Security*, London: Heinemann.

Podder, N. (1971) 'The Estimation of Equivalent Income Scales', *Australian Economic Papers*, December.

Seneca, J.J., and Taussig, M.K (1971) 'Family Equivalence Scales and Personal Income Tax Exemptions for Children', *Review of Economics and Statistics* 53: 253–62.

SWPS (1981) *Report on Poverty Measurement*, Social Welfare Policy Secretariat, Canberra: Australian Government Publishing Service.

Weir, J. (1992) *Sensitivity Testing in HBAI: An Examination of the Results*, Analytical Notes 1, London: Department of Social Security.
Whiteford, P. (1985) *A Family's Needs: Equivalence Scales, Poverty and Social Security*, Research Paper 27, Canberra: Australian Department of Social Security.

EUROPEAN RELATIVE INCOME STANDARD OF POVERTY

This is a poverty standard that depends only on a criterion of low income rather than any independent condition or state of need. The choice of the standard seems to depend just on consideration of the distribution of income, and political, as well as social, values are plainly embodied in the choice. The most common indicator is 50 or 60 per cent of the median disposable household income, or expenditure, in a country (O'Higgins and Jenkins 1990; Atkinson et al. 2002) 60 per cent is increasingly used. Townsend (1995) has proposed the epithet 'European' mainly because, from the 1970s, European agencies and research institutes (LUXEMBOURG INCOME STUDY) took the lead in using income cut-off points as means of identifying the numbers and composition of poor, in contrast to the different approaches to POVERTY LINE construction.

A variation on the relative income standard described above is the identification of income strata, such as decile groups or quintile groups, below average household income. This is the standard represented by the Households Below Average Income analyses carried out in the United Kingdom (DSS 1993). Other low-income measures have been reviewed extensively in Canadian work (especially Wolfson and Evans 1989; Canadian Council on Social Development 1984).

The strengths of this approach are that most industrialized countries conduct income and expenditure surveys and maintain administrative information about income distribution, mainly for tax purposes. These data are easily available for analysis and can be subjected to some degree of standardization for purposes of comparison. The results may vary from year to year, proportionate to population, and are therefore of more significance in relation to rates of economic growth, unemployment and employment and demographic change than fixed divisions by decile or quintile.

The European relative income standard approach has two major weaknesses. First, it relies on inequality as an indicator of poverty. The connection is limited: the Nordic countries managed for many decades with wide inequalities in the ownership and control of resources but without those at the bottom falling below the publicly accepted minimum adequacy levels. Redistributive policies in these countries prevented poverty without removing inequality. Second, the selection of a cut-off point low on the income scale is not related to any strict criteria of need or deprivation. Different choices in the construction and operational application of the cut-off points can lead to diverse results in the extent and composition of poverty in different countries.

REFERENCES

Atkinson, A.B. (2002) *Social Indicators: The EU and Social Inclusion*, Oxford: Oxford University Press.

Canadian Council on Social Development (1984) *Not Enough: The Meaning and Measurement of Poverty in Canada*, Ottawa: CCSD.

DSS (1993) *Households Below Average Income (1979–1990/91)*, Department of Social Security, London: HMSO.

O'Higgins, M., and Jenkins, S. (1990) 'Poverty in Europe Estimates for 1975, 1980 and 1985', in R. Teekins and B.M.S. van Praag (eds), *Analysing Poverty in the European Community, Policy Issues, Research Options and Data Sources*, Luxembourg: Eurostat.

Townsend, P. (1995) 'The Need for a New Poverty Line', in K. Funken and P. Cooper (eds), *Old and New Poverty: The Challenge for Reform*, London: Rivers Oram Press.

Wolfson, M.C., and Evans, J.M. (1989) *Statistics Canada's Low Income Cut Offs Methodological Concerns and Possibilities*, Research Paper Series, Ottawa: Statistics Canada.

EUROPEAN UNION DEFINITION OF POVERTY

In 1975 the Council of Europe adopted a relative definition of poverty as:

> individuals or families whose resources are so small as to exclude them from the minimum acceptable way of life of the Member State in which they live. (EEC 1981)

On 19 December 1984, the European Commission extended the definition as:

> the poor shall be taken to mean persons, families and groups of persons whose resources (material, cultural and social) are so limited as to exclude them from the minimum acceptable way of life in the Member State in which they live. (EEC 1985)

These definitions are very similar to the RELATIVE POVERTY definitions advocated by Townsend (1970, 1979), though they also have clear
relational elements.

REFERENCES

EEC (1981) *Final Report from the Commission to the Council on the First Programme of Pilot Schemes and Studies to Combat Poverty*, Brussels: Commission of the European Communities.
EEC (1985) 'On Specific Community Action to Combat Poverty (Council Decision of 19 December 1984), 85/8/EEC', *Official Journal of the EEC* 2: 24.
Townsend, P. (ed.) (1970) *The Concept of Poverty*, London: Heinemann.
Townsend, P. (1979) *Poverty in the United Kingdom*, Harmondsworth: Penguin.

EXCLUSION

People are 'excluded' if they are not adequately integrated into
society. The definition of the concept varies among countries and
different school of thought. (Silver 1994). The primary forms of exclusion cover

- circumstances in which people are left out of society, through
  non-inclusion in systems of social protection;
- circumstances, like poverty and disability, when they are unable
  to participate in ordinary activities;
- circumstances in which people are shut out, through stigma or
  discrimination.

From its initial development in France, the discourse of social exclusion has spread across the rest of Europe. The Commission of the
European Communities started to use the concept in the 1980s and
it is now widely applied by both social scientists and politicians. The
World Bank has used the idea as a multidimensional concept covering
access to goods and services, discrimination, denial of rights, and
inequality (Perry 2003).

The roots of the idea in France are based in the concept of
SOLIDARITY, which is the guiding principle of the social security
system (Dupeyroux and Ruellan 1998). The French social security
system developed after 1944 through a principle of *généralisation*, or
the progressive extension of solidarity to people who were otherwise
unprotected. This process was completed in the early 1970s but still

left many people without social protection. The idea of 'exclusion' was introduced in 1974 by René Lenoir, as a means of referring to people who were failed by existing networks. For Lenoir, then, the excluded were people who were left out of the system. The term, however, accorded closely with other conceptions of solidarity, and it was rapidly extended to mental and physical handicap, the aged and invalids, drug addicts, delinquents, suicidal individuals, single parents, abused children, or multi-problem households. Solidarity identifies society as a series of complex, overlapping networks of mutual responsibility and duty. People are marginal when they are insufficiently integrated into such networks; they are excluded when they are not part of them.

The concept of social exclusion is, in some cases, used as a substitute for poverty. Townsend specifically defined the poor by reference to their exclusion:

> individuals, families and groups in the population [whose] resources are so seriously below those commanded by the average individual or family that they are, in effect, excluded from ordinary living patterns, customs and activities. (Townsend 1979: 31)

Others have tried to establish a distinction between poverty and social exclusion. Sometimes it is argued that poverty is a narrow concept dealing with problems that are directly related to economic resources, while social exclusion deals with a broad range of questions dealing with an individual's integration in the society. This means that 'exclusion includes poverty, poverty does not include exclusion' (Delors, cited in Abrahamson 1996). It is also argued that poverty is a static phenomenon, dealing solely with people's economic situation at one point in time, while social exclusion represents a dynamic perspective focusing on the processes that lead to a situation of exclusion and, for that matter, poverty. A third distinction turns the argument the other way around, arguing that social exclusion represents an extreme form of poverty.

In so far as exclusion refers to problems associated with poverty, there seems to be little effective distinction in the approach that is called for. When the idea of exclusion refers to social networks, however, it goes beyond the concept of poverty. The idea has been taken to include not just the poor but people with AIDS, old people and racial minorities. Exclusion stands, then, for a whole series of social problems and processes and 'combating social exclusion' has come to stand for a wide range of actions in social policy.

REFERENCES

Abrahamson, P. (1996) 'Social Exclusion in Europe: Old Wine in New Bottles', paper presented at ESF conference, Blarney, 26–30 March.
Dupeyroux, J., Reullan, R., (1998) *Droit de la sécurité sociale*, Paris: Dalloz.
Lenoir, R. (1974) *Les exclus*, Paris: Éditions du Seuil.
Perry, G. (2003) 'Prólogo a las actas del taller sobre pobreza y exclusión social en América Latina', in E. Gacitúa and C. Sojo (eds), *Exclusión social y reducción de la pobreza en América Latina y el Caribe*, San José de Costa Rica: FLACSO, World Bank.
Silver, H. (1994) 'Social Exclusion and Social Solidarity: Three Paradigms', *International Labour Review* 133/5–6: 531–78.
Townsend, P. (1979) *Poverty in the United Kingdom*, Harmondsworth: Penguin.

EXPLANATIONS FOR POVERTY

Holman (1978) identifies four classes of explanation for poverty:

- *Pathological* explanations attribute poverty to the characteristics of the people who are poor. These include explanations attributing poverty to individuals, genetic characteristics and families.
- *Sub-cultural* explanations imply that the values of poor people are in some sense different from others.
- *Agency* explanations attribute poverty to the failure of agencies and, in particular, the state to act to prevent it. Because poverty is necessarily produced by other factors outside the agency, this is not a true 'explanation' of poverty.
- *Structural* explanations attribute poverty to the structures or power, resources or opportunities available to different groups in society, and to the way in which social processes create deprivations or block opportunities for escape from poverty for some groups or individuals. Structural poverty may result from the casualties of a competitive society (Titmuss 1968: ch. 11); from inequality; from structured DISADVANTAGE; or from the exercise of POWER.

REFERENCES

Holman, R. (1978) *Poverty: Explanations for Deprivation*, Oxford: Martin Robertson.
Titmuss, R.M. (1968) *Commitment to Welfare*, London: Allen & Unwin.

EXTENDED POVERTY MINIMUM

An extended poverty minimum (*ligne de pauvreté minimale élargie*) has been developed at the University of Ottawa, Canada (Genné 1992), building on the UN HUMAN DEVELOPMENT INDEX (UNDP 1991). The extended poverty minimum consists of minimum expenditure on food plus essential expenditure on non-food items plus government expenditure on needs (BASIC NEEDS).

REFERENCES

Genné, M. (1992) 'Réflexion sur les indicateurs de dévelopment humain', *Canadian Journal of Development Studies* 13/1: 81–90.

UNDP (1991) 'Mesurer le dévelopment humain et la liberté humaine', in *Rapport sur le dévelopment humain*, Paris: Economica.

EXTREME POVERTY

There is no generally agreed use of the term 'extreme poverty', which is variously identified with minimum SUBSISTENCE requirements (UN Commission on Human Rights 1994), the denial of basic ENTITLEMENT (Hunt 1994), and the experience of EXCLUSION. The World Bank defines extreme poverty as an income of under $275 per annum.

Boltvinik (1990, 1991) defines extreme poverty as the situation of those households which, although they devote all their income to food, do not appear able to satisfy their needs in this area. This is because food cannot be consumed without being prepared, for which at least fuel and a few kitchen utensils are required; because food is not consumed with one's hands straight from a saucepan, at least a few utensils are required to consume it; because nudity in public places is a punishable offence in all countries; and because without some form of transport it is impossible to get to work, at least in large cities – to mention only the most obvious contradictions.

REFERENCES

Boltvinik, J. (1990) *Pobreza y Necesidades Básicas. Conceptos y Métodos de Medición*, Regional Project to Overcome Poverty, Caracas: UNDP.

Boltvinik, J. (1991) 'La medición de la pobreza en América Latina', *Comercio Exterior* 41/5.

Commission on Human Rights (1994) *Interim Report on Human Rights and Extreme Poverty*, ref. GE94–12944 (E), New York: United Nations.

Hunt, P. (1994) 'Extreme Poverty and Human Rights', UN seminar paper presented in New York, 12–14 October.

F

FAMILY WAGE

This idea suggests that wages should be sufficient to support a 'typical' family at a reasonable standard. It arose in nineteenth-century Britain, when the formal labour market began developing and the individual replaced the family as the unit of labour. Land (1981) points out that behind the concept of the family wage lie assumptions about the respective roles of women and men in both the home and the labour market: men's wages should be sufficient to support an entire family, whereas women's wages should only be supplementary or at most need be sufficient to support only one adult. Whilst the labour movement has defended the family wage on the basis of protecting men's pay, opportunities and incentives, it has come under heavy criticism from feminists (Barrett and McIntosh 1980; Land 1980). There is concern that the family wage would make equal pay between men and women more difficult, whilst exacerbating the dependence of married women on men. Concern has also been raised at the extent to which the wage would be shared equally by family members. Hartman (1976) views the family wage as 'the cornerstone' of the present GENDER DIVISION OF LABOUR, since women are not expected to make an economic contribution to the household and that women's priority is to domestic responsibility.

REFERENCES

Barrett, M., and McIntosh, M. (1980) 'The "Family Wage": Some Problems for Socialists and Feminists', *Capital and Class* 11: 51–72

Hartman, H. (1976) 'Capitalism, Patriarchy and Job Segregation by Sex', in M. Blaxall and B. Reagen (eds), *Women and the Workplace: The Implications of Occupational Segregation*, Chicago: University of Chicago Press.

Land, H. (1980) 'The Family Wage', *Feminist Review* 6: 55–77.

Land, H. (1981) 'The Family Wage', *New Statesman*, 18 December: 16–18.

FAMINE

A famine occurs in circumstances where many people die from lack of food. Crow (1992) distinguishes this from chronic hunger:

> In many parts of the world where famine has not occurred in recent years, sustained nutritional deprivation is, nevertheless, experienced by a significant proportion of the population.

Drèze and Sen (1989) argue that famine is the result of lack of ENTITLEMENT, rather than lack of food in itself: they give several examples of famine in circumstances where food continues to be produced and exported. They also claim that no famine has occurred in a democratic state. See also FOOD SHORTAGES; MALNUTRITION.

REFERENCES

Crow, B. (1992) 'Understanding Famine and Hunger', in T. Allen and A. Thomas (eds), Poverty *and Development in the 1990s*, Oxford: Oxford University Press.
Drèze, J., and Sen, A. (1989) *Hunger and Public Action*, Oxford: Clarendon Press.

FEMALE POVERTY

Women in both 'developed' countries and in 'developing' countries are more likely to suffer poverty than men (Scott 1984; George 1988; Daly 1989; Payne 1991). According to Payne, 'throughout their lives women are more vulnerable to both poverty and deprivation, whilst there are more women than men living in conditions of poverty and deprivation at any one time'. This is primarily related to the GENDER DIVISION OF LABOUR, by which men are held to require an adequate or FAMILY WAGE and women are not (see INTRA-HOUSEHOLD TRANSFERS). Some commentators have argued that a process of feminization of poverty is taking place, causing an overrepresentation of women among the world's poor.

Despite the fact that a disproportionate number of women live in poverty, female poverty is often underrepresented in poverty statistics. Whilst traditional methods have examined poverty between households, contemporary feminist analyses have focused on poverty within the household (Daly 1989; Pahl 1989; Volger 1989). Feminist scholars have also highlighted the causes of women's poverty (Glendinning and Millar 1992).

If poverty is a consequence of an inability to generate sufficient resources to meet needs, then for women this is often a consequence of the gender division of labour (Payne 1991; Glendinning and Millar 1992). Whilst women's primary role is assigned to the home, men's primary role is assigned to the labour market. A major underpinning of the gender division of labour is women's economic dependence on men. Payne (1991) argues that the 'heroic assumption' of women's ability to depend on the economic support of men is the immediate cause of women's poverty. She says, 'in terms of poor households, women as lone parents and lone older women suffer poverty because there is no man with higher earning power or pension rights on whom to depend, whilst state benefits are paid at levels which assume there should be. In addition, opportunities for women to move out of this dependence on state benefit or poor pensions are restricted by the assumption about the role of women – the low earnings of women and the scarcity and cost of alternative forms of childcare.

Payne (1991) argues that in terms of women's poverty within the household, the earnings of men cannot be assumed to be shared equally between men and women.

REFERENCES

Daly, M. (1989) *Women and Poverty*, Dublin: Attic Press/Combat Poverty Agency.
George, V. (1988) *Wealth, Poverty and Starvation: An International Perspective*, Brighton: Harvester Wheatsheaf.
Glendinning, C., and Millar, J. (1992) *Women and Poverty in Britain in the 1990s*, London: Harvester Wheatsheaf.
Pahl, J. (1989) *Money and Marriage*, London: Macmillan Education.
Payne, S. (1991) *Women, Health and Poverty*, London: Harvester Wheatsheaf.
Scott, H. (1984) *The Feminization of Poverty: Women, Work and Welfare*, London: Pandora.
Volger, C. (1989) *Labour Market Change and Patterns of Financial Allocation within Households*, Working Paper 12, ESRSC Social Change and Economic Life Initiative, Oxford: ESRSC.

FEMINIZATION OF POVERTY

This thesis holds that as a result of recession and cuts in public spending, women are increasingly represented among the world's poor (Pearce 1978; Scott 1984; Rein and Erie 1988). Particularly affected are single-parent families but also elderly single person households. Scott (1984) cites official government figures showing that 36 million (or 15 per cent) of the US population were living in poverty in 1982. She argues that not only is poverty more widespread but women are becoming more visible among the poor because a process of feminization of poverty is taking place. Whilst women have helped keep two-earner families out of poverty, they have also become the sole earner in an increasing number of families with dependent children. The income earned by single parents is often insufficient to support their families.

The idea that poverty has only recently become feminized has been challenged on the grounds that it ignores the extent to which women have traditionally been much poorer than men (Payne 1991; Lewis and Piachaud 1992; Garfinkel and McLanahan 1988). It has been shown that British women constitute a roughly similar proportion of the poor today as in 1900 (Lewis and Piachaud 1992).

It is further argued that women's actual experience of poverty has also remained remarkably similar over the course of the last century. For instance, the habit of going without, where women ignore or sacrifice their own needs to fulfil the needs of children or husbands, existed at the start of this century just as is does in present society (Payne 1991). Critics of the thesis argue that it is the composition of female poverty which has changed, resulting in an increased visibility in women's poverty. Nowadays, women are less often poor within large poor households, because demographic changes have resulted in female poverty being concentrated among lone women, especially women with dependent children and elderly women. The increased visibility of female poverty means that poor women are more easily counted, although the extent of poverty suffered by women within households still remains hidden, just as it did in the last century.

REFERENCES

Garfinkel, I., and McLanahan, S. (1988) 'The Feminization of Poverty', in D. Tomaskovic-Devey (ed.), *Poverty and Social Welfare in the United States*, Boulder CO: Westview Press.

Glendinning, C., and Millar, J. (1992) *Women and Poverty in Britain in the 1990s*, London: Harvester Wheatsheaf.

Lewis, J., and Piachaud, D. (1992) 'Women and Poverty in the Twentieth Century', in C. Glendinning and J. Millar (eds), *Women and Poverty in Britain in the 1990s*, Hemel Hempstead: Harvester Wheatsheaf.

Payne, S. (1991) *Women, Health and Poverty*, Hemel Hempstead: Harvester Wheatsheaf.

Pearce, D. (1978) 'The Feminization of Poverty: Women, Work and Welfare', *Urban and Social Change Review*, February.

Rein, M., and Erie, S. (1988) 'Women and Welfare State', in C.M. Mueller (ed.), *The Politics of the Gender Gap 2*, London: Sage.

Scott, H. (1984) *Working Your Way to the Bottom: the Feminization of Poverty*, London: Pandora.

FOOD SHORTAGES

The Food and Agricultural Organization of the United Nations (FAO) has an international responsibility to monitor and identify countries and regions where serious food shortages and worsening nutritional conditions are imminent and make an early assessment of possible emergency food requirements, including food imports, food aid requirements, and emergency needs. Details of food shortages are publicized through the Global Information and Early Warning System on Food and Agriculture (GIEWS).

The FAO identifies three levels of food shortage:

1. *Unfavourable prospects for current crops* This refers to prospects of a shortfall in production of current crops as a result of a reduction of the area planted and/or adverse weather conditions, plant pests, diseases and other calamities, which indicates a need for close monitoring of the crops for the remainder of the growing season

2. *Shortfalls in food supplies in current marketing year requiring exceptional external assistance* This refers to an exceptional shortfall in aggregate supplies or a localized deficit as a result of crop failures, natural disasters, interruption of imports, disruption of distribution, excessive post-harvest losses, other supply bottlenecks and/or an increased demand for food arising from population movements within the country or an influx of refugees. In the case of an exceptional shortfall in aggregate food supplies, exceptional and/or emergency food aid may be required to cover all or part of the deficit.

3. *Distribution of local and/or exportable surpluses requiring external assistance* This refers to a situation of an exceptional surplus existing in a particular area of a country which needs to be transported to deficit areas in the same country or the neighbouring countries, for which purpose external assistance is required.

REFERENCES

FAO, www.fao.org/waicent/faoinfo/economic/giews/engllsh/giewse.htm.

FOSTER, GREER AND THORBECKE (FGT) INDEX

Foster, Greer and Thorbecke (FGT) developed a class of poverty measures that facilitates the exposing of more poverty with greater inequality among the poor. Considering two incomes below the POVERTY LINE, poverty is then more severe if one income is 1 per cent below the poverty line and one income is 99 per cent below the poverty line, compared with a situation with two incomes of 50 per cent below the poverty line.

The class of poverty measures is defined by FGT as:

$$P_\alpha = \frac{1}{n}\sum_{i=1}^{q} \left(\frac{z - y_i}{z}\right)^\alpha$$

where:

P_α is the level of poverty;
n is the population size;
q is the number of poor;
z is the poverty line;
y_i is the per capita household income; and
α has a normative value that can be set at different levels according to the importance attached to the lowest living standards.

The FGT measure becomes the HEAD-COUNT RATIO H if $\alpha = 0$. The degree of poverty is equal for all the poor no matter the size of their POVERTY GAP (see Figure). The FGT measure becomes the poverty gap index PGI if $\alpha = 1$. The degree of poverty increases in a linear way with the size of the poverty gap (see Figure 1). With $\alpha > 1$, a poorer person gets a higher than linear poverty weight than a less poor person. With $\alpha = 2$, the weight of each person is equal to its proportionate poverty gap. A person 75 per cent below the poverty line gets a weight of .56, a person 50 per cent below the poverty line gets a weight of .25. The FGT index with $\alpha = 2$ is sometimes called the squared POVERTY GAP INDEX.

ALTERNATIVE VALUES OF FGT

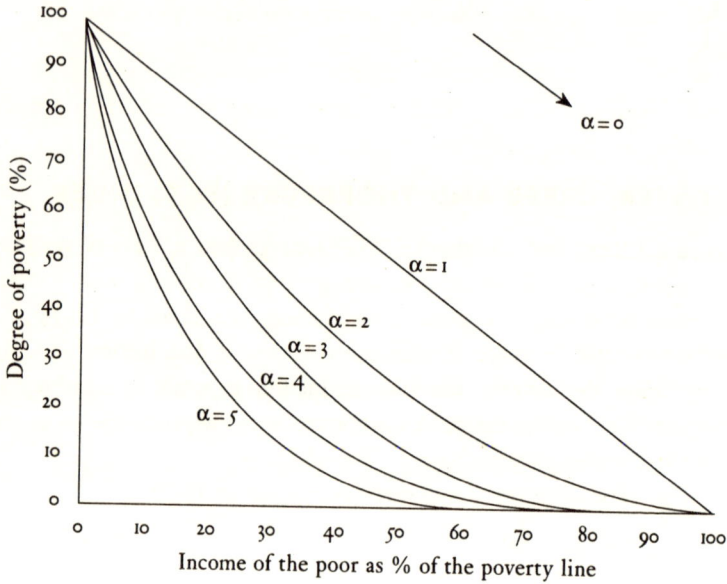

The figure presents the degree of poverty according to various values of α. The value of P_α ranges between zero (the case where all incomes of the poor are equal to the poverty line) and H (the case where all the poor have zero income.) A higher α gives more weight to the poorest and less weight to persons near the poverty line, and the gap between more poor and less poor households becomes larger. As α becomes very large, the FGT measure approaches a situation where poverty is completely determined by the income of the poorest. A person with an income of 50 per cent below the poverty line gets a poverty weight of 100 per cent if $\alpha=0$. That means that he is considered as poor as a person with zero income. With $\alpha=1$, a person whose income is 50 per cent below the poverty line gets a poverty weight of 50 per cent of the weight of a person with zero income. With $\alpha=2$, he gets a poverty weight of .25, with $\alpha=5$, he gets a weight of only .015.

An example of the FGT index in practice is available in Hagenaars et al., 1994. This presents results calculated for European countries side by side with the head-count ratio and the poverty gap. The results of the three measures are likely to be similar, because they are based on common core elements, but there is also some degree of variation. By comparison with the SEN INDEX, the FGT index has the advantages of continuity and decomposability, and the ability to model the impact of normative assumptions on the distribution of resources between poor people.

REFERENCES

Foster, J., Greer, J., and Thorbecke, E. (1984) 'A Class of Decomposable Poverty Measures', *Econometrica* 52/3, May.

Fields, G. (1995) 'Poverty Changes in Developing Countries', in R. van der Hoeven and R. Anker, *Poverty Monitoring: An International Concern*, New York: St Martin's Press.

Foster, J. (1994) 'Normative Measurement: Is Theory Relevant?', *American Economic Review*, May: 365–9.

Hagenaars, A., de Vos, K. and Zaidi, M. (1994) *Poverty Statistics in the late 1980s*, Luxembourg: European Community.

FOURTH WORLD

This is a term used by the French organization ATD–Quart Monde to refer to people in chronic poverty in developed countries. It is linked, but not confined to, to the concept of EXCLUSION.

> Among the Fourth World we find all the disadvantages, inequalities and injustices of society compounded among people, families and communities at the very bottom of the social scale. Their situation is one of serious financial insecurity, appalling housing, lack of basic education and training, isolation from the job market, lack of social and political representation, chronic bad health ... and the humiliation of being dependent on and misunderstood by society as a whole, and by other people who are in only a marginally better situation themselves. (Williams 1986: 21)

REFERENCES

Williams, S. (1986) 'Exclusion: The Hidden Face of Poverty', in P. Golding (ed.), *Excluding the Poor*, London: Child Poverty Action Group.

FUEL POVERTY

Fuel, for heating, cleaning or the preparation of food, is usually treated as an essential item for the purposes of subsistence. A lack of fuel (through lack of resources or entitlement) is consequently a major indicator of poverty, and a central part of the experience. The term 'fuel poverty', used principally in the UK (Cooper 1981; Boardman 1991), suggests that the lack of fuel is considered a form of poverty in itself (analogous to hunger or famine), though typically fuel poverty consists of sacrificing some resources for others (like warmth for food, or vice-versa).

REFERENCES

Boardman, B. (1991) *Fuel Poverty*, London: Belhaven.
Cooper, S. (1981) *Fuel Poverty in the United Kingdom*, London: Policy Studies Institute.

G

GENDER DIVISION OF LABOUR

Women's primary role is assigned to the home whilst men's primary role is assigned to the labour market. Payne (1991: 9) notes the all-encompassing nature of the gender division of labour:

> women's low pay (and educational opportunities), women's inferior pension rights, women's position in social policy, and in particular the payment, or lack of payment, of state benefits to women, whilst also justifying higher male earnings, higher male pensions, and the lack of childcare facilities.

Feminist approaches have argued that the gender division of labour is of central importance in understanding the underlying and immediate causes of women's poverty. Daly (1989) argues that this division is connected with women's poverty in two ways. First, many women are without an earned income of their own since they are involved in full-time work within the home which is unpaid. Second, women are confined to areas of employment which mirror the type of work they perform within the home. This type of work is low-paid and women often earn less than men for the same job.

Feminists have further identified a number of consequences that this division of labour has for women and men (Daly 1989; Millar and Glendinning 1991; Payne 1991). Women's unpaid work within the home means that they have no independent income of their own, leaving them financially dependent on men or on the state. Where women live with men in couple households, women's work within the home allows men to pursue employment. Whilst traditional poverty studies assume that the income obtained from men's employment is shared equally among household members, studies which have looked at INTRA-HOUSEHOLD TRANSFERS have demonstrated that women are often denied equal access to resources (Pahl 1989; Nyman 1996). Not being in paid employment also increases women's poverty in another way: by the fact that women's earnings from paid work often help keep the whole family out of poverty. Unpaid work within the home does not confer the same kind of rights and benefits usually offered to paid employment. Particularly significant is women's lack of a contributory pension and the effect that this has in old age.

REFERENCES

Daly, M. (1989) *Women and Poverty*, Dublin: Attic Press/Combat Poverty Agency.
Millar, J., and Glendinning, C. (1992) 'It All Really Starts in the Family: Gender Divisions and Poverty', in C. Glendinning and J. Millar (eds), *Women and Poverty in Britain in the 1990s*, Hemel Hempstead: Harvester Wheatsheaf.
Nyman, C. (1996) 'Inside the Black Box: Intra-household Distribution of Consumption in Sweden', in E. Bihagen, C. Nyman and M. Strand, *Three Aspects of Consensual Poverty in Sweden – Work Deprivation, Attitudes towards the Welfare-state and Household Consumptional Distribution*, University of Umeå.
Pahl, J. (1989) *Money and Marriage*, London: Macmillan.
Payne, S. (1991) *Women, Health and Poverty*, Hemel Hempstead: Harvester Wheatsheaf.

GENETIC EXPLANATIONS

Genetic explanations for poverty take it that the structure of rewards in society in some way reflect either the innate capacity or the inherited behaviour of the citizens. At the end of the nineteenth century, social problems – like crime, social immorality and drunkenness – were considered by some to be the consequence of mental handicap. These characteristics were called the 'degeneracies'.

> We believe it is established beyond controversy that criminals and paupers both, are degenerate; the imperfect, knotty, knurly, worm-eaten, half-rotten fruit of the race. (Boies 1893: 266)

The school of thought that this represents led eventually to the advocacy of eugenics (or selective breeding) as a longer-term policy to deal with social problems. Genetic explanations for poverty, and eugenic policies, were largely discredited through their association with Nazism (Weindling 1989).

Modern genetics is not deterministic; the identification of a genetic strain (or 'genotype') is not equivalent to identification of a developed pattern or 'phenotype', which may vary with environmental influences.

REFERENCES

Boies, H.M. (1893) *Prisoners and Paupers*, New York: Knickerbocker Press.
Weindling, P. (1989) *Health, Race and German Politics between National Unification and Nazism, 1870–1945*, Cambridge: Cambridge University Press.

GINI COEFFICIENT

The Gini coefficient is the most widely used single measure of income inequality and it is often incorporated into poverty indices (for example: the SEN INDEX). It ranges between 0 (everyone has the same income) and 1 (one person has all the income). The simplest and most intuitive interpretation of the Gini coefficient is:

> If we choose two people at random from the income distribution, and express the difference between their incomes as a proportion of the average income, then this difference turns out to be (on average) twice the Gini coefficient: a coefficient of 0.3 means that the expected difference between two people chosen at random is 60 per cent (2 x 0.3) of the average income. If the Gini coefficient is 0.5 then the expected difference would be the average income itself. (Raskall and Matherson 1992)

Most texts interpret the Gini coefficient in a much more complex manner and by reference to Lorenz curves. For example, Goodman and Webb (1994) state that the Gini coefficient can be understood by looking at the Lorenz curve, which plots the proportion of total income held by each percentile of the population, ranked in order of income.

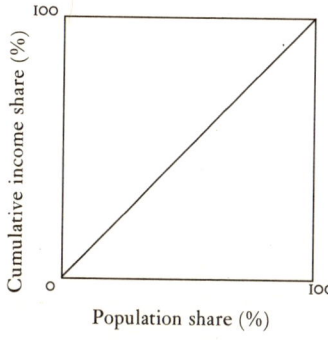

A   COMPLETE INCOME EQUALITY

Cumulative income share (%)

Population share (%)

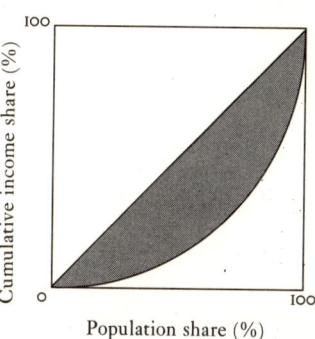

B   LORENZ CURVE FOR A TYPICAL INCOME DISTRIBUTION

Cumulative income share (%)

Population share (%)

The Lorenz curve of diagram A represents complete equality of income. Here, the bottom 10 per cent of the population receives 10 per cent of total income; the bottom 20 per cent receives 20 per cent of the total income; and so on. Diagram B shows the Lorenz curve for a typical income distribution. The curve lies below the line of complete equality.

The Gini coefficient is the ratio of the area between the Lorenz curve and the 45-degree line – that is, the shaded area in diagram B, to the total area under the 45-degree line. If incomes become more unequally distributed, the Lorenz curve bulges further away from the complete equality line and the area between the curve and the 45-degree line increases. Thus the Gini coefficient rises with rising inequality and falls with falling inequality.

REFERENCES

Goodman, A., and Webb, S. (1994) *For Richer, for Poorer: The Changing Distribution of Income in the United Kingdom, 1961–91*, London: Institute of Fiscal Studies.
Raskall, P., and Matheson, G. (1992) 'Understanding the Gini Coefficient', *SPRC Newsletter* 46: 11.

GNP PER CAPITA

This is the gross national product (or national income) divided by the total population, which gives an average income for a country as a whole. This is widely used as an indicator of development and national poverty. GDP, or gross domestic product, is also used. The difference between the terms is that GNP includes income received from foreign exchange, and GDP does not.

There are severe statistical problems such as those regarding the informal sector and exclusion of the household sector in GNP. Todaro (1994: 160–63) also points out that the indicator is biased towards those engaged in economic activity and, in particular, to the upper reaches of the income distribution. It is possible, in theory, for all the increase in national income to benefit the better-off and for this to be taken as an indication of a reduction in national poverty. (The point is particularly relevant to poverty in South American countries.) To counter this, Todaro proposes either an *equal-weights index*, assigning equal weight to growth in income for each quintile in a population, or a *poverty-weighted index* which gives extra weight to the lowest 40 per cent of the income distribution.

REFERENCES

Todaro, M. (1994) *Economic Development*, New York: Longman.

H

HEAD-COUNT RATIO OR HEAD-COUNT INDEX H

This is probably the most common measure of poverty; it refers to the proportion of individuals, households or families that falls under the poverty line. If q is the number of people identified as poor and n the total number of people in the community, then the head-count ratio measure H is q/n. The head-count ratio ranges from zero (nobody is poor) to one (everybody is poor).

This simple indicator provides useful information on the incidence of poverty and the distribution of poverty among the population. However, the head-count ratio does not capture the intensity of poverty – that is, how far the poor fall below a given poverty line (Sen 1981; Hagenaars 1986).

The head-count ratio has been under severe attack for thirty years (Atkinson 1989). In 1968, Watts (1968: 326) noted that it had 'little but its simplicity to recommend it' and Sen (1979: 295) has remarked that, considering its inadequacies, the degree of support commanded by this measure is 'quite astonishing'. The head-count ratio can be dangerous for monitoring the effectiveness of pro-poor policies. Successful policies aimed at raising the well-being of the poorest of the poor will not affect the head-count ratio if their new living standard is still below the poverty line. On the other hand, successful pro-poor policies aimed at persons just below the poverty line will reduce the head-count ratio.

REFERENCES

Atkinson, A.B. (1989) *Poverty and Social Security*, New York: Harvester Wheatsheaf.
Hagenaars, A.J.M. (1986) *The Perception of Poverty*, Amsterdam: North Holland.
Sen, A. (1979) 'Issues in the Measurement of Poverty', *Scandinavian Journal of Economics* 81: 285–307.
Sen, A. (1981) *Poverty and Famines: An Essay on Entitlement and Deprivation*, Oxford: Clarendon Press.
Watts, H.W. (1968) *An Economic Definition of Poverty*, in D.P. Moynihan (ed.), *On Understanding Poverty*, New York: Basic Books.

HEALTH AND POVERTY

The 1995 *World Health Report* (WHO 1995) states that the world's most ruthless killer and the greatest cause of suffering on earth is listed in the latest edition of WHO's *International Classification of Diseases*, an A-to-Z of all ailments known to medical science, under the code Z59.5. It stands for extreme poverty. Poverty is the main reason why babies are not vaccinated, clean water and sanitation are not provided, curative drugs and other treatments are unavailable, and why mothers die in childbirth. Poverty is the main cause of reduced life expectancy, of handicap and disability, and of starvation. Poverty is a major contributor to mental illness, stress, suicide, family disintegration and substance abuse.

In the industrialized world, there is strong evidence that poverty is an important factor in health. There are clear differences in the incidence of ill health by social class. People in lower social classes, including children, are more likely to suffer from infective and parasitic diseases, pneumonia, poisoning or violence. Adults in lower social classes are more likely, in addition, to suffer from cancer, heart disease and respiratory disease. There are also gender-related problems. Men in lower social classes are more likely to suffer from malignant neoplasms (cancer), accidents, and diseases of the nervous system. Women in lower social classes suffer more from circulatory diseases, and endocrine or metabolic disorders.

There are several possible explanations for these inequalities:

1. Artefact explanations. Both 'health' and 'social class' are artificial categories constructed to reflect social organization.
2. Natural and social selection, including genetic inheritance. This would depend on the view that people who are fittest are most likely to succeed in society, and classes reflect this degree of selection.
3. Poverty leads to ill-health through poor nutrition, housing and environment.
4. Cultural and behavioural explanations.

REFERENCES

WHO (1995) *The World Health Report 1995: Bridging the Gaps*, Geneva: World Health Organization.

HOMELESSNESS

Homelessness is often referred to as being without shelter (or 'roofless-ness'). In many societies people without shelter are able to construct their own, through SQUATTING (Aldrich and Sandhu 1995); in societies in which squatting is not permitted, people have to remain with no shelter. Although the restriction of squatting is most commonly associated with developed countries, the problems also extend to cities in poorer countries which have settled patterns of land tenure (Gilbert 1992). Homelessness is, then, produced by lack of entitlement rather than lack of housing in itself.

The term 'homelessness' is also used to indicate that people have no home of their own. On that basis, people may have some form of shelter – hostels, foyers, or temporary accommodation with friends or relatives – but still be said to be homeless (see e.g. Greve 1991).

REFERENCES

Aldrich, B., and Sandhu, R. (eds) (1995) *Housing the Urban Poor*, London: Zed Books.
Gilbert, A. (1992) 'The Housing of the Urban Poor', in A. Gilbert and J. Gugler, *Cities, Poverty and Development*, Oxford: Oxford University Press.
Greve, J. (1991) *Homelessness in Britain*, York: Joseph Rowntree Trust.

HOUSING

Housing is a major issue in the study of poverty as material depriva-tion, both because it is a major resource in its own right, and because it is often a precondition for the receipt of other resources. In devel-oping countries, issues are closely involved with squatting, because the urban poor often lack entitlements to land tenure (Aldrich and Sandhu 1995). Squatter settlements often lack basic amenities and services and are characterized by poor physical conditions.

In developing countries, the principal issues in housing poverty are access and deprivation. Problems of access arise because housing resources are commanded in a market in which poor people are relatively disadvantaged. This disadvantage implies that poor people are likely to be homeless, or situated in the least desirable properties, which are often of a low physical standard.

REFERENCES

Aldrich, B., and Sandhu, R. (eds) (1995) *Housing the Urban Poor*, London: Zed Books.

HUMAN DEVELOPMENT

Human development is defined by the United Nations Development
Program as follows:

Human development is a process of enlarging people's choices. In
principle, these choices can be infinite and can change over time. But
at all levels of development, the three essential ones are for people
to lead a long and healthy life, to acquire knowledge and to have
access to the resources needed for a decent standard of living. If these
essential choices are not available, many other opportunities remain
inaccessible.... Additional choices, highly valued by many people,
range from political economic and social freedom to opportunities
for being creative and productive and enjoying personal self-respect
and guaranteed human rights.

Human development thus has two sides. One is the formation of
human capabilities – such as improved health, knowledge and skills.
The other is the use people make of their acquired capabilities for
productive purposes for leisure or for being active in cultural, social
and political affairs....

The concept of human development is much broader than the
conventional theories of economic development. Economic growth
models deal with expanding GNP rather than enhancing the quality
of human lives. (UNDP 1995)

The Human Development Index (HDI) is a composite index based
on three indicators: longevity as measured by life expectancy at
birth; educational attainment, as measured by a combination of adult
literacy (two thirds weight) and combined primary secondary and
tertiary enrolment ratios (one-third weight); and standard of living,
as measured by real GDP per capita (PPP$). However there have
been a number of changes made to the way the HDI is constructed
since it was first produced in 1990 (UNDP 1990; 1995).

REFERENCES

UNDP (1990) *Human Development Report 1990: Concepts and Measurement of Human Develop-
ment*, Oxford: Oxford University Press.
UNDP (1995) *Human Development Report 1995: Gender and Human Development*, Oxford:
Oxford University Press.

HUMAN POVERTY INDEX (HPI)

The United Nations Development Program's 1997 *Human Development Report* introduced the Human Poverty Index. This drew heavily
on Sen's CAPABILITIES concept and defined poverty as 'the denial of
choices and opportunities for a tolerable life'. The Human Poverty
Index (HPI) attempted to operationalize this concept by focusing on
those groups whose choices are heavily constrained in each of the
three areas used in the HUMAN DEVELOPMENT Index (HDI). While
the HDI focuses on the average achievements of a country, the HPI
focuses on the most deprived. The HPI is made up of five weighted
components (UNDP 1997):

1. the percentage of people expected to die before age 40 (60 in
   developed countries);
2. the percentage of adults who are illiterate;
3. the percentage of people with access to health services;
4. the percentage of people with access to safe water;
5. the percentage of children under 5 who are malnourished.

Aspects of human poverty that are excluded from the index due to
lack of data or measurement difficulties are lack of political freedom,
inability to participate in decision-making, lack of personal SECURITY,
inability to participate in the life of the community and threats to
sustainability and intergenerational equity.

REFERENCES

UNDP (1997) *Human Development Report 1997: Human Development to Eradicate Poverty*,
   Oxford: Oxford University Press.

HUMAN RIGHTS AND POVERTY

Human rights are general RIGHTS held by every person as a human
being. In principle, human rights are moral tenets which apply to all.
The Universal Declaration of Human Rights includes several rights
to welfare (WELFARE RIGHTS), including 'the economic, social and
cultural rights indispensable for [the individual's] dignity and the
free development of his personality' (Article 22).

The establishment of concepts relating poverty to lack of ENTITLEMENT has led to an increasing emphasis on rights-based approaches as a means of ensuring BASIC SECURITY. The Office of the United Nations High Commissioner for Human Rights (OHCHR) has promoted the initiative of the *Human Rights Approach to Poverty Reduction* (OHCHR 1998, 2004a). This approach links poverty reduction to matters of rights and obligations (OHCHR 2004b), reinforcing the fusion between social, cultural and civil, political and economic rights and the modification of discrimination structures which generate and sustain poverty situations. One of the central ideas in this approach is that 'the rationale of poverty reduction no longer derives merely from the fact that the poor have needs but also from the fact that they have rights – entitlements that give rise to legal obligations on the part of others. Poverty reduction then becomes more than charity, more than a moral obligation – it becomes a legal obligation' (OHCHR 2004b).

CROP has argued that the concept of poverty as a denial of human rights 'shifts the focus from poverty reduction as question of economic development'. The language of rights challenges the utilitarian language of economics, moving the focus to entitlements and obligations enshrined within the formal legal system, while retaining the moral authority that other approaches lack. This shift also removes the emphasis on personal failure to focus on the failure of macro-economic structures and policies implemented by nation-states and international bodies. Hence, poverty in this context is no longer described as a 'social problem' but as 'a structural human rights violation, where relations of dominance and control deprive people of having their basic human rights fulfilled' (CROP 2003: 2, 4, 5).

The human rights approach has implications for the role of government. Government cannot use progressive improvement as an excuse for deferring or relaxing its efforts. First, the state must take immediate action to fulfil any rights that are not seriously dependent on resource availability. Second, it must prioritize its fiscal operations so that resources can be diverted from relatively non-essential uses to those that are essential for the fulfilment of rights that are important for poverty reduction. Third, to the extent that fulfilment of certain rights will have to be deferred, the state must develop, in a participatory manner, a time-bound plan of action for their progressive realization. Finally, the state will be called to account if the monitoring process reveals less than full commitment on its part to realize the targets (Hunt et al. 2003); thus 'a human rights approach adds value because it provides a normative framework of obligations that has the legal power to render governments accountable' (Robinson 2002).

REFERENCES

CROP (2003) *Abolishing Poverty through the International Human Rights Framework: Towards an Integrated Strategy for the Social and Human Sciencies*, consultation organized by CROP for UNESCO Sector for the Social and Human Sciences, Bergen, 5–6 June.

Hunt, P., Osmani, S., and Nowak, M. (2003) 'Summary of the Draft Guidelines on a Human Rights Approach to Poverty Reduction', OHCHR, www.ohchr.org/english/issues/poverty/docs/SwissSummary1.doc.

OHCHR (1998) 'Derechos Humanos y pobreza extrema', Resolution 25, 1998.

OHCHR (2004a) *Los derechos humanos y la reducción de la pobreza: un marco conceptual*, New York: United Nations.

OHCHR (2004b) *Human Right in Development, Draft Guidelines: A Human Rights Approach to Poverty Reduction Strategies*, New York: United Nations.

Robinson, M. (2002) World Summit on Sustainable Development, Plenary Session, www.un.org/events/wssd/statements/stat29.htm.

UN (1948) *Universal Declaration of Human Rights*, New York: United Nations, www.un.org/Overview/rights.html.

I

IMPOVERISHMENT

Impoverishment refers to the process of becoming poor, through 'slow processes' or sudden shocks, faced by individuals, households and communities. Examples include degradation of productive resources (pasture, fisheries, fields), erosion of commodity prices (cash crops, cattle, fish, labour), lack of employment, deprivation of means of subsistence such as land and water, and the weakening of local solidarity. Also the shock of starving and massive impoverishment is related to the weakness or lack of entitlements (Sen 1981). There are some situations in which individuals, households and communities are slowly driven towards poverty, like long-term illness or ageing, when the social security system doesn't work or doesn't exist.

As a concept, impoverishment was introduced in Latin America studies in the 1990s, to take into account the conditions of severe vulnerability and poverty experienced by countless households (Salama 1999; Toye 2004, cited in Barba Solano et. al 2005: 40). The concept is believed, in the context of structural adjustment implementation policies, to overcome the static effect generated by excessive emphasis on studies of poverty-line measurement, and takes account of poverty dynamics and economic volatility. In Argentina and in others countries of Latin America, impoverishment refers to the loss of income and social security coverage of large middle-class groups, called **NEW POOR**, middle class in transition, or pauper groups, as a consequence of the employment crisis created by the new regional neoliberal economics model (Minujin and Kessler 1995; Minujin et al. 1995; Murmis and Feldman 1995).

REFERENCES

Barba Solano, C., Brito Leal Ivo, A., Valencia Lomeli, E., and Ziccardi, A. (2005) 'Research Horizons: Poverty in Latin America', in E. Øyen et al., *The Polyscopic Landscape of Poverty Research, 'State of the Art' in International Poverty Research. An*

Overview and 6 In-depth Studies, report prepared for the Research Council of Norway, Bergen: CROP Secretariat, www.crop.org.

Minujin, A., and Kessler, G. (1995) *La nueva pobreza en la Argentina*, Buenos Aires: Ed. Temas de Hoy.

Minujin, A., et al. (1995) *Cuesta abajo. Los nuevos pobres: efectos de la crisis en la sociedad argentina*, Buenos Aires: UNICEF/LOSADA.

Murmis, M., and Feldman, S. (1995) 'La heterogeneidad social de las pobrezas', in A. Minujin et al., *Cuesta abajo. Los nuevos pobres: efectos de la crisis en la sociedad argentina*, Buenos Aires: UNICEF/LOSADA.

Salama, P. (1999) *Riqueza y pobreza en América Latina. La fragilidad de las nuevas políticas económicas*, México: Fondo de Cultura Económica and Universidad de Guadalajara.

Sen, A. (1981) *Poverty and Famines: An Essay on Entitlement and Deprivation*, Oxford: Clarendon Press.

Toye, J. (2004) 'Nacionalizar la agenda contra la pobreza', in J. Boltvinik and A. Damián (eds), *La pobreza en México y el Mundo*, México: Siglo XXI.

INCENTIVES TO WORK

In ordinary language, an incentive is a way of stimulating and encouraging someone to do something, like a competition prize or a reward for good behaviour. In economics, an incentive is usually seen more simply as a potential gain. Describing an action as an incentive implies four elements:

1. *Prospective gain* – that the supposed incentive implies a desired change in future outcomes.
2. *Choice* – that people have a choice, and that the incentive is capable of being chosen.
3. The influence on *motivation* – whether a factor acts as an incentive depends on whether it affects motivation overall.
4. *Marginal effect* – that the factor has a marginal influence in the context where it is applied.

The suggestion that social benefits have an incentive effect on work depends on a series of assumptions:

1. *Prospective gain: that being unemployed is a desirable outcome.* There is considerable contrary evidence. The costs of unemployment include stigma, boredom, lack of direction, and the consequences of unemployment for ill health, exclusion and poverty (Gallie 1994). There is some evidence of detachment from the labour

market for a minority of older men, but this is not true of most people of working age. (Alcock et al. 2003)

2. *Choice: that people choose to be unemployed.* UNEMPLOYMENT is structured and conditioned by a range of economic factors. Some unemployment may be voluntary, but much is not. The forms of non-voluntary unemployment include, among others, frictional, seasonal, casual, demand-deficient, structural and exclusionary unemployment.

3. *Motivation: that benefits for unemployment have a discernable effect on the motivation to work.* Unemployment benefits tend to be limited both in financial terms and through a series of conditions imposed on receipt (for example, suspension of benefit on leaving work without 'good cause' or on refusal of employment opportunities: Atkinson 1995). There is evidence to suggest that there may be a marginal influence on the position of low-paid wives of men who are in receipt of benefits (Davies et al. 1994). In relation to long-term unemployed people, however, 'the level of unemployment benefit has no explanatory value in considering the labour market behaviour of the long-term unemployed' (Dawes, cited in Alcock et al. 2003: 13).

4. *Marginal effect: that the influence of unemployment benefit outweighs other factors.* Where people are able to make decisions about work, there are many other factors besides benefits that influence decisions – typically financial rewards in employment, social status, social pressure and the desirability of roles related to work. The evidence on incentive effects is that they tend to be very limited in practice (Atkinson and Mogensen 1993).

In practice, arguments about incentives to work tend to be related less to economic or social analysis or evidence than the assumption that people need to be punished for not working. 'People respond to incentives and disincentives … Sticks and carrots work' (Murray, 1984).

REFERENCES

Alcock, P., Beatty, C., Fothergill, S., Macmillan, R., and Yeandle, S. (2003) *Work to Welfare*, Cambridge: Cambridge University Press.

Atkinson, A.B. (1995) *Incomes and the Welfare State*, Cambridge: Cambridge University Press.

Atkinson, A.B., and Mogensen, G. (1993) *Welfare and Work Incentives*, Oxford: Clarendon Press.

Davies, R., Elias, P., and Penn, R. (1994) 'The Relationship between a Husband's Un-
employment and his Wife's Participation in the Labour Force', in D. Gallie, C.
Marsh and C. Vogler (eds), *Social Change and the Experience of Unemployment*, Oxford:
Oxford University Press.

Gallie, D. (1994) 'Unemployment and Social Exclusion in the EU', *European Societies*
1/2: 139–67.

Murray, C. (1984) *Losing Ground*, New York: Basic Books.

INCOME

Income is a key concept in almost all definitions and studies of
poverty. However, 'income' is an extremely difficult concept to define
and agree upon. The term is sometimes used loosely to refer only to
the main component of monetary income for most households – that
is, wages and salaries or business income. Others use the term to
include all receipts including lump-sum receipts and receipts that
draw on the household's capital.

Classically, income has been defined as the sum of consumption
and change in net worth (wealth) in a period. This is known as the
Haig–Simons approach (see Simons 1938 in Atkinson and Stiglitz
1980: 260). Unfortunately, this approach fails to distinguish between
the day-to-day 'living well' and the broader 'getting rich' aspects
of individual or household finances (in technical terms, it fails to
distinguish between current and capital receipts).

A number of international organizations have provided guidelines
on defining and measuring income. The United Nations provides
two frameworks: the 1993 *System of National Accounts* (UN 1992) and
guidelines on collecting micro-level data on the economic resources
of households (UN 1977 and 1989). The International Labour Organization (ILO) has also produced guidelines on the collection of
data on income of households, with particular emphasis on income
from employment (ILO 1971, 1992, 1993). In January 1997 the Australian
Bureau of Statistics (ABS) tried to get an international agreement
on definitions of income, consumption, saving and wealth. The ABS
(1995) has proposed the following definition:

> income comprises those receipts accruing (in cash and in-kind)
> that are of a regular and recurring nature, and are received by the
> household or its members at annual or more frequent intervals. It
> includes regular receipts from employment, own business and from
> the lending of assets. It also includes transfer income from govern-

ment, private institutions and other households. Income also includes the value of services provided from within the household via the use of an owner-occupied dwelling, other consumer durables owned by the household and unpaid household work. Income excludes capital receipts that are considered to be an addition to stocks, and receipts derived from the running down of assets or from the incurrence of a liability. It also excludes intra-household transfers.

Townsend (1979, 1993) has argued that broad definitions of income should be used, particularly if international comparisons are to be made. It is crucial, when comparing individual or household incomes of people in different countries, that account is taken of the value of government services in, for example, the fields of health, education and transport. Unfortunately, many economic studies of poverty use relatively narrow definitions of income, such as wages and salaries or business income. International comparisons based on narrow definitions of this kind can be misleading and of only limited use.

REFERENCES

Atkinson, A., and Stiglitz, J. (1980) *Lectures on Public Economics*, London: McGraw-Hill.

ABS (1995) *A Provisional Framework for Household Income, Consumption, Saving and Wealth*, Canberra: Australian Bureau of Statistics.

ILO (1971) *Scope, Methods and Users of Family Expenditure Surveys, Report III, Twelfth International Conference of Labour Statisticians*, Geneva: ILO.

ILO (1992) *Report 1: General Report, Fifteenth International Conference of Labour Statisticians*, Geneva: ILO.

ILO (1993) *Report of the Conference: Fifteenth International Conference of Labour Statisticians*, Geneva: ILO.

Townsend, P. (1979) *Poverty in the United Kingdom*, Harmondsworth: Penguin.

Townsend, P. (1993) *The International Analysis of Poverty*, Milton Keynes: Harvester Wheatsheaf.

UN (1977) *Provisional Guidelines on Statistics of the Distribution of Income, Consumption and Accumulation of Households*, Studies in Methods, Series M, No. 61, New York: United Nations, http://unstats.un.org/unsd/publication/SeriesM/SeriesM_61E.pdf.

UN (1989) National *Household Survey Capability Program Household Income and Expenditure Surveys: A Technical Study*, New York: United Nations.

UN (1992) *Revised System of National Accounts (Provisional), August 1992 (to be presented to and adopted at the 27th session of the Statistical Commission, February–March 1993*.

INCOME DISTRIBUTION

The allocation of national income between persons or households. The distribution of income is an indicator of economic and social inequality, and the dispersion of income is frequently used as a measure of poverty in itself, although income distribution alone cannot identify the ability of any particular percentile to achieve a minimally acceptable standard of living. The Leyden study, for the European Commission, experimented with various definitions of poverty as a relationship to median income and family size (Hagenaars et al. 1980); other work for the European Community has experimented with levels at 40 per cent, 50 per cent or 60 per cent of average income (Hauser et al. 1980; Hauser and Semerau 1990). The LUXEMBOURG INCOME STUDY refers to people as poor when they have an income of less than 50 per cent of the median equivalent income (Smeeding et al. 1990).

REFERENCES

Hagenaars, A., van Praag, B. and van Weeren, H. (1980) *Poverty in Europe*, Leiden: University of Leiden.
Hauser, R., Cremer-Shaefer, H. and Nouvertné, U. (1980) *National Report on Poverty in the Federal Republic of Germany*, Frankfurt: University of Frankfurt.
Hauser, R., and Semerau, P. (1990) 'Trends in Poverty and Low Income in the Federal Republic of Germany 1962/3–1987', in R. Teekens and B. van Praag (eds), *Analysing Poverty in the European Community, Eurostat News Special Edition* 1–1990, Luxembourg: European Communities.
Smeeding, T.M., O'Higgins, M., and Rainwater, L. (eds) (1990) *Poverty, Inequality and Income Distribution in Comparative Perspective*, New York: Harvester Wheatsheaf.

INCOME ELASTICITY OF THE POVERTY LINE

This technical term is used in the USA to refer to the phenomenon that successive 'absolute' poverty lines show a pattern of rising in real terms over time as the real income of the general population rises. In the USA, minimum subsistence budget standards developed between 1905 and 1960 rose by 0.75 per cent in real terms for each 1.0 per cent increase in the real disposable income per capita of the general population (Ornati 1966; Kilpatrick 1973). A similar pattern appears when one turns from expert-devised standards to responses from the general population. Between 1946 and 1992, the Gallup Poll repeatedly asked the following question: 'What is the smallest amount of money a family of four (husband, wife, and two children) needs each week to get along in this community?' The average response to this 'get along' question rises by between 0.6 and 1.0 per cent for every 1.0 per cent increase in the income of the general population (Kilpatrick 1973; Rainwater 1974; Vaughan 1993; Fisher 1995).

The income elasticity of the poverty line is the result of social processes that operate in industrialized (and industrializing) societies. As technology progresses and the general standard of living rises, new consumption items are introduced. They may at first be purchased and used only by upper-income families; however, they gradually diffuse to middle- and lower-income levels. Things originally viewed as luxuries – for instance, indoor plumbing, telephones and automobiles – come to be seen as conveniences and then as necessities. In addition, changes in the ways in which society is organized (sometimes in response to new 'necessities') may make it more expensive for the poor to accomplish a given goal – as when widespread car ownership and increasing suburbanization lead to a deterioration in public transportation, and the poor are forced to buy cars or hire taxis in order to get to places where public transit used to take them. Finally, the general upgrading of social standards can make things more expensive for the poor – as when housing code requirements that all houses have indoor plumbing add to the cost of housing (Hamilton 1962; President's Commission on Income Maintenance Programs 1969).

REFERENCES

Fisher, G.M. (1995) *Is There Such a Thing as an Absolute Poverty Line Over Time? Evidence from the United States, Britain, Canada, and Australia on the Income Elasticity of the Poverty Line*, Poverty Measurement Working Paper, US Census Bureau website.

Hamilton, D. (1962) 'Drawing the Poverty Line at a Cultural Subsistence Level', *Southwestern Social Science Quarterly* 42/4: 337–45.

Kilpatrick, R.W. (1973) 'The Income Elasticity of the Poverty Line', *Review of Economics and Statistics* 55/3: 327–3?

Ornati, O. (1966) *Poverty Amid Affluence*, New York: Twentieth Century Fund.

Rainwater, L. (1974) *What Money Buys: Inequality and the Social Meanings of Income*, New York: Basic Books.

President's Commission on Income Maintenance Programs (1969) *Poverty Amid Plenty: The American Paradox*, Washington DC: US Government Printing Office.

Vaughan, D.R. (1993) 'Exploring the Use of the Public's Views to Set Income Poverty Thresholds and Adjust Them Over Time', *Social Security Bulletin* 56/2: 22–46.

INCOME INELASTICITY OF DEMAND

People who have met their minimum needs for goods can be expected to spend proportionately less on those items as income rises (Lipton 1995: 140). This can be used as a method in order to establish a minimum income. The best known example is the ENGEL COEFFICIENT.

REFERENCES

Lipton, M. (1995) 'Growing Points in Poverty Research: Labour Issues', in G. Rodgers (ed.), *The Poverty Agenda and the ILO*, Geneva: ILO.

INCOME MAINTENANCE

Income maintenance is a general term for the provision of financial resources when personal income is interrupted or insufficient. The term is often identified with SOCIAL SECURITY, but the idea of social security is used both more widely (including non-financial support and health insurance) and more narrowly (referring specifically to social insurance).

There are five main types of income maintenance benefit:

- SOCIAL INSURANCE, where benefits depend on previous contributions;
- means-tested benefits, which depend on a test of income, capital or resources (MEANS-TESTING);
- 'non-contributory' benefits, which have no test of contribution or means, but which may be subject to other tests of needs (e.g. industrial injuries benefits);
- universal or categorical benefits, given to everyone in a broad category, e.g. elderly people or children (universality);
- Discretionary benefits, which may be subject to the decision of an official or social worker. SOCIAL ASSISTANCE bridges these categories, because it may be means-tested, discretionary or both.

Income maintenance benefits are liable, beyond the issue of design, to be conditional on them meeting certain requirements. For example, family benefits may be conditional on families complying with terms about their children's education and health, such as school attendance (Rawlings 2004).

REFERENCES

Rawlings, L.B. (2004) *A New Approach to Social Assistance: Latin America's Experience with Conditional Cash Transfer Programs*. Social Protection Discussion Paper No. 0416, Washington DC: World Bank, http://wbln0018.worldbank.org/HDNet/HDdocs.nsf/vtlw/4BB6997285F65EF585256EE5005E3A75?OpenDocument.

INCOME SMOOTHING

Income smoothing refers to the redistribution of income over time. On an individual level, both saving (in the form, for example, of an occupational pension) and borrowing (for example for property owner-ship) may have the effect of relocating costs and benefits across an individual life cycle. Systems of social insurance similarly redistribute the income and consumption of a contributor over time. By extension, at the level of the economy, the term is associated with redistribution between people of different age groups, or 'solidarity between generations' (Barr 1991). The process of horizontal REDISTRIBUTION, and the obligations associated with it, can be reinterpreted as a form of distribution over time (Falkingham et al. 1993).

At the level of the household, income smoothing refers to an adjustment by households to protect themselves from adverse income shocks *before* they occur by making conservative production or employment choices and diversifying economic activities (Morduch 1995). The concept of income smoothing in this context is typically applied to the farm and village households of low-income economies. Agriculture, and income derived from it, is dependent on various factors like weather, labour input, fertilizer use and commodity prices. For example, delaying farming in anticipation of certainty about weather, applying less fertilizer and using more labour are typical strategies to decrease variability in income – that is, to smooth income.

Income smoothing is differentiated from consumption smoothing – that is, strategies like borrowing – adopted *after* income shocks occur.

REFERENCES

Barr, N. (1991) 'The Objectives and Attainments of Pension Schemes', in T. Wilson and D. Wilson (eds), *The State and Social Welfare*, London: Longman.

Falkingham, J., Hills, J., and Lessof, C. (1993) *William Beveridge versus Robin Hood: Social Security and Redistribution over the Lifecycle*, London: London School of Economics Welfare State Programme.

Morduch, J. (1995) 'Income Smoothing and Consumption Smoothing', *Journal of Economic Perspectives* 9/3: 103–14.

INDICATORS

The term 'indicators' is generally used to show that quantitative information about social issues represents not simple 'facts' but rather ways of putting together complex and uncertain information. Indicators are sometimes represented as summary factors: for example, a social indicator can be seen as

> a statistic of direct normative interest facilitating concise, comprehensive and balanced judgement about the condition of major aspects of society. (US Department of Health, Education and Welfare, cited in Carley 1981)

It has been argued, however, that this simply describes an operational definition of an issue: an indicator is a statistic which is taken to mean something else besides the core information it contains (Midgely and Piachaud 1984: 39). An 'indicator' points in a direction; it has to be interpreted. Typical problems include:

- the selection of indicators which are easily available and quantifiable, in preference to others which may be difficult or expensive to collect;
- the inclusion of normative judgements as if they were 'facts': for example, the use of monetary values to estimate the social value of labour, or distinctions between unemployment and non-employment;
- the problems of treating issues, once quantified, as if they were numbers; figures for mortality cannot meaningfully be added together with figures for income to construct INDICES OF DEPRIVATION.

REFERENCES

Carley, M. (1981) *Social Measurement and Social Indicators*, London: Allen & Unwin.
Midgley, J., and Piachaud, D. (1984) 'Social Indicators and Social Planning', in *The Fields and Methods of Social Planning*, London: Heinemann.

INDICES OF DEPRIVATION

An index consists of a set of indicators which are compiled in order to produce a composite measure. Spicker (2004) outlines the main issues as:

- *Validity*: indices have to measure what they are supposed to measure, and cross-validation is difficult. (In the UK, benefit rates have frequently been used as the main test.)
- *Reliability*: indices which are reliable within a particular social context, or at a certain period, are not necessarily transferable to other circumstances.
- *Quantification* (cf. INDICATORS); the construction of indices tends to presume linear mathematical relationships.
- *Inclusion* and exclusion of relevant factors: exclusions lead to important issues being ignored. Over-inclusion can lead to excessive weight being given to particular factors; the high level of multicollinearity in social phenomena related to deprivation makes multivariate analysis difficult.
- *Weighting*: factors have to be given appropriate weights, which depends on appropriate quantification.

REFERENCES

Spicker, P. (2004) 'Developing Indicators: Issues in the Use of Quantitative Data about Poverty', *Policy and Politics* 32/4: 431–40.

INDIGENCE

A person who is indigent is in need, and in mot uses of the term lacks the means for SUBSISTENCE. The United Nations Economic Commission for Latin America has referred to an indigence line, which at half the value of the poverty line is supposed to cover only basic nutritional requirements (cited in Golbert and Kessler 1996). An example is its use in BRAZILIAN DEFINITIONS OF POVERTY.

In early-nineteenth-century texts on political economy, particularly the British Poor Law Report of 1834, a distinction was often made between 'indigence' and 'poverty'. Indigence was a condition of abject destitution: it was 'the state of a person unable to labour, or unable to obtain, in return for his labour, the means of subsistence' and should thus be met with relief provision. Poverty on the other hand, was inexorably woven into society, being a part of inequality: it was 'the state of one who, in order to obtain a mere subsistence, is forced to have recourse to labour' (Checkland and Checkland 1974: 334) and was thus a consequence of differential earning power.

REFERENCES

Checkland, S., and Checkland, O. (eds) (1974) *The Poor Law Report of 1834*, Harmondsworth: Penguin.

Golbert, L., and Kessler, G. (1996) *Latin America: Poverty as a Challenge for Government and Society*, in E. Øyen, S.A. Samad and S.M. Miller (eds), *Poverty: A Global Review. Handbook on Poverty Research*, Oslo and Paris: Scandinavian University Press and UNESCO.

INFORMAL SECTOR OF THE ECONOMY

The distinction between formal and informal engagement in the economy is mainly concerned with the dynamics of the labour market. The conceptualization of the informal economy has two main characteristics. First, informality includes residual activities – in the sense that they are productive activities, not conforming to capitalist production forms, which in general are not registered using the standard measurement techniques. Second, informality has to do with activities which are not subject to conventional norms or regulation.

The informal sector is identified by its heterogeneity, manifest in technological diversity, market segmentation, the uneven distribution of income and welfare, difference in lifestyles, and even in the intergenerational transmission of opportunities. The sector is directly associated with poverty, even though the focus is on the type of non-capitalist rationale of the economic activities.

The Regional Programme of Employment for Latin America and the Caribbean (PREALC) laid the foundation for a definition of the informal sector as the sum of activities characterized by a logic of production different from that in force in the visible part of the economy. This research identifies the main economic rationale for the sector as a means of maintaining family livelihoods (Raczynski 1979; Tockman and Souza 1976). The informal sector consists of a wide range of alternative ways of generating income. This includes direct livelihood activities: self-employed individuals producing or trading goods and services in the market; domestic exchange; production in small companies; and the employment of marginal or hidden paid workers without the protection of legal rights.

Portes (1964) sees the formal sector as characterized by contractual employment featuring explicit rights and responsibilities, line management, and terms for hiring and firing. He argues that legality has been the result of workers' social struggle, seeking to set limits to the various forms of capital exploitation. Informality, by contrast, is associated with working relationships that are illegal or that fall outside the scope of legal agreements. These are associated with the processes of labour flexibility, breakdown of the permanent and contractual paid model, and deregulation and privatization of state activities.

REFERENCES

Portes, A. (1964) 'El sector informal: definición, controversias, relaciones con el desarrollo nacional', in *Ciudades y Sistemas Urbanos*, Buenos Aires: CLACSO.

Raczynski, D. (1979) 'Sector informal urbano, algunos problemas conceptuales', in *El subempleo en América Latina*, Buenos Aires: El Cid.

Tockman, V., and Souza, R. (1976) *El empleo en América Latina, problemas económicos, sociales y políticos*, Buenos Aires: Siglo XXI.

INSERTION

Insertion is an attempt to incorporate people who are excluded into the pattern of solidaristic social networks that is part of normal social life: EXCLUSION. This is often understood in terms of insertion into the labour market, but the focus of insertion goes beyond economic issues into questions of conduct and social relationships. Thévenet (1989: 181–4) applies a broad conception of the term, covering provisions that are associated with social work support, housing provision, community development, health and education.

The French Revenu Minimum d'Insertion makes provision for benefit recipients to sign a 'contract of insertion'. The pattern of contracts has been characterized generally as social, professional or economic (Euzeby 1991: 85–6).

Social insertion refers to the situation of people who are excluded by virtue of social disadvantage, for example disability or single parenthood. Professional insertion is for people who require some kind of training or preparation for work. Economic insertion is for people who are unemployed but who would be in a position to move directly to employment.

REFERENCES

Euzeby, C. (1991) *Le revenu minimum garanti*, Paris: Éditions la Découverte.

Thévenet, A. (1989) *RMI Théorie et pratique*, Paris: Centurion.

INSTITUTIONAL WELFARE

The term 'institutional welfare' was first used by Wilensky and Lebeaux (1958) to describe a model of welfare in which the collective provision of social protection is an accepted and normal part of social life. It is generally contrasted with the 'residual' model of welfare, which is confined to people who are otherwise unable to provide for themselves.

REFERENCES

Wilensky, H., and Lebeaux, C. (1958) *Industrial Society and Social Welfare*, New York: Free Press.

INTEGRATED POVERTY (*PAUVRETÉ INTÉGRÉE*)

The term *pauvreté intégrée* in France is used to refer to poverty which affects people who are in salaried employment, or whose poverty is concealed because they are otherwise part of existing social networks. Poverty ordinarily is associated with EXCLUSION; Paugam (1996) contrasts integrated poverty with the poverty of DISQUALIFICATION. Integrated poverty also occurs where there is mass poverty, which does not imply exclusion; there may be no identifiable group of poor people who are distinguishable from the rest of the population.

REFERENCES

Paugam, S. (1996) 'Pauvreté et exclusion: la force des contrastes nationaux', in S. Paugam (ed.), *L'exclusion: l'état des savoirs*, Paris: Éditions la Découverte.

INTEGRATED POVERTY LINE

This term has been used to describe a POVERTY LINE that draws together information from a range of sources, rather than relying on a single indicator like INCOME. The Economic Commission for Latin America and the Caribbean refers to the combination in urban Chile of minimum food requirements with a range of indicators; for example, 'the sewerage system, the availability of water and electricity, the type of housing, standard of construction, crowding within the dwelling.'

REFERENCES

Wratten, E. (1995) 'Conceptualizing Urban Poverty', *Environment and Urbanization* 7/1 (April): 11–36.

INTERGENERATIONAL CONTINUITY

This refers to the belief that poverty is maintained from generation to generation within certain families; it is associated with pathological modes of explanation, including genetic and familial explanations. Research in the UK has raised doubts as to the validity of the belief (CYCLE OF DEPRIVATION) (Brown and Madge 1982). Kolvin et al. (1990) studied the progress of 1,000 poor families from the early 1950s through to the late 1980s. In each generation, risks and vulnerability to poverty were greater among those whose parents were poor. However, the combined effect over time of economic cycles, life-cycle changes, marriage and social mobility meant that there were no visible continuities that lasted across four generations. In their conclusion the researchers speculated that there may be evidence of continuity at the level of the individual family which their method was unable to detect. However, the related study, by Coffield and Sarsby (1980), did not find continuities in specific families either.

REFERENCES

Brown, M., and Madge, N. (1982) *Despite the Welfare State*, London: Heinemann.
Coffield, F., and Sarsby, J. (1980) *A Cycle of Deprivation?* London: Heinemann.
Kolvin, I., Miller, F.J.W., Scott, D.M., Gatzanis, S.R.M., and Fleeting, M. (1990) *Continuities of Deprivation? The Newcastle 1000 Family Study*, Aldershot: Avebury.

INTERNATIONAL AID

Also known as foreign aid or overseas development assistance, international aid refers to the transfer to countries of middle or low income of financial resources, equipment, knowledge or technical assistance. It is aimed at alleviating poverty or extreme poverty, promoting economic growth, fighting epidemics, minimizing the effects of natural disasters or armed conflicts.

In general, this aid is provided by government, multilateral agencies or non-governmental organizations (NGOs). From the mid-1980s development assistance has been subjected to CONDITIONALITY or incentives such as an optimum government, reduced corruption, the privatization of state companies, as a requirement on the part of applicant countries for access to resources. The effectiveness of development assistance under these conditionalities and incentives is an matter of controversy, for it not only breaks the sovereignty of the poor nations but creates relations of dependency (see DEPENDENCY THEORY) and places the reduction of poverty within a rhetoric of objectives that are difficult to attain.

Furthermore, there is evidence to show that in many cases the placing of aid has tended to give high priority to criteria such as the quality of institutions and the consistency of public policies, thereby relegating aid to the poorest countries with weakened institutions (Collier 1999; McGillivray 2005). On the other hand, the policies of structural adjustment promoted by the World Bank and IMF have shown the ineffectiveness of this conditionality in promoting growth and reduced poverty.

Recently, new instruments have emerged to coordinate and provide rules regarding access and availability of resources for development assistance (Rogerson et al. 2004), such as the US Millennium Challenge Account, the Global Fund to Fight AIDS, TB and malaria, and the International Financing Facility. Together with the setting of goals such as the MILLENNIUM DEVELOPMENT GOALS, these approaches aim to reorganize the system of international aid at a global level and whose advance and outcome are still uncertain.

REFERENCES

Collier, P. (1999) *Target Aid to Performance Not Promises*, Washington DC: World Bank.

IMF (2001) *Conditionality in Fund-Supported Programs – Overview*, Policy Development and Review Department, Washington DC: International Monetary Fund, 20 February.

McGillivray, M. (2005) 'Aid Allocation and Fragile States', background paper for OECD Senior Level Forum on Development Effectiveness in Fragile States, London, 13–14 January.

Rogerson, A., Hewitt, A., Waldenberg, D. (2004) *The International Aid System 2005–2010: Forces For and Against Change*, London: Overseas Development Institute.

INTERNATIONAL FUND FOR AGRICULTURAL DEVELOPMENT DEFINITIONS OF POVERTY

The IFAD is one of three international organizations, along with the World Bank and the United Nations Development Programme, that produces internationally comparative estimates of poverty for developing countries (see WORLD BANK POVERTY LINES and HUMAN POVERTY INDEX). The IFAD, one of the world's foremost authorities on rural poverty, has constructed four poverty indices that are designed to measure rural poverty and deprivation (Jazairy et al. 1995).

1. The *food security index* (FSI), which attempts to measure the composite food security situation of a country. This index combines relevant food production and consumption variables, including those reflecting growth and variability. The index can take values zero and above, with one being a cut-off point between countries which are relatively food secure and those which are not.

2. The *integrated poverty index* (IPI) is an economic index which is calculated by combining the head-count measure of poverty with the income-gap ratio, income distribution below the poverty line, and the annual rate of growth of per capita GNP. According to the IFAD the HEAD-COUNT INDEX represents the percentage of the rural population below the poverty line. The income-gap ratio is a national measure, the difference between the highest GNP per capita from among the 114 developing countries and the individual country GNP per capita expressed as a percentage of the former. Life expectancy at birth is used as a surrogate measure of income distribution below the poverty line. The IPI follows Amartya Sen's composite poverty index (Sen 1976) and can take values between zero and one, closer to one indicating a relatively worse poverty status.

3. The *basic needs index* (BNI) is designed to measure the social development of rural areas. It is composed of an education index and a health index. The education index covers adult literacy and primary school enrolment, while the health index includes population per physician, infant mortality rate and access to services such as health, safe water and sanitation. The BNI can take values between zero and one. The closer the value is to one, the higher the basic needs status of the population of a country.

4. The *relative welfare index* (RWI) is the arithmetic average of the other three indices (FSI, RWI, BNI). The FSI is normalized to take values between zero and one; the RWI takes value within the same range.

The IFAD also produces a women's status index (WSI), which is designed to measure the situation of women in order to derive concrete policy recommendations to help improve the status of poor rural women in developing countries. The indicators used in the WSI are: maternal mortality rate, percentage of women using contraceptives, female adult literacy rate, gross female primary school enrolment, gross female secondary school enrolment, female–male wage ratio in agriculture, and female labour-force participation rate. The WSI can take a value between zero and one; the closer the value is to one the higher the status of women.

The Food Security Index demonstrates that there was a general decline in food security in many developing countries between the mid-1960s and mid-1980s, particularly in sub-Saharan Africa. The twenty lowest ranked countries on the relative welfare index are consistent with those considered poorest using the HUMAN DEVELOPMENT Index method of the UNDP (UNEP 1995).

REFERENCES

Jazairy, I., Alamgir, M., and Panuccio, T. (1995) *The State of World Rural Poverty*, London: IFAD.

Sen, A. (1976) 'Poverty: An Ordinal Approach to Measurement', *Econometrica* 44/2: 219–31.

UNEP (1995) *Poverty and the Environment*, Nairobi: United Nations Environment Programme.

INTRA-HOUSEHOLD TRANSFERS

Pahl (1989) argues that traditional poverty studies see the household as a black box. By focusing on the household as a single homogenous unit, poverty studies tend to ignore the transfer of resources within the household and the impact of this division on the experience of poverty. Behind this notion of the household as a single economic unit lies the assumption that there is equal access to household resources. Research which goes inside the black box has demonstrated that, as a result of differences in power, household resources cannot be assumed to be shared equitably (Nyman 1996). The effect of ignoring intra-household transfers is that those living in poverty may be misrepresented. Feminist scholars have argued that women may be experiencing poverty, even when they live in households with aggregate incomes well above the poverty line (Payne 1991). Furthermore, in situations of poverty, women may be exposing themselves to a higher degree of poverty in order to protect their family from its worst effects.

REFERENCES

Cowell, F. (1986) *Micro-economic Principles*, Oxford: Philip Allan.

Nyman, C. (1996) 'Inside the Black Box: Intra-household Distribution of Consumption in Sweden', in E. Bihagen, C. Nyman and M. Strand, *Three Aspects of Consensual Poverty in Sweden – Work Deprivation, Attitudes towards the Welfare-state and Household Consumptional Distribution*, University of Umeå.

Pahl, J. (1989) *Money and Marriage*, London: Macmillan.

Payne, S. (1991) *Women, Health and Poverty*, Hemel Hempstead: Harvester Wheatsheaf.

INVERSE CARE LAW

Although poor people tend to have worse health, they also are liable to receive less health care. In many countries this is related to the deterrent effects of pricing, but the situation also applies in the UK National Health Service, which is nominally free at the point of delivery. The Black Report in the UK identified two main classes of explanation. The first are cultural: the demand for health care is different among different groups. People in lower social classes are said to be less able to explain complaints to middle-class doctors, less able to demand resources and more willing to tolerate illness. The second are practical problems. Working-class people are less likely to have access to a telephone, less likely to have cars, and less free to take time off work without losing pay. Doctors' surgeries are more likely to be in salubrious areas, and so difficult to reach (Townsend et al. 1988).

The term 'inverse care law' was coined by Tudor Hart to describe the general observation that 'the availability of good medical

care tends to vary inversely with the need of the population served'
(Tudor Hart 1971).

REFERENCES

Townsend, P., Davidson, N., and Whitehead, M. (1988) *Inequalities in Health*, Harmondsworth: Penguin.
Tudor Hart, J. (1971) 'The Inverse Care Law', *Lancet* 1: 405–12.

ISLAMIC DEFINITIONS OF POVERTY

Poverty, in the Islamic perspective, is the state of inadequacy of
goods, means or both, that are necessary for the continued well-being
of the human being. It implies a state where the individual lacks the
resources to meet the needs necessary, not only for continued survival but also for a healthy and productive survival (Ul Haq 1996).

The Qu'ran denotes two levels of poverty: the destitute poor and
the needy poor.

The destitute poor, *al fuqara* (sing. *fakir*) are persons who lack
material means, possessions or income to support themselves. The
destitute poor, are persons in involuntary poverty who are unable to
satisfy their necessary needs. They may be disabled or handicapped,
unable to fend for themselves, without assets or incomes, without
capital for trade or self-employment, landless, unskilled, old, orphans
or poor widows (Ul Haq 1996).

The needy poor, *al masakin* (sing. *miskin*), live in misery, dependent
on others, either unable to work or not earning enough to maintain
themselves and their family, humble and in straitened circumstances.
The needy *masakin* are the working poor, the underemployed who
work long and hard hours, or the non-working but income-possessing
individuals, who face inadequacy of income/assets due to a large
number of dependants or low-level productivity.

While *miskin* implies a state of involuntary poverty, the Qu'ran
mentions one category of *masakin* who chooses poverty voluntarily. Those were the people who in the Prophet's time had devoted
themselves completely to learning, teaching and meeting priority
social needs. As a consequence, they could not work and support
themselves (Qu'ran 2: 273).

Beside the destitute and the needy poor, the Qu'ran points to other groups who need temporarily monetary assistance. The overburdened, *al gharimun*, include two kinds. The first are those overwhelmed by debts contracted in good faith which they are subsequently unable to repay. The debts can be for consumption needs or for business needs, or for people who are simply in chronic debt. They become poor, and get poorer, while trying to pay back their debts. The second are those who lose their properties due to natural catastrophes: floods, fire, agricultural epidemic, and so on.

The wayfarer, *ibn al sabil* (literally, son of the road), denotes any person far from home who lacks sufficient means to meet the needs on the journey or stay, and consequently faces hardship. Nowadays, this includes the category of people who, for some valid reason, are unable to return home, temporarily or permanently.

REFERENCES

Mashhour, N. (1998) 'Potential Impact of the Application of the "Basic Needs" Concept vis-à-vis the "Sufficiency Level" Concept of Poverty Alleviation and Social Development', paper presented at CROP/INSEA workshop in Morocco, February.

Ul Haq, I. (1996) *Economic Doctrines of Islam*, Kuala Lumpur: International Institute of Islamic Thought.

K

KUZNETS INVERTED U CURVE; KUZNETS RATIO

The U curve is a hypothesis of the relationship between income growth and inequality. It states that at very low levels of income, income inequality must also be low as nearly everybody is close to a subsistence level of income. As the momentum of growth (rate of increase of GNP) picks up, income inequality increases. People migrate from the traditional (agricultural) to the modern (industrial/manufacturing) sector where wages as well as their differential are higher. At the early stages of development, both physical and human capital are scarce and unequally distributed. Their owners command high returns on both (scarcity premium). As both types of capital accumulate and become less concentrated, the rate of return on physical capital tends to decline, while wage differentials between skilled and unskilled labour narrow. Income distribution gets more equal.

The Kuznets ratio refers to the proportion of output produced in agriculture relative to the rest of the economy. On the basis of the U curve hypothesis, this can be taken to provide a functional indicator of the distribution of income in developing countries (Samad 1996).

REFERENCES

Samad, S.A. (1996) 'The Present Situation in Poverty Research, in E. Øyen, S.A. Samad and S.M. Miller (eds), *Poverty: A Global Review. Handbook on Poverty Research*, Oslo and Paris: Scandinavian University Press and UNESCO.

L

LAEKEN INDICATORS

At the Nice Summit in December 2000, European Union countries agreed to produce National Action Plans on Social Inclusion (NAP-incl) designed to promote social inclusion and combat poverty and social exclusion. The Laeken European Council subsequently argued that establishing a set of common indicators was an important element

> for eradicating poverty and promoting social inclusion, taking in health and housing. The European Council stresses the need to reinforce the statistical machinery and calls on the Commission gradually to involve the candidate countries in this process. (Laeken 2001)

The eighteen indicators of poverty and social inclusion which have been agreed to date are listed below – they are sometimes referred to as the 'Laeken' indicators.

Primary indicators

1. Low-income rate after transfers with low-income threshold set at 60 per cent of median income (with breakdowns by gender, age, most frequent activity status, household type and tenure status; as illustrative examples, the values for typical households).
2. Distribution of income (income quintile ratio).
3. Persistence of low income.
4. Median low-income gap.
5. Regional cohesion.
6. Long-term unemployment rate.
7. People living in jobless households.
8. Early school leavers not in further education or training.
9. Life expectancy at birth.
10. Self-perceived health status.

Secondary indicators

11. Dispersion around the 60 per cent median low-income threshold.
12. Low-income rate anchored at a point in time.
13. Low-income rate before transfers.
14. Distribution of income (Gini coefficient).
15. Persistence of low income (based on 50 per cent of median income).
16. Long-term unemployment share.
17. Very long term unemployment rate.
18. Persons with low educational attainment.

REFERENCES

Laeken Summit (2001) www.europarl.eu.int/summits/pdf/lae_en.pdf.

LANDLESSNESS

Landlessness constitutes one of the key deprivations faced by the poor. It encompasses varied situations like absolute deprivation of land, but also insecure tenancy, informal occupancy, lack or negation of rights of property faced by rural workers, the rural poor and indigenous people, but also by the urban poor, the urban dweller and the informal urban population occupying informal settlements.

The problems of land tenure have been important in very dissimilar situations, such as the de-collectivization and privatization processes in Eastern Europe or the legacy of colonial administration. In Africa, the issues have been compounded by traditional patterns of land holding (IFAD 2001; World Bank 2003), and in particular the limited rights of women to hold land (Sachs 2005). These situations indicate what access to land represents, since it is related not only to property rights but also to aspects such as access to natural resources, identity and culture.

Recently, landlessness and the problem of land distribution have became more prominent as a consequence of the social and political demands of the Movemento dos Trabalhadores Rurais Sem Terra (MST) of Brazil. In its early stages, the MST demanded land access and occupied state-owned farms, but subsequently it has taken on new responsibilities like credit access. It has extended the demand for land rights beyond rural areas to peri-urban and urban settlements. (Coletti 2003; Carter 2003).

REFERENCES

Carter, M. (2003) *The Origins of Brazil's Landless Rural Workers' Movement (MST): The Natalino episode in Rio Grande do Sul (1981–84)*, Working Paper CBS-43–2003, University of Oxford Centre for Brazilian Studies.

Coletti, C. (2003) 'Avancos e Impasse do MST e da Luta per la Terra no Brasil nos Anos Recentes', in J. Seona (ed.), *Movimientos Sociales y Conflicto en América Latina*, Buenos Aires: CLACSO–Ocsal.

IFAD (2001) *Rural Poverty Report 2001: The Challenge of Ending Rural Poverty*, International Fund for Agricultural Development, Oxford: Oxford University Press.

Sachs, J. (2005) *Investing in Development: Overview*, New York: United Nations Development Programme.

World Bank (2003) *Land Policies for Growth and Poverty Reduction. A World Bank Policy Research Report*, Oxford: Oxford University Press.

LESS ELIGIBILITY

The English POOR LAW Report of 1834 set the principle that the condition of the pauper should be 'less eligible' (that is, less to be chosen) than that of the independent labourer: a pauper's situation should 'not be made really or apparently so eligible as the situation of the independent labourer of the lowest class' (Checkland and Checkland 1974: 335). Essentially the less eligibility principle stipulates that those in receipt of benefit should not be better off (materially and psychologically) than those in the lowest-paid employment. It is thus a device to enforce work incentives and labour supply.

The principle of less eligibility has operated in most social security systems around the world and has usually been the criterion by which benefit levels have been fixed, rather than by notions of 'subsistence'. The principle has a direct descendant in present-day concerns with the maintenance of INCENTIVES TO WORK, which in the UK and USA are judged not by the replacement ratio of income for individuals but by a comparison of the position of the benefit recipient with the lowest wage that another person might earn.

REFERENCES

Checkland, S., and Checkland, O. (eds) (1974) *The Poor Law Report of 1834*, Harmondsworth: Penguin.

LIVING STANDARDS MEASUREMENT STUDY

The LSMS Program is an initiative of the World Bank to obtain high-quality household and community survey data from developing countries. It provides comparable (and in many ways superior) data on developing countries to that provided on the industrialized countries by the LUXEMBOURG INCOME STUDY (LIS). Despite the relative ease of access and huge potential that LSMS data has for poverty studies, they have been relatively underused by academic researchers.

The Living Standards Measurement Study was launched in 1980 and the first surveys were implemented in Côte d'Ivoire in 1985 and in Peru in 1985–86. Since then, over forty LSMS surveys have been conducted in nineteen countries and new LSMS surveys are currently in the field or being planned in nine additional countries.

LSMS surveys provide data on several aspects of household welfare. They have a modular design, with

- *Household questionnaire* covering household composition, durables, CONSUMPTION, INCOME, dwelling characteristics, asset ownership and economic and agro-pastoral activities. Sectoral modules from each household include health, education, fertility, anthropometrics and migration. The sectoral modules are designed to measure a few key outcomes (such as nutritional status, vaccination rates, incidence of diarrhoea among children, and enrolment rates) and to measure the use of services that might affect those outcomes.
- *Community questionnaire* covering information on local conditions that are common to all households in the area. This questionnaire is typically used only in rural areas, where local communities are easier to define. The information covered by the questionnaire typically includes the location and quality of nearby health facilities and schools, the condition of local infrastructure such as roads, sources of fuel and water, availability of electricity, means of communications, and local agricultural conditions and practices.
- *Price questionnaire* In countries where prices vary considerably among regions, it is important to gather information on the prices that households actually pay for goods and services. The price questionnaires compile information on the prices of the most important items that a household (particularly a poor household) must buy and that are widely available throughout the country.

The prices are gathered in markets or shops in the communities where the households live.

- *Special facility questionnaire*   Sometimes special questionnaires are designed to gather detailed information on schools or health facilities.

LSMS surveys are useful for understanding household economic decisions and the effects of social and economic policies. The use of LSMS data in poverty assessments helps to ensure that efforts to reduce poverty can be guided by quantitative information on levels, causes and consequences of poverty. Governments have used the data in various direct and indirect ways. In Bolivia, LSMS data were used to help the government evaluate its public employment programme. In Jamaica, the government used data from its LSMS survey to reformulate the food stamps programme. In South Africa, the government used the data in designing its tax reform programme.

LSMS surveys have evolved over time. Originally they were motivated primarily to support research; now they are more often driven by policy needs. The contents of the questionnaires have accordingly changed over the years and from country to country. In 1995, Tanzania became the first country to allow data from its LSMS survey to be put on the Internet for easy access by scholars worldwide.

REFERENCES

Grosh, M.E., and Muñoz, J. (1996) *A Manual for Planning and Implementing the Living Standards Measurement Study Survey*, Living Standards Measurement Study Working Paper 126, Washington DC: World Bank.

LOW INCOME CUT-OFFS

Low Income Cut-Offs (LICOs) are used in Canada to analyse poverty. LICOs were devised by Jenny Podoluk and have been published regularly by Statistics Canada since 1969. Podoluk (1965) found from the Survey of Family Expenditures for 1959 that, on average, urban families spent about 50 per cent of their income on 'essentials' – food, shelter, and clothing. She assumed that families spending a significantly higher proportion (70 per cent) of their income on these necessities were probably 'in straitened circumstances', with little discretionary income left after meeting basic living requirements.

She picked the income levels at which families of various sizes spent 70 percent of income on these necessities as the LICOs. Methodologically her figures resembled food-ratio poverty lines determined without reference to the cost of any specific subsistence diet.

LICOs have been subject to progressive revisions to reflect changes in expenditure patterns. As real incomes rise, the proportion spent on food, shelter and clothing decreases, resulting in higher LICOs. As of 2004, 1992-based LICOs were still being used, adjusted for price changes only since the base year.

In 1991 Statistics Canada introduced a new measure, the Low Income Measure (LIM), calculated as half of median family income after adjustment for family size. The LIM, unlike the LICOs, was not adjusted for size of area of residence (Statistics Canada 1991). Two further variants, LICO-IAT and the LIM-IAT, were introduced in 1992, both based on income after tax (IAT) (Statistics Canada 1992).

REFERENCES

Podoluk, J.R. (1965) 'Characteristics of Low Income Families', unpublished paper prepared for the Federal-Provincial Conference on Poverty and Opportunity, Ottawa.

Statistics Canada (1992) *Income after Tax, Distributions by Size in Canada, 1990*, Ottawa: Statistics Canada.

LUXEMBOURG INCOME STUDY; LUXEMBOURG EMPLOYMENT STUDY

The Luxembourg Income Study is an attempt to compile data on the distribution of income in several developed countries to produce standardized and directly comparable information (Smeeding et al. 1990; Mitchell 1991). The LIS project is the prime source of comparative data on income inequality in industrialized countries. Over 150 papers have been published, the majority of which are concerned with the characteristics of low income/expenditure households. Much of this research on income inequality, equates low income with poverty and/or SOCIAL EXCLUSION despite the fact that a relatively narrow definition of income is used and little additional information is available on standard of living. The study has been able effectively to compare disparate benefit systems through examination of the 'income package' available to people in similar circumstances.

The LIS began in 1983 under the joint sponsorship of the government of Luxembourg and the Centre for Population, Poverty and Policy Studies (CEPS) in Walferdange. The LIS Project has four goals:

1. To test the feasibility for creating a database containing social and economic data collected in household surveys from different countries.
2. To provide a method allowing researchers to use the data under restrictions required by the countries providing the data.
3. To create a system that would allow research requests to be received and returned to users at remote locations.
4. To promote comparative research on the economic status of populations in different countries.

Since its beginning in 1983, the experiment has grown into a cooperative research project with a membership that includes countries in Europe, North America, the Far East and Australia. The database now contains information for more than twenty countries for one or more years. Negotiations are under way to add data from additional countries, including Korea, Russia, Portugal and Mexico. The LIS databank has a total of over sixty data-sets covering the period 1968–92.

In 1994, a new project associated with LIS was set up the Luxembourg Employment Study (LES), funded by the Human Capital and Mobility Programme of the European Commission and the Norwegian Research Council. It contains labour-force survey micro-data from the early 1990s for Austria, the Czech Republic, Finland, Hungary, Luxembourg, Norway, Poland, Slovenia, Spain, Sweden, the United Kingdom and the United States (additional countries are being added). Many LES studies are concerned with unemployment and social exclusion.

REFERENCES

de Tombeur, C. (ed.) (1995) *LIS/LES Information Guide*, LIS Working Paper 7, Luxembourg: LIS.
Mitchell, D. (1991) *Income Transfers in Ten Welfare States*, Aldershot: Avebury.
Smeeding, T., O'Higgins, M., and Rainwater, L. (eds) (1990) *Poverty, Inequality and Income Distribution in Comparative Perspective: The Luxembourg Income Study*, New York: Harvester Wheatsheaf.

M

MALAWI POVERTY PROFILE

In 1990 a World Bank paper outlined a strategy for growth in Malawi through poverty reduction. The profile identifies a poverty line of US$ 40 per capita per annum based on minimum nutrition requirements. Using this line, 55 per cent of the population was classified as poor with a further line drawn for the 'core poor' 20 per cent of the population. Poverty was found to be predominantly rural, in the smallholder sector (85 per cent) and in the estate subsector (10 per cent). A third of the poor were in female-headed households.

In 1995 a poverty profile was built on the fortieth and twentieth percentiles of household distributions of income or expenditures. However, poverty is so severe in Malawi that households above the cut-off point cannot be said to be non-poor.

REFERENCES

World Bank (1990) *Malawi: Growth through Poverty Reduction*, Washington DC: World Bank.
World Bank (1995) *Malawi: Human Resources and Poverty, Profile and Priorities for Action*, Washington DC: World Bank.

MALNUTRITION

Pryer and Crook (1988) argue that people are malnourished if there is evidence that their present or future health status or physical function is impaired due to insufficient supplies of nutrients in their bodies. In practice, there is often insufficient knowledge to achieve this, and therefore malnutrition tends to be graded according to international conventions. The term 'malnutrition' tends to be applied to a wide range of different conditions. These can be briefly summarized as follows:

- *Protein energy malnutrition* This is a state in which (in its severest form) the physical function of an individual is reduced due to inadequate quantities of food. Functional impairment in this context includes inability to maintain an adequate level of performance for such things as physical growth, resisting and recovering from disease, the states of pregnancy and lactation, and physical work.
- *Specific nutrient deficiency* This occurs when present or future health status is impaired due to a deficiency of a specific nutrient. For example, nutritional anaemia is usually due to a deficiency of either iron or folate, rickets is due to deficiencies of vitamin D and/or calcium, and severe deficiencies of vitamin A can cause blindness.

It is generally accepted that undernutrition or protein energy malnutrition, resulting from disease and inadequate food supply, is the most widespread nutritional problem in developing countries. Specific nutrient deficiencies – especially vitamin A deficiency, and iron and folate anaemias – are also widely prevalent; however, they frequently occur in conjunction with protein energy malnutrition.

The technique of measuring body size and growth is called anthropometry. Anthropometric measurements of body size and growth may be taken regularly or intermittently in order to assess the nutritional status of individuals and communities. The three main indicators are: *wasting* (being underweight for one's height); *stunting* (being a low height for one's age); and *underweight* (being a low weight for one's age). Stunting is the most prevalent problem, affecting about a third of children in developing countries.

Attempting to measure malnutrition in young children can be problematic, and in practice children are described as malnourished if their body size or rate of growth is below international growth standards, which are based on 'healthy' American or European children. For regular routine assessments of the nutritional status of individuals in a community, the most common method is to record the weight of an individual child and to plot it against the child's age on a weight record (sometimes called 'Road to Health Charts' or 'Growth Charts'). Failure to gain weight, often referred to as 'faltering', suggests that either the child's diet is inadequate or that he or she is ill, or both.

For intermittent assessments, by contrast, judgements have to be made on the basis of observations and measurements made on one single occasion. The measurements most frequently used for this purpose are weight, height or length, and mid-upper arm circumference, which are then compared with international growth standards. A 'nutritional index' is thus obtained – for example, the percentage of expected weight for age, or the percentage of expected weight for height. The degree of deficit – that is, the difference between the measured and the expected value – is used to grade the child's nutritional status.

The measurement of weight or mid-upper arm circumference in relation to height is used to indicate the degree of thinness or current undernutrition that the child may be suffering. The measurement of height or length in relation to age is used to indicate chronic or long-term undernutrition, which is reflected in retarded bone growth. Whereas the measurement of weight in relation to age used on its own is a composite indicator of both long-term malnutrition (i.e. deficit in height) and current malnutrition (i.e. deficit in weight), it does not distinguish between the two.

REFERENCES

Pryer, J., and Crook, N. (1988) *Cities of Hunger: Urban Malnutrition in Developing Countries*, Oxford: Oxfam.

MARGINALITY

Marginality is sometimes used to refer to a process of being pushed to the margins of society, or in relation to the economic process, in both senses equivalent to EXCLUSION. This is the primary use in the European Union.

> For some years now we have used the terms 'marginalization' and 'social exclusion' to denote the severest forms of poverty. Marginalization describes people living on the edge of society whilst the socially excluded have been shut out completely from conventional social norms. (Burnel Report 1989)

The distinction is sometimes made between 'marginalization' and 'marginality' to distinguish the process of being marginalized from the status of marginality, but this use is not consistent.

The term is, however also used in the sense of deviance. The concept of marginality has been used to designate those groups which, according to functionalist sociology, manifested cultural expressions and ways of life that were pushed to the margins of what it called 'normality'. People are deviant not if they are different but if their conduct breaches social norms (Cohen 1966). The populations left outside these margins showed an anomic, pathological or deviant behaviour and were considered to be 'marginal'.

A third approach, influential in Latin America, focuses on marginality as the product of both industrialization processes and the dichotomy between the 'traditional' and 'modern' stages. Modern society would cover and assimilate the 'traditional' spaces in the social sectors considered to be poor and 'left behind', via the spread of values and cultural patterns of modern and Western society, especially in the case of those ways of life unable to adjust. Marginality is believed to be the product of segregation first produced in industrialization, but these maladjustments would be corrected after the incorporation of initial paupers in the industrialization processes (Hoselitz 1964). According to these authors, the development of 'underdeveloped' societies was hindered by the aftermath of 'traditional' and 'archaic' cultural expressions and behaviours featured by those 'marginalized' or by the so-called 'folk societies'. These obstacles were to be overcome – by modifying their behaviour patterns – in order to promote that 'development' and the anticipated modernity, which would bridge the gap between both types of societies (Germani 1973).

Marxist writers have argued that urban marginality in underdeveloped countries is structural. In classical Marxist theory, marginality is a product of the generation of a 'reserve industrial army' in a setting of unequal development (Amin 1973). Writers in the field of DEPENDENCY THEORY have argued for 'structural dualism' (e.g. Nun 1970). Marginality has been seen as a product of social relationships and relative overpopulation. The surplus population is not a reserve, but the product of 'peripheral capitalism'. This has led to the generation of a non-productive sector, the 'marginal mass' or 'marginal pole', which is not integrated into the formal labour market.

These concepts may overlap in practice. DESAL, a Catholic foundation based in Santiago de Chile, has argued that urban 'marginalized' populations are unable to provide intra-group solidarity help or promote it or use the economic recourses of society because of 'traditional' behavioural patterns. Marginality for these groups implied an internal disruption of those social groups struck by family breakdowns, anomie, ignorance, and so on (Veckemans and Venegas 1966). This analysis combines elements of economic exclusion, the marginalization of traditional society and deviance.

REFERENCES

Amin, S. (1973) *El desarrollo desigual. Ensayo sobre las formaciones sociales del capitalismo periférico*, Barcelona: Editorial Fontanella.
Burnel Report (1989) *Poverty*, Economic and Social Consultative Assembly, Brussels: European Communities Economic and Social Committee.
Cohen, A.K. (1966) *Deviance and Control*, Englewood Cliffs NJ: Prentice Hall.
Germani, G. (1973) *El concepto de marginalidad*, Buenos Aires: Ed. Nueva Visión.
Hoselitz, B. (1964) 'A Sociological Approach to Economic Development', in D. Novack and R. Lekachman (eds), *Development and Society*, New York: St Martin's Press.
Nun, J. (1970) 'Superpoblación relativa, ejército industrial de reserva y masa marginal', *Revista Latinoamericana de Ciencias Sociales* 4/2: 178–236.
Veckemans, R., and Venegas, R. (1966) *Seminario de promoción popular*, Santiago de Chile: Ed. Desal.

MATERNAL MORTALITY AND MORBIDITY

In 1995 the World Health Organization (WHO) and the United Nations Children's Fund (UNICEF) revised their estimates of maternal mortality and morbidity. Around 585,000 women are estimated to die each year in pregnancy and childbirth and 15 million each year incur injuries and infections. There are several hundred million women in the world today who have suffered or are suffering from the untreated and uncared-for consequences of injuries arising during pregnancy and childbirth (Adamson 1996).

The WHO defines maternal mortality as a death during or within forty-two days of a pregnancy from causes related to or aggravated by the pregnancy or its management. The biggest killers are haemorrhage, infection, toxaemia, obstructed labour and unskilled abortion, which between them account for 75 per cent of all maternal deaths. However, narrowing the focus to the last hours of a woman's life gives a very incomplete picture of the causes of maternal mortality. In many developing countries, maternal death rates are significantly higher in rural than in urban areas and this underlines a crucial point: that lack of access to hospital for routine delivery or in emergencies is often a root cause of death (Armstrong and Royston 1989; Armstrong 1990).

The overwhelming majority of women who die or suffer from untreated injuries of pregnancy and childbirth are poor. The rates of maternal mortality in rich and poor countries show a greater disparity than any other public health indicator, frequently more than 200 times higher in the developing countries than in Europe and North America. In developing countries, death in childbirth accounts for about a quarter of all deaths of women of childbearing age, whereas the figure for the USA is less than 1 per cent. However, alleviating individual poverty among women will not by itself solve this problem. Only good-quality family planning and obstetric care combined with poverty alleviation can rapidly reduce maternal risk. In the United Kingdom, there was very little fall in maternal mortality before the 1930s despite the rapid advances in standards of health, nutrition, education and hygiene. It was only when skilled midwifery made deliveries safer and cleaner that dramatic falls in maternal morbidity and mortality resulted. High-quality obstetric care is also important for reducing CHILD MORTALITY, as about half of all infant deaths occur in the first month of life – and most of those in the first week.

REFERENCES

Adamson, P. (1996) 'A Failure of Imagination', in UNICEF, *The Progress of Nations 1996*, New York: UNICEF.

Armstrong, S. (1990) 'Labour of Death: The World is Slowly Waking Up to a Hidden Tragedy – in the Third World, Giving Birth Kills Half a Million Mothers Each Year', *New Scientist* 125/1710 (March).

Armstrong, S., and Royston, E. (1989) *Preventing Maternal Deaths*, Geneva: World Health Organization.

MEANS-TESTING

Tests of means are used to identify individuals and households on low incomes or resources as the basis for entitlement to benefit. Means tests have been extensively criticized on the basis of:

- low take-up, because such benefits often fail to reach the population at which they are targeted (Van Oorschot 1995);
- the POVERTY TRAP;
- STIGMA, through the identification of dependent poor people.

REFERENCES

Spicker, P. (1993) *Poverty and Social Security*, London: Routledge.

Van Oorschot, W. (1995) *Realizing Rights*, Aldershot: Avebury.

MIGRATION AND POVERTY

Migration refers to movement of people from one locality to another. People migrate, voluntarily or involuntarily, into the same country or from country to another, due to diverse and complex causes. They do it in search of better opportunities and chances, or they are forced by political or economic crises, wars or natural disasters. Even if to be a migrant does not imply being poor, migration and poverty are closely linked.

The classical approach tends to associate the migrant with marginality and poverty (Park 1928; Gordon 1964). From this perspective, the assimilation and integration of migrant groups, through a progressive process of their incorporation into 'modern' society, consisted in achieving native-born levels of education, employment and income. This view suggests that migrants represent a problem based on a 'lack' or deficiency explained not only by migrant's material condition, but the peculiarities of the culture they have brought, as in Oscar Lewis's idea of a CULTURE OF POVERTY. An opposite view, in Latin America, is that urban migrants develop survival strategies to adapt to this new reality and to cope with violence, unemployment and lack of housing and amenities in the city (Adler de Lomnitz 1975). Lourdes Arizpe (1979) argues that rural–urban migration in Latin America is not a question of the lack of capacity or culture of the migrant poor. Migration is, on the one hand, linked with process of impoverishment in the rural areas, including the process of expulsion and impoverishment of peasants, the development of a formal agricultural economy including salaries, mechanization of social production in rural areas and monopolist commercialization of subsistence economy production; on the other hand, it also reflects the special characteristics of industrialization, urbanization and attraction to the city. This has led to the settlement of migrants in precarious and very vulnerable conditions. This phenomenon has also been one of the powerful issues concerning urban growth and one of the fundamental problems in the analysis of 'modernity' and 'tradition' in the explanation of poverty in the so-called 'underdeveloped' countries.

Similarly, other studies find that migrant and ethnic groups are the main groups affected by discrimination in their access to the labour market (Bovenkerk 1992; Bovenkerk et al. 1995), or when they get a job they are confined to zones which are ethnically bounded (Portes and Zhou 1993). A. Sayad (1991), in his study on Algerian migration in France, observes that migration has to be considered in its dual dimension, since those who migrate are both immigrant and emigrant, and suggests that migration has to be analysed in terms of the two societies involved. In this case of migration from a former colony to the colonial metropolis, migration is seen as the result of the historical relation of inter-national domination affecting both societies. The 'problems', commonly defined in terms of employment, housing, schooling and health, that migrants pose for the advanced societies which attract them need to be reconsidered in light of the persistent inequality that connects and relates poor and rich societies.

Remittances from migrants have an impact on poverty in the place or country of origin. In some countries the remittances received from migrants become an important source of income (GCIM 2005). Others point out that this resource involves uprooting family members, with its attendant suffering (both the migrants and those who remain in the original country).

REFERENCES

Adler de Lomnitz, L. (1975) *Como sobreviven los marginados*, Madrid: Siglo XXI.
Arizpe, L. (1979) 'Migración y marginalidad', in H. Díaz Polanco et al., *Indigenismo, modernización y marginalidad, una revisión crítica*, México: Juan Pablos Ed.
Borja, J., and Castells, M. (1998) *Local y Global. La gestión de las ciudades en la era de la información*, Madrid: Taurus.
Bovenkerk, F. (1992) *A Manual for International Comparative Research on Discrimination on the Grounds of 'Race' and Ethnic Origin*, Geneva: ILO.
Bovenkerk, F., Gras, M.J.I., and Ramsoedh, D. (1995) *Discrimination against Migrant Workers and Ethnic Minorities in Access to Employment in the Netherlands*, Geneva: ILO.
CEPAL (2003) *Derechos humanos y trata de personas en las Américas*, Santiago de Chile: Centro Latinoamericano y Caribeño de Demografía (CELADE), Organización Internacional para las Migraciones (OIM), Fondo de Población de las Naciones Unidas (UNFPA).
GCIM (2005) *Migration in an Interconnected World*, Geneva: Global Commission on International Migration, October.
Gordon, M.M. (1964) *Assimilation in American Life: the Role of Race, Religion and National Origins*, Oxford: Oxford University Press.
Park, R. (1928) 'Human Migration and the Marginal Man', *American Journal of Sociology* 33: 881–93.
Portes, A., and Zhou, M. (1993) 'The new Second Generation: Segmented Assimilation and Its Variants', *Annals of the American Academy of Political and Social Science* 530: 74–96.
Sayad, A. (1991) *L'Immigration ou les paradoxes de l'altérité*, Brussels: Editions Universitaires De Boeck.

MILLENNIUM DEVELOPMENT GOALS

The Millennium Development Goals (MDGs), stated in the 2000 United Nations Millennium Declaration, are eight goals that UN member states promise to achieve by the year 2015. Targets are associated with each goal, and indicators are associated with each target, as a way to define goals and provide verifiable measures of achievement (UNDP 2005). The MDGs are:

1. Eradicate extreme poverty and hunger:
   - halve, between 1990 and 2015, the proportion of people whose income is less than $1 a day;
   - halve, between 1990 and 2015, the proportion of people who suffer from hunger
2. Achieve universal primary education:
   - ensure that all boys and girls complete a full course of primary schooling.
3. Promote gender equality and empower women:
   - eliminate gender disparity in primary and secondary education preferably by 2005, and at all levels by 2015.
4. Reduce child mortality:
   - reduce by two-thirds, between 1990 and 2015, the under-5 mortality rate.
5. Improve maternal health:
   - reduce by three-quarters, between 1990 and 2015, the maternal mortality rate.
6. Combat HIV/AIDS, malaria, and other diseases:
   - halt, by 2015, and begin to reverse the spread of HIV/AIDS;
   - halt, by 2015, and begin to reverse the incidence of malaria and other major diseases.
7. Ensure environmental sustainability:
   - integrate the principles of sustainable development into country policies/programmes; reverse loss of environmental resources;
   - halve, by 2015, the proportion of the people without sustainable access to safe drinking water and basic sanitation;
   - achieve significant improvement in lives of at least 100 million slum dwellers, by 2020.
8. Develop a global partnership for development:
   - develop further an open trading and financial system that is

rule-based, predictable and non-discriminatory. Includes a commitment to good governance, development and poverty reduction – nationally and internationally;

- address the least developed countries' special needs, including tariff- and quota-free access for their exports, enhanced debt relief for heavily indebted poor countries, cancellation of official bilateral debt, and more generous official development assistance for countries committed to poverty reduction;
- address the special needs of landlocked and small-island developing states;
- deal comprehensively with developing countries' debt problems through national and international measures to make debt sustainable in the long term;
- in cooperation with the developing countries, develop decent and productive work for youth;
- in cooperation with pharmaceuticals companies, provide access to affordable essential drugs in developing countries;
- in cooperation with the private sector, make available the benefits of new technologies – especially information and communications technologies.

There are different views as to the importance, expectation and feasibility of these goals. Some views emphasize the role of MDGs in providing a precise framework for the accountability of development-providing guidelines and timetable to achieve measurable goals (Vandemoortele 2002). Others claim that the goals are impossible to meet because the international economic and political conditions that generate global poverty and inequality are not under discussion. This critical view, associated with some NGOs and social movements, argues that the MDG approach is based on the interests and organizations dominated by the North, when poverty eradication and global justice should result from a South and North compromise (WFUNA–NSI 2005).

Some criticisms are based on the scope and universal character of the goals. Some targets apply to certain countries but not to others. A case in point is malaria incidence, which is particularly important in parts of Asia and sub-Saharan Africa but not in other developing countries (UN 2003). Another issue is the use of the notional poverty level of $1 a day, which has a different impact among poor or less developed, and developing countries, and is aimed at reducing absolute poverty. In addition, a common criticism, pointed out by the *Human Development Report 2005* (UNDP 2005) is that MDGs do not fully take into account distributive effects among generational groups in a given country or among countries. Consequently, inequality resulting not only from income but from gender, generational, geographical and ethnic background is not directly addressed by many of the MDGs.

Since the acceptance of the MDGs there have been concerns regarding the 'slow and uneven implementation of the internationally agreed development goals', as it is stated in the draft document by the UN secretary-general showing the difficulties and slow progress of this initiative (UN 2005). Even if there are some advances in water provision, absolute poverty reduction and significant advances in debt relief, some goals – for example, mortality-rate reduction, poverty reduction and guaranteeing universal education – are, according to the *Human Development Report 2005* (UNDP 2005: 5), unlikely to be met by 2015 if the current pattern prevails.

REFERENCES

Black, R., and White, H. (2003) *Targeting Development: Critical Perspective on Millennium Development Goals*, London: Routledge.

Maxwell, S. (2005) The *Washington Consensus is Dead! Long Live the Meta-narrative!*, ODI Working Paper No. 243, January, Overseas Development Institute.

Reddy, S., and Pogge, T. (2002) *How Not to Count the Poor*, Version 6, New York: Columbia University, www.columbia.edu/~sr793/count.pdf.

UN (2003) *Incorporación de las estrategias de lucha contra la pobreza en los objetivos de desarrollo del Milenio*, United Nations, Consejo Económico y Social, 13 February, E/C.16/2003/5.

UN (2004) *Implementation of the United Nations Millennium Declaration*, Report of the Secretary-General, A/59/282.

UN (2005) Revised Draft Outcome Document of the High-level Plenary Meeting of the General Assembly of September 2005, submitted by the President of the General Assembly, A/59/HLPM/CRP.1/Rev.2.

UNDP (2005) *Human Development Report 2005: International Cooperation at a Crossroads*, New York: United Nations Development Programme, http://hdr.undp.org/reports/global/2005/.

UN Millennium Project (2005) *Investing in Development: A Practical Plan to Achieve the Millennium Development Goals*, New York: Earthscan.

Vandemoortele, J. (2002) *Are the MDGs Feasible?* New York: United Nations Development Programme.

WFUNA–NSI (2005) *We the Peoples 2005: Mobilizing for Change: Messages from Civil Society*, Ottawa: World Federation of United Nations Associations and North–South Institute.

MINIMUM INCOME STANDARDS

Minimum income standards are used by governments as political criteria of the adequacy of income levels. The standard of adequacy is primarily a political reflection of that government's values, ideology and electoral considerations (Veit-Wilson 1994). These are prescriptive standards and need to be distinguished from the descriptive POVERTY LINE used by social scientists to identify the income levels or bands associated with high levels of deprivation.

Governments use minimum income standards for three main purposes:

* as *guidelines* towards setting some level of the different tiers of the income maintenance system, such as minimum wage rates, income tax thresholds and judicial minimum inalienable incomes, contributory social security benefits or means-tested social assistance and related benefits. Formulae are commonly used to express various benefits as proportions of the MIS;
* as *criteria* of the adequacy of various parts of the income maintenance system to achieve politically acceptable levels of living;
* as *measures* for identifying and counting population groups 'in poverty' for statistical purposes and calculating the POVERTY GAP by this measure, and also for establishing eligibility for income maintenance or other programmes for low-income households.

The instruments or constructs used by different governments to symbolize or embody minimum income standards include statutory minimum wage provisions, minimum state pension levels, and empirical measures of the cost of low levels of living (Veit-Wilson 1998).

REFERENCES

Veit-Wilson, J. (1994) *Dignity Not Poverty*, London: Institute for Public Policy Research.
Veit-Wilson, J. (1998) *Setting Adequacy Standards: How Governments Define Minimum Incomes*, Bristol: Policy Press.

NEEDS

'Needs' commonly refer to the kinds of problem that people experience: for example, people who suffer from mental or physical impairments are deemed to have 'needs' on that basis. 'In a general sense', Feinberg writes, 'to say that S needs X is to say simply that if he doesn't have X he will be harmed' (Feinberg 1973: III).

Doyal and Gough interpret harm primarily in terms of an impaired ability to participate in society, and argue that needs can be seen as objective interests. (1991: 2, 50–51). People who are in need are not simply people who have a problem; they lack something which will remedy that problem. This implies that problems have to be interpreted, or operationalized, as requiring a particular kind of response; and, properly speaking, the definition of a 'need' is determined by the relationship between functional problems and possible responses. Spicker argues that 'if needs entail responses, there are no needs which are not in some sense claims' (Spicker 1993).

Bradshaw (1972) distinguishes four main categories of need: normative, comparative, felt and expressed:

- *Normative need* is need which is identified according to a norm (or set standard); such norms are generally set by experts. Benefit levels, for example, or standards of unfitness in houses, have to be determined according to some criterion.
- *Comparative need* concerns problems which emerge by comparison with others who are not in need. One of the most common uses of this approach has been the comparison of social problems in different areas in order to determine which areas are most deprived.
- *Felt need* is need which people feel – that is, need from the perspective of the people who have it.
- *Expressed need* is the need they say they have. People can feel need which they do not express and can express needs they do not feel.

REFERENCES

Bradshaw, J. (1972) 'A Taxonomy of Social Need', *New Society*, March: 640–43.
Doyal, L., and Gough, I. (1991) *A Theory of Human Need*, London: Macmillan.
Feinberg, J. (1973) *Social Philosophy*, Englewood Cliffs NJ: Prentice Hall.
Spicker, P. (1993) 'Needs as Claims', *Social Policy and Administration* 27/1: 7–17.

NEO-PHILANTHROPY

Philanthropy nowadays takes new forms, referred by some authors as neo-philanthropy. It includes different forms of private and public social intervention with the poor that have a moral, symbolic and economic purpose. Neo-philanthropy includes contributions by: (1) non-governmental organizations or the third sector; (2) new forms of governmental social intervention; (3) expansion of a new entrepreneurial philanthropy; (4) international aid.

The role of neo-philanthropy has been conceived, first, to play a main role in the poverty-reduction initiatives in the face of the state withdrawing from social protection (World Bank 2005). The third sector, the NGOs, usually operates as a non-profit provider, based on volunteering, developing a particular type of non-political association that usually provides social services and resources, mostly to the poor, not based on rights (World Social Forum 2005).

Second, neo-philanthropy refers to new forms of governance anchored in compassion, sympathy and moral duty displacing previous forms based on social rights (Fix and Arantes 2004). In this regard, emergent notions like charity and humanism, along with a view of the poor as victims, is changing the practice of social work into neo-philanthropy (Aquín 1999). Robert Castel (1995) considers insertion and TARGETING policies as examples of neo-philanthropy since they reflect the ancient distinction between the deserving and the undeserving.

Third, advocates of neo-philanthropy entrepreneurship emphasize the pitfalls of government involvement in social problems related to poverty, health, infancy, education and environment, criticizing the scope and effectiveness of official expenditures. At the same time, some governments introduce fiscal incentives, through tax reductions, in order to promote philanthropic activities and donations among companies (Di Donato 2004). This suggests that philanthropy is not always driven by charitable or moral imperatives but also has an economic logic.

Fourth, neo-philanthropy is also shaping international aid, as the case of Interamerican Initiative for Social Capital, Ethics and Development, supported by the Inter-American Development Bank, suggests (IADB 2005). In this case, international aid to poor countries is driven by philanthropic principles such as the promotion of ethical values, community participation, private solidarity, business ethics with social responsibility, support and promotion of volunteer associations, and development of solidarity in general (Kliksberg 2004: 20–21).

REFERENCES

Aquín, N. (1999) 'Hacia la construcción de enfoques alternativos para el trabajo social para el nuevo Milenio', *Revista de Servicio Social* 1/3 (June–December).

Castel, R. (1995) 'El advenimiento del individualismo negativo', interview with F. Ewald, *Revista Debats* 54 (December).

Di Donato, P.A. (2004) El estado de la filantropía empresarial, www.hivatwork.org.

Fix, M., and Arantes, P. (2004) 'Cidade Aberta, São Paulo: metrópole–ornitorrinco', *Revista Cidade Aberta Rebele-se*, www.correiocidadania.com.br.

IADB (2005) *Interamerican Initiative on Social Capital, Ethics and Development*, Inter-American Development Bank, www.iadb.org//etica/index.cfm?language= English.

Kliksberg, B. (2004) *Más ética, más desarrollo*, Buenos Aires: Editorial Temas.

World Bank (2005) *Organizaciones gubernamentales y sociedad civil*, www.bancomundial.org/ong.html.

World Social Forum (2005) 'Democracia, límites y posibilidades del cambio en la región', seminar, Porto Alegre, 28 January, Red Encuentro de Entidades no Gubernamentales para el Desarrollo, www.alop.or.cr/trabajo/Argentina_Mesa Articulaci%F3n.doc.

NEW POOR

The term 'new' poverty has been used to describe the effect of changing economic and social conditions on the relative vulnerability to poverty of different social groups. The new poor are 'the direct victims of structural adjustment measures' (Samad 1996). Golbert and Kessler describe them as 'former members of different countries middle classes' who descended below the poverty line as a consequence of the crisis, stabilization and adjustment processes. The new poverty is characterized by the heterogeneity of its members, since they come from different occupational and sociocultural backgrounds (Golbert and Kessler 1996: 24).

Although the term has no precise or accepted meaning, its occurrence in the debates of the European Union has led to it being associated with the relational views of poverty which are also a part of those debates.

REFERENCES

Golbert, L., and Kessler, G. (1996) 'Latin America as a Challenge for Government and Society', in E. Øyen, S.A. Samad and S.M. Miller (eds), *Poverty: A Global Review. Handbook on Poverty Research*, Oslo and Paris: Scandinavian University Press and UNESCO.

Samad, S.A. (1996) 'The Present Situation in Poverty Research', in E. Øyen, S.A. Samad and S.M. Miller (eds), *Poverty: A Global Review. Handbook on Poverty Research*, Oslo and Paris: Scandinavian University Press and UNESCO.

NON-CONTRIBUTORY BENEFITS

Non-contributory benefits may refer either to benefits that are not insurance-based, and so have no requirement for contributions, or to benefits that have no test of contributions or of means. The latter use distinguishes them from MEANS-TESTED BENEFITS.

NORMATIVE STANDARDS

Norms are standards that are used as the basis for judgements about the adequacy of resources. The term 'normative' is consequently used to refer to both the imposition of expert judgements about standards and the use of moral judgements.

Normative standards are of two main kinds. There are, first, norms identified by experts, which relate to the capacity of people to function in society. Rowntree's (1922) or Piachaud's (1980) measurement of minimum standards are attempts not to impose arbitrary personal definitions, but to describe a minimum necessary to social functioning. Normative approaches are sometimes considered to be linked with ABSOLUTE POVERTY, but there is no necessary link, and

Rowntree, who is usually cited as the example of this approach, did not hold to such a view (Veit Wilson 1986).

Second, there are socially established norms, a commonly held set of expectations and values. The derivation of CONSENSUAL METHODS is based in such norms.

REFERENCES

Piachaud, D. (1980) *Children and Poverty*, London: CPAG.

Rowntree, B.S. (1922) *Poverty: A Study of Town Life*, London: Longman.

Veit Wilson, J. (1986) 'Paradigms of Poverty: A Rehabilitation of B.S. Rowntree', *Journal of Social Policy* 15/1: 69–99.

OVERALL POVERTY

In the final Copenhagen Declaration of the World Summit for Social Development 1995, overall poverty was defined in the following terms to differentiate it from absolute poverty:

> Poverty has various manifestations, including lack of income and productive resources sufficient to ensure sustainable livelihoods; hunger and malnutrition; ill health; limited or lack of access to education and other basic services; increased morbidity and mortality from illness; homelessness and inadequate housing; unsafe environments; and social discrimination and exclusion. It is also characterized by a lack of participation in decision-making and in civil, social and cultural life. It occurs in all countries: as mass poverty in many developing countries, pockets of poverty amid wealth in developed countries, loss of livelihoods as a result of economic recession, sudden poverty as a result of disaster or conflict, the poverty of low-wage workers, and the utter destitution of people who fall outside family support systems, social institutions and safety nets.
>
> Women bear a disproportionate burden of poverty, and children growing up in poverty are often permanently disadvantaged. Older people, people with disabilities, indigenous people, refugees and internally displaced persons are also particularly vulnerable to poverty. Furthermore, poverty in its various forms represents a barrier to communication and access to services, as well as a major health risk, and people living in poverty are particularly vulnerable to the consequences of disasters and conflicts. Absolute poverty is a condition characterized by severe deprivation of basic human needs, including food, safe drinking water, sanitation facilities, health, shelter, education and information. It depends not only on income but also on access to social services.

REFERENCES

The Copenhagen Declaration and Programme of Action, World Summit for Social Development, 6–12 March 1995, New York: United Nations.

OVERCROWDING

Overcrowding refers to the relationship between the number of people within a dwelling or home and the space or number of rooms available. Because poor people have a limited command over resources, the housing facilities they are able to occupy are likely to be less suitable than facilities available for other people. Typically this relates to location, housing AMENITIES and space. The idea of overcrowding depends on a normative judgment about appropriate levels of occupancy, density and privacy. However, the norms which are applied vary considerably between different societies.

Occupancy is determined by establishing the numbers of persons per unit of accommodation. Where multiple occupants from different households have to share facilities, this may be interpreted either as a problem of space or as evidence of 'hidden households', a form of homelessness. Because facilities are shared, high levels of occupancy can imply problems relating to hygiene and sanitation.

Density may be determined in terms of space (persons per square metre) or of room occupancy (persons per room). The number of persons per room is widely used in national statistics as a simple basic indicator of enforced proximity, usually with a limit of 1.5 or 2 persons per room, but in developed countries this crude measure has been supplemented by additional standards. The UN uses floor area for its indicators of sustainable development (UN 2001), while its statistics division uses persons per room (UN 2005).

Standards on *privacy* also vary, but many norms would additionally imply separation of unmarried people of different sexes before a defined age. The UK government uses a 'bedroom standard', initially devised in the 1960s, which avoids requiring unmarried males and females above the age of 10 to share bedrooms (ODPM 2001).

REFERENCES

ODPM (2001) *Allocation of Housing Capital Resources*, Office of the Deputy Prime Minister, www.odpm.gov.uk/stellent/groups/odpm_housing/documents/page/odpm_house_ 601668–05.hcsp.

UN (2001) *Indicators of Sustainable Development: Guidelines And Methodologies*, New York: United Nations, www.un.org/esa/sustdev/natlinfo/indicators/isdms2001/isdms2001socialB.htm.

UN (2005) Advisory Committee on Indicators, http://unstats.un.org/unsd/indicator-foc/indsearchpage.asp?cid=114.

P

PARTICIPATION

Participation refers primarily to the process of involvement in decision-making (though note, in the context of writing on poverty, the importance of 'participation in society' as the alternative to EXCLUSION). It is seen, after Freire (1972), as both an empowering and educative process.

> The participatory approach argues that the only way the poor can overcome their difficulties is by directly participating in the process of development including formulation of social policy, development of programs, their implementation at the ground level and sharing in the benefits of such programs. The participatory approach has the dual goal of promoting growth and equity while also ensuring the development of democratic processes in the grass-roots. (Silva and Athukorala 1996)

The emphasis on political participation is of particular importance in developing countries, where it is associated with important material gains. In developed countries, it has passionate adherents, though there may also be reservations about pursuit of special interests and the scope of participatory action for those who are excluded (Taylor 1996: part II).

REFERENCES

Freire, P. (1972) *Pedagogy of the Oppressed*, Harmondsworth: Penguin.
Silva, K.T., and Athukorala, K. (1996) 'South Asia: An Overview', in E. Øyen, S.A. Samad and S.M. Miller (eds), *Poverty: A Global Review. Handbook on Poverty Research*, Oslo and Paris: Scandinavian University Press and UNESCO.
Taylor, D. (ed.) (1996) *Critical Social Policy*, London: Sage.

PARTICIPATORY RESEARCH

Participatory research is a research paradigm that seeks to enable people providing information to identify the issues, terms and methods employed themselves. The primary purpose is to promote the EMPOWERMENT of research respondents, replacing the role of the expert researcher with an emphasis on the VOICE of participants.

Although there are earlier examples of the principle (Lewin 1946), the development of the principle of participative research is probably attributable to the influence of Paolo Freire (1972), who argues for empowerment through allowing people who are disadvantaged to define issues and problems for themselves. Colombian sociologist Orlando Fals Borda, among other Latin Americans, promotes Participative Action Investigation (PAI). Borda holds that research is not neutral, that knowledge is power, and that the goal of research 'is subject to knowledge building', and should therefore be included. Since this type of knowledge is emancipating, it may generate a change in social structures and because of it participation must encompass awareness, organization and mobilization of popular sectors by changing the character of public action from a technical matter to a political one (Fals Borda 1982).

The World Bank has sponsored a large number of Participatory Poverty Assessments, or PPAs (Narayan et al. 2000a, 2000b, 2002). PPAs are based on the views and voices of poor people. Poor people are encouraged to 'define, describe, analyse and express their perceptions' of poverty (World Bank 1999: 3). The studies identify poverty through a participative process of research aimed at gaining insight into poverty in local, institutional and political social contexts. Explicit objectives include engaging local people as partners in research, developing capacity, and linking research to other work relating to poverty (World Bank 1999). The approach is a multidimensional examination of the problems afflicting the poor and those institutions that the poor are faced with. The studies point to four main conclusions about the experience of poverty as perceived by the poor themselves.

> First, poverty is multidimensional. Second, the household collapses under the stress generated by poverty. Third, the state has long been ineffective in reaching the poor. Fourth, the role of the NGO in the lives of the poor is limited and thus they depend primarily on

their own informal networks. Finally, the poor believe the bonds of solidarity and trust are fading. (Narayan 2000a: 7–9)

REFERENCES

Fals Borda, O. (1992) 'La ciencia y el pueblo: nuevas reflexiones, in M.C. Salazar, *La investigación acción participativa: inicios y desarrollos*, Bogota: Cooperativa Editorial Magisterio.

Freire, P. (1972) *Pedagogy of the Oppressed*, Harmondsworth: Penguin.

Lewin, K. (1946) 'Action Research and Minority Problems', *Journal of Social Issues* 2: 34–46.

Narayan, D., with Patel, R., Schafft, K., Rademacher, A., and Koch-Schulte, S. (2000a) *Voices of the Poor: Can Anyone Hear Us?*, New York: Oxford University Press for the World Bank.

Narayan, D., Chambers, R., Kaul Shah, M., and Petesch, P. (2000b) *Voices of the Poor: Crying Out for Change*, New York: Oxford University Press for the World Bank.

Narayan, D., and Petesch, P. (2002) *Voices of the Poor: from Many Lands*, New York: Oxford University Press for the World Bank.

World Bank (1999) *Consultations with the Poor: Methodology Guide*, Washington DC: World Bank Poverty Group/PREM.

PAUPERISM

A 'pauper' was a recipient of assistance under the laws which existed for the poor prior to modern welfare systems. Pauperism was the state of being poor or pauper requiring support from the community. The term 'pauperism' was generally used in political debates before the development of modern welfare systems to refer to dependent poverty (Poynter 1960). In English usage particularly the word 'pauper' was an administrative term for people who received assistance under the POOR LAW. A person to be relieved under the Poor Law had to be destitute person. Paupers incurred certain civil disabilities, including, where applicable the loss of the right to vote.

Nineteenth-century debates strongly identified pauperism with other aspects of social change. The Industrial Revolution led to the development of towns, rapid population growth, and the first experience of modern unemployment and the trade cycle. All this caused considerable changes to both the number and incomes of paupers. For example, in 1688 there were about 1.3 million people classified as 'paupers' or 'cottagers' (the lowest feudal class of peasant) in England. They had an average family income of £5 per year, which was approximately equivalent to 16 per cent of average family income. By

1803, the number of paupers had fallen to 1.04 million in England and Wales and the incomes of pauper families had increased, in both absolute and relative terms, to £26 per family, which was approximately equivalent to 23 per cent of average family income. The relatively comprehensive data for 1812 include Ireland (which had a population of 7–8 million before the famine of the 1840s) and show that there were 1.5 million people in pauper families with an average family income of £25 per year, which was approximately equivalent to 21 per cent of average family income (Stone 1997; Pantazis et al. 2005).

The key explanations were those of Morton Eden (Pyatt and Ward 1999) Malthus, Bentham and Ricardo (Poynter 1960). Morton Eden saw poverty as an 'unfortunate but necessary evil' required by 'divine will', which was required to ensure the continuation of civilisation itself. Malthus argued that population was increasing beyond the ability of the country to feed it. The Poor Law was seen as an encouragement to illegitimacy, and this would lead in turn to mass starvation. Ricardo's 'iron law of wages' was believed to show that the Poor Law was undermining the wages of independent workers. Together with the 'roundsman system', where paupers were hired out at cheap rates to local employers, the SPEENHAMLAND SYSTEM was thought to depress wages. Ricardo's work on unemployment was a major influence on the reform of the Poor Law, where the principle of 'less eligibility' was seen as a way to protect the position of the independent labourer. It was also a strong influence on Marx, who considered that capitalism would lead to accumulation, concentration of capital and 'progressive immiseration'. Jeremy Bentham argued that people did what was pleasant and would not do what was unpleasant – so that if people were not to claim relief, it had to be unpleasant. This was the core of the argument for 'the stigma of pauperism' – making relief deliberately shameful and humiliating.

REFERENCES

Pantazis, C., Gordon, D., and Levitas, R. (eds) (2005) *Poverty and Social Exclusion in Britain: The Millennium Survey*, Bristol: Policy Press.
Poynter, J. (1960) *Society and Pauperism*, London: Routledge & Kegan Paul.
Pyatt, G., and Ward, M. (eds) (1999) *Identifying the Poor: Papers on Measuring Poverty to Celebrate the Bicentenary of the Publication in 1797 of the State of the Poor by Sir Frederick Morton Eden*, Amsterdam: IOS Press.
Stone, R. (1997) *Some British Empiricists in the Social Sciences, 1650–1900*, Cambridge: Cambridge University Press.

PHILANTHROPY

Philanthropy refers to the giving or transfer of money or other resources, especially to the poor on the part of private sectors and groups – particularly middle- and upper-class sectors – for artistic, religious, instructional and humanitarian purposes. What defines philanthropy is not the transfer of resources alone, but the moral or symbolic purpose that guides that transfer. Someone who practises philanthropy is known as a philanthropist.

By the nineteenth century, philanthropy promoted, beside gifts and charitable aid, autonomy through work, savings, advice and education on the poor. At that time, the term was associated with hygienist ideas promoting preventive and educational measures, and establishing behaviours among the poor in order to 'civilize' them. Accordingly, one of the biggest subjects of social intervention was the control over the 'vagrancy' of children through a moralizing process which would produce *free* citizens (Donzelot 1997). These trends were also extrapolated to the colonies or former colonies, encouraged by positivist and hygienist thinking, and resulted in various philanthropic societies, serving in most instances as a prelude to public institutions of social welfare. In this context, philanthropy features a strong component of social control through its civic education discourse, claiming a *conversion* role among the subject population.

Philanthropy strives to integrate social aspects into moral and affective ones, leaving aside the concept of rights. The term also refers to a dependence based upon charity and affection, while shunning political ties and limiting the scope of democracy. In addition, philanthropy can pave the way for the representation of solidarity and produce demands for an expanded democracy (Rojas 2000: 5). Current forms of private and public social intervention with the poor that have a moral or symbolic purpose are termed neo-philanthropy.

REFERENCES

Donzelot, J. (1997) *The Policing of Families*, trans. Robert Hurley, Baltimore MD: Johns Hopkins University Press.

Rojas, C. (1999) 'Corporate Philanthropy and Democratic Governance: The Case of Colombia', in C. Rojas, G. Morales, C. Saldías, E. Caro and J. Jaramillo (eds), *Filantropía y Cambio Social: El Caso de las Fundaciones Empresariales Filantrópicas en Colombia*, Bogota: CCRP.

PHILIPPINES DEFINITION OF POVERTY

In a review of the literature, the ILO (1995) identified three definitions of poverty used by Philippine sociologists and economists:

1. The amount of money required by a person to subsist (SUBSISTENCE concept of poverty).
2. The life below a minimum subsistence level and living standard prevalent at a given time and in a given place (RELATIVE DEPRIVATION concept of poverty).
3. The comparative state of well-being of a few and ill-being of the majority of society.

However, in the Philippines, the most widely used definition of poverty is the minimum amount of income below which a person cannot attain a predetermined consumption bundle of goods and services, as deemed necessary for the fulfilment of certain basic consumption needs or minimum basic needs.

The National Statistics Office (NSO), in its estimation of the incidence of poverty in the country, identified the basic needs of the households as: (a) food, and (b) non-food requirements, namely clothing and footwear, housing, medical care, education, transportation and communication, non-durable furnishings, household operations and personal care and effects. As defined, the poor are those families whose income falls below the identified threshold level – those who are excluded from acquiring even the basic consumption needs.

From 1985 to 1991, the incidence of poverty – that is, the percentage of poor families compared to total number of families – decreased from 44.2 per cent to 40.7 per cent. However, in terms of the number of poor families, there was an increase from 4.3 million to 4.8 million (National Statistics Co-ordination Board, quoted in ILO 1995). Moreover, the national poverty incidence of 40.7 per cent in 1991 conceals the wide disparity in the magnitude of the poverty situation across the different provinces. In thirty-eight provinces of the country, more than 50 per cent of the total families were considered poor.

The overwhelming majority (92 per cent) of poor people were working; only 7.7 per cent of the poor were unemployed. The five groups of people at greatest risk of poverty were:

1. *Lowland landless agricultural workers* work in agriculture but have neither ownership nor farming rights. They earn most of their

income from the sale of labour, either to plantations or to smaller
farms. Their engagement in rural or agricultural activities does
not sufficiently characterise them, however: the main division is
the lack of rights to till the land.

2. *Lowland small farm owners and cultivators* own the land they till or
have a recognized right to till the soil. They own land of less than
3 hectares. This group includes lessees and tenants.

3. *Upland farmers* Subsistence farmers of marginal land on rolling
hills and steep mountain slopes. Subgroups may be distinguished
as tribal or cultural communities; *kaingeros* or slash-and-burn shifting farmers; and rice and corn farmers who have resettled.

4. *Artisanal fisherfolk*, alternatively referred to as municipal, small-scale
or subsistence fishermen. They are broadly regarded as 'self-
employed' in agriculture.

5. *Industrial labourers, hawkers, micro-entrepreneurs and scavengers* Principal
poverty groups characteristic of 'urban' poverty. Industrial wage
labourers are found under the category of production workers
in both urban and rural areas, as well as the unemployed. By
class of worker, labourers are found under those who work for
private establishments, especially in urban areas; hawkers and
micro-entrepreneurs correspond largely to sales and service workers in both urban and rural areas and are included under the
self-employed; scavengers are classified under service workers and
self-employed.

REFERENCES

ILO (1995) *Social Exclusion in the Philippines: A Review of the Literature*, Geneva: ILO.

POOR LAW

The English Poor Law was the first national system for poor relief,
introduced in 1598 and consolidated in 1601. It dominated social policy
in Britain and exercised a considerable influence in all English-
speaking countries. The Old Poor Law (1601–1834) organized a national system of poor relief, but its practice was inconsistent and
dependent on local administration (Webb and Webb 1927). The New
Poor Law (1834–1948) was intended to combine relief for destitution
with disciplinary or punitive measures against the poor. The 1834

reform based intervention on two principles: the 'workhouse test', which meant that relief had to be confined to the workhouse, as a deterrent to receipt; and 'LESS ELIGIBILITY', the principle that paupers should be in a worse position than independent labourers outside the workhouse (Checkland and Checkland 1974).

The Poor Law has been taken as the model for deterrent and residual forms of poor relief. In the twentieth century, a range of social services were developed to avoid making recipients subject to the 'stigma of PAUPERISM'. Responsibility for the administration of services was gradually transferred to local authorities, and the Poor Law was finally abolished in 1948.

REFERENCES

Checkland, S., and Checkland, O. (eds) (1974) *The Poor Law Report of 1834*, Harmondsworth: Penguin.
Webb, S., and Webb, B. (1927) *English Local Government*, vol. 7: *The Old Poor Law*, London: Frank Cass.

POSITIONAL GOODS

Positional goods are items which are valued according to their impact on status or social position rather than their intrinsic use-value. The term was introduced by Fred Hirsch in a critique of economic growth (Hirsch 1976). The possession of certain goods, like housing and education, depends not only on their nature of commodities but on their implications for social roles. In certain cases (for example, fear of a pauper's funeral) positional goods may be no less important than other items that are commonly considered 'essential', like food.

The concept of positional goods has two implications for the analysis and measurement of poverty. First, it suggests that both 'CAPABILITIES' and 'commodities' have a relative element, beyond the issue of their social definition; part of people's capability rests in their social position. Second, it links poverty directly with inequality of resources and the concept of ECONOMIC DISTANCE. The capacity of poor people to function in society is affected not only by their own resources and income, but by other people's.

REFERENCES

Hirsch, F. (1976) *Social Limits to Growth*, Cambridge MA: Harvard University Press.

POVERTY DOMINANCE

Country B is poverty dominant over country A if there is more poverty in B than in A according to all possible poverty lines and according to all poverty indicators.

Atkinson (1987), Foster and Shorrocks (1988), and Ravallion (1992) have examined the relationship of poverty dominance between three common poverty indicators: the head-count index H, the poverty gap index PGI, and the FGT index, if we do not know the location of the poverty line z.

The first-order dominance condition analyses poverty dominance according to the head-count ratio with unknown poverty line z. Consider two countries A and B with a common poverty line z and use the head-count ratio as poverty indicator. Even if we do not know the level of poverty line z, it is clear that there is more poverty in country B than in country A according to the head-count ratio, if the cumulative population share of country B is nowhere lower than that of country A for all poverty lines z. The figure illustrates this condition. This graph is sometimes called the poverty incidence curve.

THE POVERTY INCIDENCE CURVE

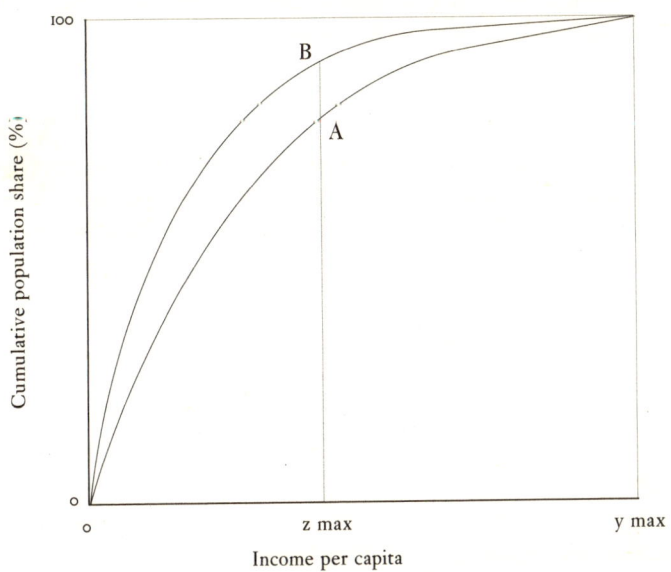

REFERENCES

Atkinson, A. (1987) 'On the Measurement of Poverty', *Econometrica* 55: 749–64.
Foster, J., and Shorrocks, A. (1988) 'Poverty Orderings', *Econometrica* 56: 173–7.
Ravallion, M. (1992) *Poverty Comparisons, A Guide to Concepts and Methods, in Living Standards Measurement Study*, Working Paper 88, Washington DC: World Bank.

POVERTY GAP

The poverty gap, sometimes called the average income shortfall of the poor, can be expressed in absolute terms or as a proportion of the poverty line. In absolute terms:

$$I_{abs} = \frac{1}{q}\sum_{i=1}^{q} z - y_i = z - \mu_q$$

As a proportion of the poverty line:

$$I = \frac{1}{q}\sum_{i=1}^{q} \frac{z - y_i}{z} = 1 - \frac{\mu_q}{z}$$

where

I_{abs} is the poverty gap,
I is the poverty gap as a ratio of the poverty line,
y_i is per capita income of household i,
z is the poverty line,
μ_q is the mean income of the poor.

The poverty gap as a ratio of the poverty line is sometimes called the proportionate average income shortfall, or the income-gap ratio, or the poverty gap ratio. It ranges from zero (nobody is poor) to one (incomes of the poor are all zero). The strength of I, like that of H, is its simplicity and its appeal.

As a poverty INDICATOR, I is a poor indicator because it not only ignores the number of the poor, but it also ignores the distribution among the poor. Further, like H, I is a dangerous poverty indicator if used for evaluating the successfulness of anti-poverty programmes. When the income of a person just below the poverty increases such that he is no longer poor, poverty according to the average income shortfall will *increase* instead of decline.

REFERENCES

Lipton, M., and Ravallion, M. (1995) 'Poverty and Policy', *Handbook of Development Economics* 3B, Amsterdam: North Holland.

POVERTY GAP INDEX (PGI)

The poverty gap index has been defined as the proportionate poverty gap normalized to the total population size.

$$PGI = \frac{1}{n}\sum_{i=1}^{q}\frac{z - y_i}{z} = H^*I$$

The poverty gap index includes both the incidence of poverty, the head-count index H, and the depth of poverty, the poverty gap I. The value of the index ranges between zero (nobody is poor) and H (all incomes of the poor are zero). The poverty gap index can also be interpreted as a manifestation of the potential for eliminating poverty by targeting transfers to the poor. Thus interpreted, it is the ratio of the minimum costs of eliminating poverty with perfect TARGETING

$$\sum_{i=1}^{q} z - y_i$$

to the maximum costs with no targeting (z.n). Some drawbacks of the partial poverty indicators H and I persist in the aggregate poverty indicator PGI, especially the insensitiveness for inequalities among the poor.

Lipton and Ravallion illustrate this by the following example:

A drawback of PGI and I is that they neglect inequality among the poor; they may not capture differences in the severity of poverty. For example, consider two distributions of consumption for four persons; The A distribution is (1, 2, 3, 4) and the B is (2, 2, 2, 4). For a poverty line z=3, A and B have the same value of PGI = 0.25 (=[(3–1)/3 +(3–2)/3]/4 for A). However, the poorest person in A has only half the consumption of the poorest person in B. The poverty gap will be unaffected by a transfer from a poor person to someone who is less poor.

REFERENCES

Lipton, M., and Ravallion, M. (1995) 'Poverty and Policy', *Handbook of Development Economics* 3B, Amsterdam: North Holland.

POVERTY LINE

A poverty line is generally taken to be a threshold, in terms of income or wealth, below which people can be considered to be 'poor'. Poverty lines can be identified prescriptively, in accordance with some norm, or descriptively, on the basis that people who fall below the line appear to be poor.

Poverty lines may be identified on the basis of observation or the assessment of needs, but some poverty lines have been adopted primarily because they provide a useful or plausible indicator of need. The World Bank's estimate of $372 per annum is not based on a precise assessment of needs; it has been multiplied up from the arbitrary figure of $31 per month, a dollar a day (see WORLD BANK POVERTY LINES). Abel-Smith and Townsend's (1965) use of lines related to the level at which state benefits were set in Britain is another example.

Poverty lines are generally seen as indicators of poverty, rather than precise measures, because lack of income is not usually thought of as a sufficient definition of income. Attempts to apply poverty lines with greater precision, for example to the position of women within households or the special needs of people with disabilities, make the application of poverty lines progressively more complex; there is a trade-off between sensitivity and applicability.

Poverty lines are sometimes confused with the MINIMUM INCOME STANDARDS which some governments use as a criterion of the adequacy of their minimum wage or social security provisions. Such measures are based on political consideration of acceptability and not necessarily on any evidence about the minimum incomes which are necessary for people in that country to live decently.

REFERENCES
Abel-Smith, B., and Townsend, P. (1965) *The Poor and the Poorest*, London: Bell.

POVERTY PRODUCTION

The search for causal explanations of poverty has always been part of the research process. Although much has been done in understanding the relationship between causes and effects, relatively little effort has been invested in understanding the common nature of the causes and the way they interrelate. It is a missing link in the research process. A different kind of vocabulary may instigate this process. In scientific language the term 'causes' of poverty is used to refer both to EXPLANATIONS FOR POVERTY and to the circumstances in which people are liable to become poor; in the latter sense the idea of 'causation' is politically neutral. It is not neutral to speak of 'production' of poverty since the wording suggests some kind of action to produce poverty (Øyen 2002). One way to understand the complexity of poverty formation may be to look closer at those 'actions' and the actors involved in the process, as well as the fact that certain interests are actually served by upholding poverty. The interests vary from economic and political to social and emotional gains. It can be argued that poverty has certain positive functions for a society (Gans 1973). This is a picture that strongly contradicts the consensus model, within which anti-poverty strategies avoid taking into account conflicts of interest.

Øyen defines poverty production in these terms:

characteristics of a poverty producing process can be identified as (a) an enduring phenomenon, (b) that follows a repetitive pattern, (c) where certain actors behave in such a way that poverty increases or is sustained, and (d) where the victims/poor people are placed within a structure that gives few or no opportunities to change the situation. (Øyen 2004)

If poverty production is placed within a human rights framework (see HUMAN RIGHTS AND POVERTY), a wide definition of poverty is the violation of an individual's basic human rights; a narrow definition of poverty is the violation of one or several elements in the spectrum of human rights. If we follow the human rights language, the actors are defined as perpetrators; depending on their role in the poverty-producing process they can be identified as first-order perpetrators, second-order perpetrators, and so on (Øyen 2002).

Poverty production is currently an underresearched field which lacks theoretical examination and comprehensive empirical documentation. As a consequence it is necessary to be open to a diversity of approaches and to invite a variety of studies from different subfields and settings. Comparative studies are preferable (Alvarez Leguizamón 2005).

REFERENCES

Alvarez Leguizamón, S. (2005) *Trabajo y producción de la pobreza en Latinoamérica y el Caribe. Estructuras, discusos y actores*, Buenos Aires: CLACSO–CROP.

Gans, H.J. (1973) 'The Positive Functions of Poverty', *American Journal of Sociology* 78/2.

Øyen, E. (2002) 'Poverty Production: A Different Approach to Poverty Understanding', in N. Genov (ed.), *Advances in Sociological Knowledge over Half a Century*, Paris: International Social Science Council; also available on www.crop.org.

Øyen, E. (2004) 'Knowledge about Poverty Production as a Key Word to Poverty Reduction', paper presented at NFU conference, Bergen, 30 September.

POVERTY PROFILE

The UNDP's guidance for the construction of profiles suggests that

> Poverty profiles are analytical tools that summarize poverty-related information and attempt to answer the following questions:
> - who are the poor?
> - where do they live?
> - what are the main characteristics of poverty?
> - why are they poor?
> ... Poverty profiles should provide information on the extent, depth and severity of poverty. (Lok-Desallien, n.d)

This does little, however, to distinguish poverty profiles from other types of poverty research. A poverty profile is a set of descriptive information, usually in the form of aggregate indicators, outlining the distribution and prevalence of poverty in a defined area. Such a profile 'shows how the aggregate poverty measure can be decomposed into poverty measures for various sub-groups of the population, such as by gender, region of residence, employment sector, education level or ethnic group' (UN 1995).

REFERENCES

Lok-Desallien, R. (n.d.) *Poverty Profiles: Interpreting the Data*, UN Social Development and Poverty Elimination division, www.undp.org/poverty/publications/pov_red/Poverty_Profiles.pdf.

UN (1995) *Indicators of Sustainable Development: Guidelines and Methodologies*, Division for Sustainable Development, www.un.org/esa/sustdev/publications/indisd-mg2001.pdf.

POVERTY REDUCTION STRATEGY PAPERS

Poverty Reduction Strategy Papers (PRSPs) are documents intended to describe a country's macroeconomic, structural and social policies and programmes intended to promote growth, reduce poverty, introduce health and education reforms, and associated with external financing needs. According to the World Bank and the IMF, the PRSP approach is also expected to increase aid effectiveness by enhancing broad country ownership. PRSP, as part of the enhanced Highly Indebted Poor Countries Initiative (HIPC) promoted by the World Bank and the IMF among low-income countries receiving debt relief, proposes to be the result of a participatory process as it is understood by international agency. Policy and programmes are assumed to be the result of a process of consultation with a broad spectrum of domestic stakeholders as a way to guarantee the sustainability of strategies, and lead to better 'partnership' with donors.

Some studies (Piron 2004; Dijkstra 2005) based on the experience of PRSPs in Bolivia, Honduras and Nicaragua, among other countries, find that the results are disappointing, since the PRSP approach, designed according to what donors define as processes and goals, has unintended and sometimes harmful consequences. Other studies suggest that 'nationally owned' strategies, as the basis for international assistance, reflect international agency views on participation rather than local-based understanding. Gould (2005) argues that, even if this approach postulates participation, accountability and empowerment, PRSPs are a new kind of governance since aid availability depends on the political performance of the recipient government, along with the fact that the interventions of external actors often condition and distort domestic agendas.

Although the PRSP approach is controversial, it has become a centrepiece of international aid over the past years and is set to play an important role in the coming years in initiatives like the MILLENNIUM DEVELOPMENT GOALS.

REFERENCES

Dijkstra, A.G. (2005) 'The PRSP Approach and the Illusion of Improved Aid Effectiveness: Lessons from Bolivia, Honduras and Nicaragua', *Development Policy Review* 23/4: 443–64.
Gould, J. (2005) *The New Conditionality: The Politics of Poverty Reduction Strategies*, London: Zed Books.

Muggeridge, E., Sheehey, T., and Godfrey, S. (2000) 'Civil Society Participation in Poverty Reduction Strategy Papers (PRSPs)', background paper for *Making Globalisation Work for the Poor*, London: SGTS & Associates, www.ids.ac.uk/eldis/.

McGee, R., and Norton, A. (2000) *Participation in Poverty Reduction Strategies: A Synthesis of Experience with Participatory Approaches to Policy Design, Implementation and Monitoring*, IDS Working Paper 109, Falmer: IDS, www.ids.ac.uk/eldis/.

Piron, L.H., with Evans, A. (2004) *Politics and the PRSP Approach: Synthesis Paper*, Working Paper 237, London: Overseas Development Institute.

Robb, C.M. (1999) *Can the Poor Influence Policy? Participatory Poverty Assessments in the Developing World*, World Bank Directions in Development Series, www.worldbank.org.

POVERTY TRAP

The 'poverty trap' mainly refers to a problem in the design of income maintenance benefits, when the combined effects of taxation and withdrawal of benefits make people worse off as their earnings increase. If benefits are given to people on low incomes, they must be taken away from people whose incomes go up. Getting out of poverty, Piachaud writes, is like getting out of a well; if you can't jump up far enough you simply slide back to the bottom again (Piachaud 1973).

There have, however, been other uses of the term. Charles Booth's pioneering research used the term 'poverty trap' to denote a geographical area in which poverty had become concentrated. This use did not gain general currency. The Sachs report (UN Millennium Project 2005) uses the term 'poverty trap' to refer to factors keeping developing countries in poverty. This is described as a vicious cycle where poverty leads to low saving and investment; low savings and investment imply poor economic growth; and poor economic growth deepens poverty. This usage is broadly equivalent to the standard view of economic depression identified in Keynesian thought. Sachs broadens the list of self-reinforcing problems to include low tax revenues, low foreign investment, violent conflict, the 'brain drain', rapid population growth, environmental degradation, and low innovation.

REFERENCES

Piachaud, D. (1973) 'Taxation and Poverty', in W. Robson and B. Crick (eds), *Taxation Policy*, Harmondsworth: Penguin.

UN Millennium Project (2005) *Investing in Development*, New York: United Nations Development Programme.

POWER

Power refers to the ability to direct the conduct of others who accept that direction. Elitism is the view that power is concentrated in the hands of a few; corporatism that it is hierarchically structured through the actions of agencies; and pluralism that it is relatively diffused among competing bodies (Ham and Hill 1993).

The lack of power of poor people is important in understanding both their vulnerability to exploitation and their relative inability to change their circumstances. Analyses of power have pointed not just to the direct use of social control (e.g. Piven and Cloward 1971), but also to the importance of 'non-decisions' – where issues are kept off the agenda (Bachrach and Baratz 1970). Many strategies for changing the situation of the poor are consequently based in the idea of EMPOWERMENT.

REFERENCES

Bachrach, P., and Baratz, M. (1970) *Power and Poverty*, Oxford: Oxford University Press.

Ham, C., and Hill, M. (1993) *The Policy Process in the Modern Capitalist State*, Hemel Hempstead: Harvester Wheatsheaf.

Piven, F.F., and Cloward, R. (1971) *Regulating the Poor*, London: Tavistock.

PRECARIOUS LABOUR

Precariousness in relation to labour is defined by labour instability, absence of legal contracts (of employment abiding by legal standards), lack of protection and social benefits, collective agreements of employment, low wages.

The concept of labour precariousness was linked to the discussion on poverty since it has been associated with deteriorating labour conditions and its negative consequences on standards of living, and the risk affecting the lives of an increasing number of people. Castells (1998) sees UNEMPLOYMENT and precariousness of labour conditions – particularly that of formal paid work – as the chief consequences of the highly productive and competitive processes of capitalist reorganization and the introduction of new flexible production management methods, work organization, and standards governing their operation. This situation was considered a step backwards for workers, who strove to attain better labour conditions and have them embodied in workers' rights. Several empirical studies have shown a close association between labour precariousness and poverty, particularly among some groups such as the young, women and those with a low level of instruction.

Precarious labour conditions are not something new in Latin America and peripheral countries since the presence of an INFORMAL SECTOR OF THE ECONOMY has always been to the fore. In recent decades and due to the impact of these new processes, conditions worsened to such an extent that they took a toll even on workers from the formal and public sectors.

Labour precariousness is analysed as the new form in which Third World countries insert themselves into the world production regime. In the context of the emergence of a global production system (Milberg 1999), many firms have moved their factories or operations to less developed countries, encouraged by factors such as low labour costs. Consequently, precarious labour conditions have been characterized by an absence of contracts, run-down workplaces, and longer working days (Varley 1988; Chan 2001), which in some cases have witnessed the incorporation of peripheral countries into global production and have provoked a debate on the need to impose a labour standard on trade and global production (Elliott and Freeman 2003).

In its 90th meeting the International Labour Organization (ILO), described the strong association of informal economy and precariousness in terms of a shortage of *decent work*. This new category refers to 'recognized, protected, safe and formal' work.

REFERENCES

Beccaria, L. (2001) 'Movilidad Laboral e Inestabilidad de Ingresos en la Argentina por Luis Beccaria' (U. Nac. de General Sarmiento), Jornada Preparatoria del 1er Congreso Nacional de Políticas Sociales, October.

Castells, M. (1998) *La era de la información. Economía, sociedad y cultura*, México: Siglo XXI.

Chan, A. (2001) *China's Workers Under Assault – The Exploitation of Labor in a Globalizing Economy*, Armonk NY: M.E. Sharpe.

Elliot, K.A., and Freeman, R.B. (2003) *Can Labor Standards Improve under Globalization?* Washington DC: Institute for International Economics.

Milberg, W. (2004) 'The Changing Structure of Trade Linked to Global Production Systems: What Are the Policy Implications?', *International Labour Review* 143/1–2.

ILO (2002) *Resolutions adopted by the International Labour Conference at its 90th Session*, www.ilo.org/public/english/standards/relm/ilc/ilc90/pdf/res.pdf.

Varley, P. (1998) *The Sweatshop Quandary: Corporate Responsibility on the Global Frontier*, Washington DC: Investor Responsibility Research Center.

PRECARIOUSNESS

Precariousness refers to the loss of forms of security and lack of fundamental rights, commonly related to some conditions of labour. There are two main classes of meaning. In France, the term *précarité* is used to refer to conditions of VULNERABILITY linked to sub-employment and economic marginality. This is related to vulnerability in the labour market (PRECARIOUS LABOUR). The second is related with the absence of security experienced in terms of a constellation of deprivation including the loss of rights. The Wresinski (1987) report defines precariousness as

> the absence of one of more forms of security, notably that of employment, which allow people and families to meet their professional, familial and social obligations and to enjoy their fundamental rights. The insecurity which results may be more or less extended and can have consequences of varying severity and nature. It leads to serious poverty when it affects several aspects of existence, when it becomes persistent, and when it compromises the opportunity to reassume responsibilities and to reclaim rights by oneself, in the foreseeable future.

This links the idea of precariousness with RIGHTS and ENTITLEMENTS.

REFERENCES

Wresinski, J. (1987) 'Grande pauvreté et précarité économique et sociale', *Journal officiel de la République française* 6 (February): 6.

PRIMARY AND SECONDARY POVERTY

These ideas were proposed by Seebohm Rowntree in his study of social conditions in York, in 1899. Rowntree developed what is now termed the subsistence concept of poverty, and he defined the poor as those people 'living in obvious want and squalor' (Rowntree 1901). The poor were further subdivided into

• those in primary poverty which were families whose total earnings were insufficient to obtain the minimum necessities for the maintenance of merely physical efficiency;

- those in secondary poverty which were families whose total earnings would have been sufficient for the maintenance of merely physical efficiency were it not that some portion of it was absorbed by other expenditure, either useful or wasteful.

Rowntree found that less than half the working class were poor, and that of those living in poverty one-third had incomes below the primary poverty line. This was a very harsh poverty line which Rowntree described as follows:

> And let us clearly understand what a merely physical efficiency means. A family living upon the scale allowed for must never spend a penny on railway fare or omnibus. They must never go into the country unless they walk. They must never purchase a half penny newspaper or spend a penny to buy a ticket for a popular concert. They must write no letters to absent children, for they cannot afford to pay the postage. They must never contribute anything to their church or chapel, or give any help to a neighbour which costs them money. They cannot save nor can they join a sick club or trade union, because they cannot pay the necessary subscriptions. The children must have no pocket money for dolls, marbles or sweets. The father must smoke no tobacco and drink no beer. The mother must never buy any pretty clothes for herself or her children, the character of the family wardrobe as for the family diet being governed by the regulation 'nothing must be bought but that which is absolutely necessary for the maintenance of physical health' and what is bought must be of the plainest and most economical description.

Veit-Wilson (1986) has argued that Rowntree's work has often been misinterpreted as supporting an absolute conception of poverty.

> a clear conscious distinction between poverty (which is a relative condition defined by visible lifestyle) and the primary poverty income level runs through Rowntree's work from the onset. It is vitally important to clearly understand how Rowntree recognized the relativistic nature of the primary poverty line and his belief that such a standard was not in a general sense 'scientifically absolute'.

The central purpose of the standard of primary poverty was an attempt to put the existence of poverty beyond dispute; the classification of secondary poverty was not to suggest that such poverty was less serious or real, but to include those who were also experiencing poverty in practice. Rowntree (1901) stated that the point at which 'primary poverty' passes into 'secondary poverty' is largely a matter of opinion, depending on the standard of well-being which is considered necessary.

REFERENCES

Rowntree, B.S. (1901) *Poverty: A Study of Town Life*, London: Macmillan.
Veit-Wilson, J. (1986) 'Paradigms of Poverty – A Rehabilitation of B.S. Rowntree', *Journal of Social Policy* 15/1.

PROBLEM FAMILIES

The idea of the 'problem family' was originally linked to the eugenics movement. Definitions of a 'problem family' were many and varied, often focusing on rather vague and unquantifiable social dysfunctions such as household squalor, maternal incompetence and 'intractable ineducability'. Blacker (1952) described the characteristics of problem families as including numerous children, temperamental instability, low educational achievement and a squalid environment. The idea of the 'problem family' was strongly advocated by the Eugenics Society and some medical officers of health. Together these groups cooperated on several empirical inquiries, all of which produced results that were inconclusive or speculative. By the early 1960s the idea of the 'problem family' was being subjected to increasing criticism despite attempts to substitute a view of 'multi-problem families' which would be less judgemental (Spencer 1963).

The idea of the 'problem family' has not been supported by research (Macnicol 1997). Evidence on the dynamics of poverty is that poor people typically pass through many changes of circumstance (Kolvin et al. 1990), while studies on specific families failed to find either the persistence or consistency of patterns of problems which the idea of the 'problem family' requires (Coffield and Sarsby 1980).

REFERENCES

Blacker, C.P. (ed.) (1952) *Problem Families*, London: Eugenics Society.
Coffield, F., and Sarsby, J. (1980) *A Cycle of Deprivation?* London: Heinemann.
Kolvin, I., Miller, F.J.W., Scott, D.M., Gatzanis, S.R.M., and Fleeting, M. (1990) *Continuities of Deprivation? The Newcastle 1000 Family Study*, Aldershot: Avebury.

Macnicol, J. (1997) 'From "Problem Family" to "Underclass" 1945–95', in R. Lowe and H. Fawcett (eds), *The Road from 1945*, London: Macmillan.

Spencer, J.C. (1963) 'The Multi-problem Family', in B. Schlesinger (ed.), *The Multi-problem Family: A Review and Annotated Bibliography*, Toronto: University of Toronto Press.

R

REDISTRIBUTION

Redistribution involves a transfer of resources from some people to others. Redistribution which transfers resources between richer and poorer people is described as 'vertical'; redistribution which transfers resources between different kinds of groups (for example, between people without children and those with children) is called 'horizontal'. Vertical redistribution which benefits poor people at the expense of richer ones is said to be 'progressive'.

In his discussion of equalities, Rae outlines a number of strategies for redistribution:

- *maximin* (raising the minimum someone might have);
- *minimax* (reducing the ceiling of incomes);
- *least difference* (reducing the range of inequality);
- *ratio* (changing the ratio between rich and poor) (Rae 1981).

Raising the minimum has the most direct effect on the poor, because it directly increases the resources of those who are poorest. Imposing a ceiling has the least, because the resources which are redistributed are not necessarily made available to those who are poorest.

REFERENCES
Rae, D. (1981) *Equalities*, Cambridge MA: Harvard University Press.

RELATIVE DEPRIVATION

In the work of W.G. Runciman (1966), relative deprivation is a process in which people compare their circumstances to those of other people to determine whether or not they should consider themselves deprived. The selection of an appropriate reference group is of great importance in determining whether or not people feel a sense of relative deprivation. Runciman points to the importance of comparison both with others at the same time (synchronic reference groups) and with themselves at other times (diachronic reference groups). The concept is derived from research in the USA in the 1940s, when it was used to help explain why some objectively well-off soldiers in the US Army were discontented. There was an evident difference between feelings and reality (see, for example, Runciman 1966).

In the work of Townsend (1979), relative deprivation is a set of objective circumstances in which people may be considered to be poor. He defines relative deprivation as follows:

> People are relatively deprived if they cannot obtain, at all or sufficiently, the conditions of life – that is, the diets, amenities, standards and services which allow them to play the roles, participate in the relationships and follow the customary behaviour which is expected of them by virtue of their membership of society. If they lack or are denied the incomes, or more exactly the resources, including income and assets or goods or services in kind to obtain access to these conditions of life, they can be defined to be in poverty.
>
> People may be deprived in any or all of the major spheres of life – at work, where the means largely determining position in other spheres are earned, at home, in neighbourhood and family; in travel; in a range of social and individual activities outside work and home or neighbourhood in performing a variety of roles in fulfilment of social obligations. (Townsend 1993: 36; see also Townsend 1979: 31)

Townsend's 'relative deprivation' standard is built on the idea that in all societies there is a threshold of low income or resources marking a change in the capacity of human beings to meet the needs, material and social, enjoyed by that society. As income (or income combined with the value of other types of resources) declines, instances of deprivation steadily increase. However, below a certain level of income, the forms and instances of deprivation are hypothesized to multiply disproportionately to the fall in income. Information is collected about both material and social needs in the sense of role obligations, customs and activities. This work has been particularly influential. Among empirical investigations and demonstrations of the existence of a threshold of multiple deprivation at a particular level of income are: Desai and Shah 1988; Hutton 1989; Chow 1981; Bokor 1984; De Vos and Hagenaars 1988; Gordon and Pantazis 1997.

REFERENCES

Bokor, A. (1984) 'Deprivation: Dimensions and Indices', in R. Andork and T. Kolosi (eds), *Stratification and Inequality*, Budapest: Institute for Social Sciences.

Chow, N. (1981) *Poverty in an Affluent City*, Department of Social Work, Chinese University of Hong Kong.

Desai, M., and Shah, A. (1988) 'An Econometric Approach to the Measurement of Poverty', *Oxford Economic Papers* 40/3: 505–22.

De Vos, K., and Hagenaars, A. (1988) *A Comparison between the Poverty Concepts of Sen and Townsend*, Rotterdam: Erasmus University

Gordon, D., and Pantazis, C. (eds) (1997) *Breadline Britain in the 1990s*, Aldershot: Avebury.

Hutton, S. (1989) 'Testing Townsend: Exploring Living Standards Using Secondary Data Analysis', in S. Baldwin, C. Godfrey and C. Propper (eds), *The Quality of Life*, London: Routledge & Kegan Paul

Runciman, W.G. (1966) *Relative Deprivation and Social Justice*, London: Routledge & Kegan Paul.

Townsend, P. (1979) *Poverty in the United Kingdom*, Harmondsworth: Penguin.

Townsend, P. (1993) *The International Analysis of Poverty*, Hemel Hempstead: Harvester Wheatsheaf.

RELATIVE POVERTY

Relative poverty defines poverty in terms of its relation to the standards which exist elsewhere in society. This used to be understood primarily in terms of inequality: Roach and Roach, for example, define relative poverty as a standard applying to 'the bottom segment of the income distribution' (1972: 23), and the LUXEMBOURG INCOME STUDY measures poverty as a proportion of average personal disposable income per capita (Smeeding et al. 1990) (see ECONOMIC DISTANCE). Townsend refers to poverty as a form of RELATIVE DEPRIVATION, 'the absence or inadequacy of those diets, amenities, standards, services and activities which are common or customary in society' (Townsend 1979: 915); this has become the dominant model in discourse on relative poverty.

Relative poverty has two main elements. The first is the premiss that poverty is socially defined, the converse of a position commonly attributed to advocates of ABSOLUTE POVERTY. The second element is the use of comparative methods to determine poverty by contrast with others in the society who are not poor. This identifies poverty with disadvantage, and so with inequality (see EQUALITY).

REFERENCES

Roach, J.L., and Roach, J.K. (eds) (1972) *Poverty: Selected Readings*, Harmondsworth: Penguin.

Smeeding. T.M., O'Higgins, M., and Rainwater, L. (eds) (1990) *Poverty, Inequality and Income Distribution in Comparative Perspective*, New York: Harvester Wheatsheaf.

Townsend, P. (1979) *Poverty in the United Kingdom*, Harmondsworth: Penguin.

RESIDUAL WELFARE

Welfare that is provided as a safety net for people who are unable to cope through their own resources or by other means. It was proposed by Wilensky and Lebeaux (1958) as the alternative to the institutional model of welfare.

REFERENCES

Wilensky, H., and Lebeaux, C. (1958) *Industrial Society and Social Welfare*, New York: Free Press.

RIGHTS

Hohfield (1923) distinguishes four categories of rights: claim-rights, immunities, powers and liberties.

- *Claim-rights* are rights which imply duties on other people; many rights to the receipt of social services generally fall into this category.
- *Liberties* prevent actions by other people.
- *Powers* are a restricted form of liberty, where some people are allowed to do things which others cannot; a driving licence is an example.
- *Immunities* are also a form of liberty, which make people exempt from obligations which apply to others. An example is tax relief.

Claim-rights tend to be more important in the discussion of poverty. The basic claim-rights most often referred to in discussions of poverty are claims for social security – that is, poor relief or income maintenance; rights to housing, in the sense both of access to decent housing and avoidance of deprivation; access to health care; and the right to be educated. The basic liberties that are sought include protection from crime; protection from unsafe or unhealthy environments; the avoidance of discrimination; and legal security, meaning the protection of citizens from arrest or legal harassment, and the avoidance of injustice. Rights are not confined to the individual level as the enforcement of collective or group rights may also be an effective solution in situations where discrimination or the denial of self-determination is a cause of poverty.

Rights may be general (applying to all, like rights of citizenship) or particular (applying to specific individuals, like many pension entitlements). Strategies against poverty have relied on a complex combination of different types of individual and collective rights (Spicker, 2001).

REFERENCES

Hohfield, W. (1923) 'Fundamental Legal Conceptions'; cited in A. Weale, *Political Theory and Social Policy*, London: Macmillan, 1983.
Spicker, P. (2001) 'The Rights of the Poor', in P. Robson and A. Kjonstad (eds), *Poverty and the Law*, Oxford: Hart.

RURAL POVERTY

The United Nations International Fund for Agricultural Development (IFAD) estimates that over 75 per cent of the poor people in the world live in rural areas of developing countries. Data from the late 1980s, from 114 developing countries, showed that 939 million people were living in poverty in rural areas, as defined by the INTEGRATED POVERTY index (IPI). The rural poor constituted 36 per cent of the world's total rural population; 31 per cent in Asia, 60 per cent in sub-Saharan Africa, 61 per cent in Latin America and 26 per cent in the Near East and North Africa. In terms of absolute numbers, Asia dominates the picture of world poverty with 633 million rural poor − 371 million in India and China alone (Jazairy et al. 1992).

The groups most likely to suffer from rural poverty are (in order of numerical importance): smallholder farmers, the landless, ethnic indigenous peoples, small and artisanal fishermen, refugees and displaced people, and nomadic pastoralists. Households headed by women also represent a large vulnerable group; it is estimated that there are 76 million women heads of households in the 114 developing countries who are responsible for the well-being of 377 million household members.

A fivefold classification of rural poverty was developed by the IFAD, based on research in the Philippines, Somalia, the Near East and North Africa:

- *Interstitial poverty* Pockets of poverty surrounded by power, affluence and ownership of assets, and characterized by material DEPRIVATION and alienation. It is difficult to target resources at the rural poor without their being pre-empted by the non-poor. A lot of poverty in the industrialized world could be characterized in this way. In the Philippines, interstitial poverty is found amongst landless agricultural workers in the densely settled lowlands.

- *Peripheral poverty* is found in marginal areas mainly amongst smallholder farmers and the landless in upland areas and on marginal agricultural land. It is characterized by material deprivation combined with isolation and alienation.

- *Traumatic or sporadic poverty* is often caused by natural or social calamities such as war, drought, floods, pests and labour displacement, which can produce occasional poverty with serious incidences of MALNUTRITION. Nomadic peoples are particularly vulnerable to this kind of poverty; however, natural and social calamities can affect all kinds of people in all parts of the world and they are a major cause of world poverty. War has caused poverty in former Yugoslavia and the USSR as well as in Rwanda and Angola.

- *Overcrowding poverty* generally arises from population growth in areas of high agricultural productivity, which sustain large rural populations. In Bangladesh and eastern India, poverty is heavily concentrated in areas of high rural population density. Overcrowding poverty is characterized by material deprivation and alienation.

- *Endemic poverty* is caused by low productivity and poor resource base and results in low income, poor nutrition and poor health (see HEALTH AND POVERTY). In Africa and the Near East, the groups most vulnerable to endemic poverty are smallholders, small fishermen and small herdsmen. Isolation, alienation, technological deprivation and lack of assets are characteristics of endemic poverty.

REFERENCES

Jazairy, I., Alamgir, M., and Panuccio, T. (1992) *The State of World Rural Poverty*, London: IFAD.

S

SAFETY NETS

'Safety nets' generally refer to forms of protection which cover people in the event of failure of other systems of support. Social risks are covered through a variety of forms of social protection; vulnerability, by contrast, arises when people who are exposed to risk are unable to avoid harm in consequence. Safety nets are primarily developed to protect people in the event of vulnerability. Safety-net provision is usually based on transfer payments, means testing or some equivalent form of assistance. By contrast, the World Bank suggests,

> social insurance programs, such as contributory pensions or unemployment insurance, are largely related to earnings and need not include any transfers (though many schemes do contain an element of cross-subsidization). Social insurance programs help households manage risk, but before the fact. Safety nets take up the load where households cannot participate in social insurance schemes or when the benefits from those are exhausted. (World Bank Group 2001a)

The notion of transiently promoting 'safety' is based on the assumption that the 'safety nets' programmes are used to 'mitigate the effects of poverty' and 'other risks on vulnerable households' (World Bank Group 2001b).

Safety nets can be developed through both government and independent mechanisms. *Public safety nets* are based on formal programmes 'run by governments that aim to provide additional income or in-kind help to vulnerable households'. *Private safety nets* or *informal private safety nets* refer to obtaining safety and protection for persons through networks of local reciprocity (SOCIAL CAPITAL). These include 'community-based informal arrangements', for example when family members in different households support each other through hard times with cash, food, or labour; and public safety nets also make use of the first type of net. Safety-net programmes include:

cash transfers, food related programmes, prices and other subsidies, public works, micro-credit, school vouchers or scholarships, fee waivers for health-care services, heating in cold climates (World Bank Group, 2001a).

The World Bank identifies two main functions of safety nets (World Bank Group 2001a). The first is income maintenance. Safety nets redistribute income and resources to the needy in society, helping them to overcome short-term poverty. Although safety nets are conventionally thought to be counter-cyclical, empirical studies in Latin America suggest that the opposite may be true; safety nets may be cut during times of economic crisis. (Hicks and Wodon 2001). The other main function is social protection, linked to the aid provided to domestic units so they are able to handle risks in order to avoid the risk run by the poorest among the poor. This is especially aimed at certain poor groups (*the chronic poor, the transient poor* and *those with special circumstances* – sections of the population with vulnerability attributable to 'disability, discrimination due to ethnicity, displacement due to conflict, "social pathologies" of drug and alcohol abuse, domestic violence or crime').

The idea of safety nets is strongly advocated by those who favour RESIDUAL WELFARE, on the basis that safety nets are more efficiently targeted than other systems. Since they only aid the 'poor', they do nothing to prevent poverty. Safety nets are often costly to administer, result in poverty traps, stigmatize the recipients and have problems of incomplete take-up (Van Oorschot 2002). At the same time, some form of residual safety net, such as social assistance, also features in all universalist welfare schemes. By contrast with residual welfare, institutional benefits and service provision aid all citizens/residents and can provide an effective mechanism to prevent poverty and promote inclusion. The primary argument for residual provision within the context of institutional welfare is that it acts as a guarantee of comprehensiveness.

REFERENCES

Hicks, N., and Wodon, Q. (2001) 'Social Protection for the Poor in Latin America', *Cepal Review* 73: 93–110.
Van Oorschot, W. (2002) 'Targeting Welfare: On the Functions and Dysfunctions of Means Testing in Social Policy', in P. Townsend and D. Gordon (eds), *World Poverty: New Policies to Defeat an Old Enemy*, Bristol: Policy Press.

World Bank Group (2001a) *Social Safety Nets*, www.worldbank.org/sp/safetynets/Key-concepts.asp#What%20are%20SNPs.

World Bank Group (2001b), *Safety Nets*, www.worldbank.org/sp/safetynets/.

SCIENTIFIC DEFINITIONS OF POVERTY

Scientific definitions of poverty are those that conform to the requirements of the philosophy of science: the most important of these are that they should be testable and falsifiable. In practice theories that define poverty in industrialized countries as persons or households that have both a low standard of living and a low income are generally considered scientific. People are not poor if they have a low income and a reasonable standard of living or if they have a low standard of living but a high income.

A low standard of living is often measured by using an index of deprivation (high deprivation equals a low standard of living; see INDICES OF DEPRIVATION) or by CONSUMPTION expenditure (low consumption expenditure equals a low standard of living). Of these two methods, deprivation indices are more accurate since consumption expenditure is often only measured over a brief period and is obviously not independent of available income. This 'scientific' concept of poverty can be made universally applicable by using the broader concept of resources instead of just monetary income. It can then be applied in developing countries, where barter and 'income in kind' can be as important as cash income. Poverty can then be defined as the point at which resources are so seriously below those commanded by the average individual or family that the poor are, in effect, excluded from ordinary living patterns, customs and activities. As resources for any individual or family are diminished, there is a point at which there occurs a sudden withdrawal from participation in the customs and activities sanctioned by the culture. The point at which withdrawal escalates disproportionately to falling resources can be defined as the poverty line or threshold (Townsend 1979).

The RELATIVE DEPRIVATION concept of Townsend (1979), the CONSENSUAL METHODS approach of Mack and Lansley (1985) and the BUDGET STANDARDS approach used by Bradshaw are examples of scientific concepts of poverty (see Townsend and Gordon 1989; Gordon and Townsend 1990; Gordon and Pantazis 1997 for discussion). Veit-

Wilson (1998) differentiates between empirical scientific approaches, which draw their categories from an evidential base, and prescriptive scientific approaches, such as budget standards, which define their terms normatively.

Some authors have suggested that since poverty is a moral concept it cannot by definition also be a scientific concept (Piachaud 1981, 1987) However, there are many concepts, like 'evolution' and 'health', that are both scientific and moral.

REFERENCES

Gordon, D., and Pantazis, C. (eds) (1997) *Breadline Britain in the 1990s*, Aldershot: Avebury.

Gordon, D., and Townsend, P. (1990) 'Measuring the Poverty Line', *Radical Statistics* 47: 5–12.

Mack, J., and Lansley, S. (1985) *Poor Britain*, London: Allen & Unwin.

Piachaud, D. (1981) 'Peter Townsend and the Holy Grail', *New Society* 10 (September).

Piachaud, D. (1987) 'Problems in the Definition and Measurement of Poverty', *Journal of Social Policy* 16/2: 125–46.

Townsend, P. (1979) *Poverty in the United Kingdom*, Harmondsworth: Penguin.

Townsend, P., and Gordon, D. (1989) 'What is Enough? New Evidence on Poverty in Greater London Allowing the Definition of a Minimum Benefit', Memorandum of Evidence to the House of Commons Social Services Select Committee on Minimum Income 579, London: HMSO.

Veit-Wilson, J. (1998) *Setting Adequacy Standards: How Governments Define Minimum Incomes*, Bristol: Policy Press.

SECONDARY WORKERS

In relation to the labour market, women have been defined as secondary workers. Glendinning and Millar (1992) argue that this is so for three reasons. First, women's paid work is considered secondary to their unpaid work within the home. Women's paid employment is shaped according to their domestic duties as wives and mothers and as carers for elderly relatives, with the result that women have periods outside the labour market and/or periods of part-time employment. Second, in many couple households, women's pay is seen to be supplementing the pay of the male partner. Third, women's work is often peripheral to the labour market. It is often part-time, short-term, casual and low-skilled, and often in a service industry (Barron and Norris 1992; Rodgers and Rodgers 1989), thereby increasing the risk of female poverty.

REFERENCES

Barron, R., and Norris, G. (1992) 'Sexual Divisions and the Dual Labour Market', in C. Glendinning and J. Millar (eds), *Women and Poverty in Britain in the 1990s*, Hemel Hempstead: Harvester Wheatsheaf.

Glendinning, C., and Millar, J. (eds) (1992) *Women and Poverty in Britain in the 1990s*, Hemel Hempstead: Harvester Wheatsheaf.

Rodgers, G., and Rodgers, J. (1989) *Precarious Jobs in Labour Market Regulation*, Brussels: International Institute for Labour Studies.

SECURITY

Wresinski (1987) identifies poverty with a 'lack of basic security', understood as 'the absence of one of more factors than enable individuals and families to assume basic responsibilities and to enjoy fundamental rights' (cited in Duffy 1995: 36). This appears to be equivalent to the definition of poverty in terms of need. Security can also be understood, however, in terms of the circumstances in which people are removed from the risks associated with poverty and need.

Countries which formerly had a planned centralized economy based the organization of their societies on the principle of basic security. Ferge (1992) defines the concept as a combination of security of employment, security of income and security of accommodation. The right to employment was written into the constitution of these countries. Each citizen had a position or role in society, associated with a modest income and housing. Low wages were compensated for by various benefits and subsidies and free social services; the state redistributed a large part of the social product in the form of pensions, family benefits, food subsidies and transport. Businesses offered, for their part, a range of premiums and perquisites and services for health, education, holidays and culture and payments in kind. The funds for this came from the businesses themselves and trade unions. The breakdown of this coherent and relatively egalitarian system has played its part in the growth of poverty which has accompanied the movement to market economies in these countries.

The concept of human security (as opposed to territorial security of nations) has always been central to the United Nations and its agencies (UNDP 1994). At the founding conference of the United Nations, in San Francisco in 1945, where the UN Charter was signed, the US Secretary of State reported:

The battle for peace has to be fought on two fronts. The first is the security front where victory spells freedom from fear. The second is the economic and social front where victory means freedom from want. Only victory on both fronts can assure the world of an enduring peace. ... No provisions that can be written into the Charter will enable the Security Council to make the world secure from war if men and women have no security in their homes and their jobs.

The United Nations Development Programme (UNDP 1994) recognizes seven main categories of threat to human security:

1. economic security;
2. food security;
3. health security;
4. environmental security;
5. personal security;
6. community security;
7. political security.

REFERENCES

Duffy, K. (1995) *Social Exclusion and Human Dignity in Europe*, CDPS(95) 1 Rev., Council of Europe.
Ferge, Z. (1992) 'Marginalisation, pauvreté et institutions sociales', *Travail et société* 16/4: 447–69.
UNDP (1994) *Human Development Report 1994*, Oxford: Oxford University Press.
Wresinski, J. (1987) 'Grande pauvreté et précarité économique et sociale', *Journal officiel de la République française* 6 (February).

SELECTIVITY

Selectivity is where people receive benefits according to NEEDS. If need is interpreted solely in financial terms, then the issue is identified with MEANS-TESTING. Selectivity and means-testing are sometimes treated as equivalent (Reddin 1970), but this is not necessarily what selectivists argue; selectivity may imply a test of means or need (Seldon and Gray 1967). Some writers, then, see non-means-tested benefits for physically disabled people as selective and others do not. Selectivity is also closely related to TARGETING. These terms need to be distinguished because targeting can take place based on criteria other than need.

Selective social benefits are often associated with a RESIDUAL welfare model on the basis that such a model would need to target people according to need. However, selective benefits and services are also widely used in institutional welfare states, for which a range of methods have to be applied.

REFERENCES

Reddin, M. (1970) 'Universality versus Selectivity', in W.A. Robson and B. Crick (eds), *The Future of the Social Services*, Harmondsworth: Penguin.
Seldon, A., and Gray, H. (1967) *Universal or Selective Social Benefits?*, London: Institute of Economic Affairs.

SEN INDEX

The Sen Index is an alternative measure of poverty to the head count index and the poverty gap, intended to take into account both the depth of poverty and inequality. It can be argued that the extent of poverty in a given moment depends on:

- the fraction of the population that falls under the poverty line as measured by the HEAD-COUNT RATIO;
- the intensity of poverty – that is, the aggregate shortfall of income among the poor from the specified poverty line as measured by the POVERTY GAP;
- the distribution of income among the poor, proxied by, for instance, the GINI COEFFICIENT. Sen's argument for incorporating this third aspect is the axiom of transfers: that a transfer from a poor person to a richer person should always lead to an increase in poverty.

The Sen Index combines these three elements into a single indicator of poverty for a given poverty line by calculating:

$$S = H[I = (1 - I) G_p]$$

where S is the Sen Index, H is the head-count index, I is the poverty gap and G_p is the inequality among the poor expressed by the Gini coefficient.

The strength of the Sen Index is its incorporation of all three dimensions of poverty: incidence H, depth I, and inequality among the poor G_p. The Sen Index S increases, respectively, with increasing H, I or G_p, and S declines, respectively, with declining H, I or G_p.

A drawback of the Sen Index is its discontinuity at the poverty line. Another drawback is its lack of decomposability. An elegant poverty indicator is additively decomposable, meaning that overall poverty can be decomposed into poverty of subgroups such that the population weighted sum of poverty in the various subgroups is equal to overall poverty.

REFERENCES

Förster, M.F. (1994) 'Measurement of Low Incomes and Poverty in a Perspective of International Comparison', OECD/GD(94)10, *Labour Market and Social Policy Occasional Papers* 14.

Hagenaars, A.J.M. (1986) *The Perceptions of Poverty*, Amsterdam: Elsevier Science.

Sen, A. (1976) 'Poverty: An Ordinal Approach to Measurement', *Econometrica* 44 (March).

Sen, A. (1981) *Poverty and Famines: An Essay on Entitlement and Deprivation*, Oxford: Clarendon Press.

Shorrocks, A. (1995) 'Revisiting the Sen Poverty Index', *Econometrica* 63: 1225–30.

SOCIAL ASSISTANCE

Social assistance consists of relief for those who are poorest, in cash or kind (Atkinson 1995: ch 13). Social assistance is usually subject to some kind of MEANS-TESTING and may be subject to administrative or professional discretion.

REFERENCES

Atkinson, A.B. (1995) *Incomes and the Welfare State*, Cambridge: Cambridge University Press.

SOCIAL CAPITAL

Social capital refers to the exchange of non-marketable goods, both tangible and intangible, in networks of social relationships. The idea of 'networks' implies close relations defined by culture and characterized by loyalty and trust between exchanging partners. Social capital has to be exchanged and promoted so that the poor themselves manage their own poverty (Alvarez Leguizamón 2002).

The idea of social capital has been applied recently to the field of economy and development discourse. Economists treat social capital as *capital* or *asset*. 'Its importance in feasibility and productivity in economic activities' is acknowledged (Moser 1998: 4), as well as its value and functionality in the 'fight against poverty'. In his study of Italy, Robert Putnam defines the stock of 'social capital as mutual informal networks, trust and standards – within hierarchical and horizontal institutions – promoting cooperation and coordination aimed at securing mutual benefits' (Putnam 1993). He claims that in communities such as those found in northern Italy, where social capital is strong (active community agencies, clubs and associations), there is economic progress, in comparison with the situation in southern Italy, where 'uncivilized' communities are supported by these underdeveloped causes. According to Putman, 'civil lack of culture' is tantamount to lack of social capital and economic underdevelopment. Subsequently, Putnam has expressed further reservations: 'in established democracies, ironically, growing numbers of citizens are questioning the effectiveness of their public institutions'; therefore, an 'erosion of social capital may be under way in other advanced democracies, perhaps in different institutional and behavioral guises' (Putnam 1995: 77; 2000).

The World Bank considers social capital a crucial requirement in development initiatives and poverty reduction. Social capital is seen as a means of generating goods and services. Joseph Stiglitz refers to this process as the subsuming of social issues in economic issues (2000). Edwards (1999) states that the incorporation of this category makes it easy for international agencies to 'integrate non-commercial rationality in the economic model'. Arguably it also justifies an anti-state approach. The concept is underpoliticized.

Else Øyen questions the role of social capital in poverty reduction. For her the poor do not have the same sort of networks as the non-poor, and the poor are not allowed to have access to the networks of the non-poor. The majority of the poor are neither able to develop useful networks for increasing their own social capital on a large scale, nor given entry into those networks where social capital flourishes; therefore social capital is not an efficient instrument for poverty reduction (Øyen 2000: 28–9).

REFERENCES

Alvarez Leguizamón, S. (2002) 'Capital social y concepciones de pobreza en el discurso del Banco Mundial, su funcionalidad en la "nueva cuestión social"', in L. Andrenacci (ed.), *Cuestión política y social en el Gran Buenos Aires*, Buenos Aires: Ediciones Al Margen.
Edwards, M. (1999) *Enthusiasts, Tacticians and Sceptics: The World Bank, Civil Society and Social Capital*, www.worldbank.org/poverty/scapital/library/edwards.htm.
Moser, C. (1998) 'The Asset Vulnerability Framework: Reassesing Urban Povery Reduction Strategies', *World Development* 26/1: 1–19.
Øyen, E. (2000) 'Social Capital Formation as a Poverty Reducing Strategy?', UNESCO/MOST and CROP/ISSC symposium at the UN World Summit for Social Development, Geneva, June.
Putnam, R.D. (1993) 'The Prosperous Community: Social Capital and Public Life', *The American Prospect* 13 (Spring).
Putnam, R.D. (1995) 'Bowling Alone: America's Declining Social Capital', *Journal of Democracy* 6/1.
Putnam, R.D. (ed.) (2002) *Democracies in Flux: The Evolution of Social Capital in Contemporary Society*, New York: Oxford University Press.
Stiglitz, J. (2000) 'Formal and Informal Institutions', in P. Dasgupta and I. Serageldin, *Social Capital, A Multifaceted Perspective*, Washington DC: International Bank for Reconstruction and Development.

SOCIAL DISTANCE

Sociologically, a person's social position can be measured as a composite index of the resources that person commands. Social distance can be defined as the difference between the social position of two or more persons.

The poor are located at the lower end of one or several distributions of resources, such as income, assets, education, housing, political influence, access to public goods, and so on. Poverty reduction through transfers of one or more of these resources increases the social position of those persons receiving transfers – that is, it diminishes simultaneously the social distance between the poor and the remainder of the population.

REFERENCES

Øyen, E. (1974) 'Sosialpolitikk som manipulering av sosial avstand', *Tidsskrift for Samfunnsforskning 1974* 15: 191–208.

SOCIAL ECONOMY

Although there is a wide range of theoretical perspectives and experiences, social economy is distinguishable from other relationships of production and distribution in that it is a non-profit-oriented economy governed by the principle of SOLIDARITY. There are variants in the concept: namely, new social economy, solidarity economy, new solidarity economy, popular economy, and economy of the poor.

During the early capitalist period, social economy took two distinct forms: one was philanthropic – whereby employer patronage was established (Castel 1995; Forni et al. 2004) – and the other was tied to mutualism and cooperativism. Currently in Europe, the social economy is understood as a third sector bearing humanistic values rejecting extreme commercialization. The principles include non-profit organization, democratic management, independence from government and service to members (Eme et al. 2001; CEPES 2004; Monzón and Defourny 2004).

In Latin America, social economy is closer to concepts such as informal economy, small-scale economy, marginality and subsistence economy. This concept gave rise to two new types of programme. One is related to international agencies discourses relating to 'community participation' and TARGETING policies (UNDP 1989; UNDP et al. 1990), in which the economy of the poor or popular economy represents a boost to the growth of economy, rather than a hindrance to it. Poor people, by this account, are producers who manage and provide for their own wants and needs through the reinforcement of family ties and the solidarity both of the neighbourhood and the community, vis-à-vis the corresponding weakened state institutions (Alvarez Leguizamón 2002). For example, UNDP (1988: 46–50) and CEPAL (1990) documents focus on the main role of associations, training of the informal sector and the option of the self-employed's and small companies' commercialization. In this sense, several countries are incorporating social economy into reduction poverty and unemployment programmes through varied and contested approaches. Some common characteristics may be identified: the idea of the social economy considers the poor as beneficiaries, promotes proximity ties and community participation; favours the local setting and proposes reinstituting a particular social citizenship with the help of the state or civil society organization.

The second view promotes a greater democratization of society, proposing a mixed economy while insisting on the citizenship's autonomy and the value of work. It does not renounce the state or civil society, but underscores the summons of the citizenship itself. Profits in this economy do not play a role as do savings, accumulation and investments (Coraggio 2004).

REFERENCES

Alvarez Leguizamón, S. (2002) 'Capital social y concepciones de pobreza en el discurso del Banco Mundial, su funcionalidad en la "nueva cuestión social"', in L. Andrenacci (ed.), *Cuestión política y social en el Gran Buenos Aires*, Buenos Aires: Ediciones Al Margen.

Castel, R. (1995) *Les Métamorphoses de la question sociale. Une chronique du salariat*, Paris: Fayard.

CEPAL (1990) *Transformación productiva con equidad. La tarea prioritaria del desarrollo de América Latina y el Caribe en los años noventa*, CEPAL.

CEPES (2004) Confederación Empresarial Española de Economía Social (CEPES), www.cepes-andalucia.es/modules.php?name=News&file=article&sid=1033.

Coraggio, J.L. (2004) 'Una alternativa socio económica necesaria: La economía social', in C. Canani (ed.), *Política Social y Economía Social*, Buenos Aires: Altamira.

Eme, B., Laville, J.L., and Maréchal, J.P. (2001) *Economía Solidaria, ilusión o vía de futuro?*, Mesa redonda sobre la economía Solidaria, Universidad de Verano, Arles, www. france.attac.org/i3289.

Forni, F., Freytes, A., and Quaranta, G. (2004) *Frédéric Le Play: un precursor de la Economía Social, Instituto de Investigación en Ciencias Sociales*, Facultad de Ciencias Sociales, Facultad del Salvador, www.salvador.edu.ar/csoc/idicso/docs/sdti001.pdf.

Monzón, J., and Defourny, J. (2004) La economía social: tercer sector de un nuevo escenario, www.plataforma.uchile.cl/fg/semestre1/_2004/asocia/modulo1/clase2/doc/monzon.doc.

UNDP (1988) Base para una estrategia y un programa de acción regional (documento técnico para discusión), Conferencia regional sobre la pobreza en América Latina y el Caribe, Proyecto Regional para la superación de la pobreza RLA/86/004, May 1988, Bogotá.

UNDP (1989) Proyecto regional para la superación de la pobreza. La comunidad urbana y la vivienda productiva. Sugerencias para el desarrollo de actividades productivas, como eje del mejoramiento de los asentamientos urbanos pobres, April 1989, Cartagena.

UNDP, CLAD, AECI (1990) 'Proyecto Regional para la superación de la pobreza', Desarrollo sin pobreza, II conferencia Regional sobre la pobreza de AL y el Caribe, Quito.

SOCIAL INSURANCE

A scheme in which benefits for social protection are conditional on the payment of contributions (Atkinson 1995: ch. 11) The models of insurance which are most widely referred to are BISMARCKIAN SOCIAL INSURANCE, which relates social protection to occupational

status and contributions made from employment, and the BEVERIDGE
SCHEME, which aims to provide general coverage at basic levels. Social
insurance schemes may be administered by state agencies or on a corporate basis by independent non-profitmaking organizations; membership of a scheme is often compulsory, though not necessarily so.

REFERENCES

Atkinson, A.B. (1995) *Incomes and the Welfare State*, Cambridge: Cambridge University
Press.

SOCIAL PROTECTION

In the discourse of the European Union, the term 'social protection'
is used extensively in the discussion of social welfare services, social
insurance and the WELFARE STATE (European Commission 1991; 1992).
It refers to the general principle of protection in contingencies where
people may otherwise suffer hardship, be disadvantaged or suffer
adverse changes of circumstances. As such it may apply not only to
those who are poor but also to those who have satisfactory income
and resources but who suffer temporary adversity, such as an interruption of earnings through sickness. The term is also used to refer
to a range of services offered to provide this protection, including
SOCIAL INSURANCE, SOCIAL ASSISTANCE and health care.

REFERENCES

European Commission (1991) Council Recommendation on Social Protection: Con-
vergence of Objectives, COM (91) 228 Final, OJ C194.
European Commission (1992) *Recommendation on Common Criteria Concerning Sufficient
Resources and Social Assistance in the Social Protection Systems*, COM(91) 161 final;
COM(92) 240, OJ C163.

SOCIAL SECURITY

The term 'social security' is used in three main senses (Spicker 1993):

1. as a form of INCOME MAINTENANCE, including SOCIAL ASSISTANCE
   but excluding forms of SOCIAL PROTECTION which do not directly
   yield income for the recipients, like health insurance (UK);

2. as SOCIAL INSURANCE, including health insurance but excluding other forms of income maintenance (France);
3. as social insurance solely for the purpose of income maintenance (USA).

Although in some countries social security is identified with government activity, in other countries the term extends to include non-governmental and independent agencies.

The identification of social security with the agencies administering it can also extend the scope of the term to include a range of other activities: in Germany, for example, social security may include some aspects of industrial relations.

REFERENCES

Clasen, J. (1994) 'Social Security', in J. Clasen and R. Freeman (eds), *Social Policy in Germany*, Hemel Hempstead: Harvester Wheatsheaf.
Spicker, P. (1993) *Poverty and Social Security*, London: Routledge.

SOLIDARITY

Solidarity refers to social responsibility and support. The concept of solidarity is important in Catholic social teaching: people are born into families and communities in which they have duties to each other (Coote 1989). This social responsibility is mixed with the principle of subsidiarity to produce a sense of responsibilities which are hierarchically ordered, with the strongest duties applying to those to whom one is nearest. Alfarandi (1989: 73) writes, 'One can imagine a system of concentric circles of solidarity, wider and wider, which goes from the nuclear family to the international community.'

The idea of solidarity is used in two main ways (Spicker 1991). The first is mutualism or the principle of mutual aid. People are part of groups and networks in which each person is protected by the others. The second basic principle is collective solidarity or fraternity. The pattern of solidarity is one in which people generally have responsibility to others in a community or a nation.

The idea of solidarity was used in a restricted legal sense from the sixteenth century, and is referred to in the Napoleonic Code, but it had acquired its modern meaning by the 1830s, when it was understood as 'mutual responsibility which is established between two or several people' (Académie Française 1835, cited in Zoll 1998). Leroux, who coined the word 'socialism', used the term to 'solidarity' refer to a sense of common humanity (Leroux 1840), and Hippolyte Renaud, who popularized the term, identified it with a utopian vision of society (Renaud 1845). Much later, the popular term was reinterpreted by Durkheim (1893). By that time, the concept was also the root of 'solidarism', a political movement in France (Bourgeois 1896), and the Code de Sécurité Sociale identifies solidarity as the central principle of the social security system.

Discourse on solidarity is fundamental to the concepts of EXCLUSION and INSERTION, both of which developed in French social policy. The central aim of French social policy has been gradually to extend the range and scope of these networks. This has led to a patchwork quilt of services, provided on many different terms but seeking to ensure that nearly everyone is included. The main approach to policy has centred on two strategies: trying to identify and work within existing patterns of support (Baldwin 1990) and seeking to integrate or 'insert' people at the margins into the available networks (Lejeune 1988; Alfarandi 1989; Donzelot 1991).

REFERENCES

Alfarandi, E. (1989) *Action et aide sociales*, Paris: Dalloz.
Baldwin, P. (1990) *The Politics of Social Solidarity*, Cambridge: Cambridge University Press.
Bourgeois, L. (1896) *Solidarité*, Paris: Colin.
Coote, N. (1989) 'Catholic Social Teaching', *Social Policy and Administration* 23/2: 150–60.
Donzelot, J. (1991) *Face à l'exclusion*, Paris: Éditions Esprit.
Durkheim, E. (1893) *De la division du travail*, Paris: Alcan.
Lejeune, R. (1988) *Réussir l'insertion*, Paris: Syros-Alternatives.
Leroux, P. (1840) *De l'humanité*, Paris: Perrotin.
Renaud, H. (1845) *Solidarité: vue synthétique sur la doctrine de Charles Fourier*, http://visualiseur.bnf.fr/Visualiseur?Destination=Gallica&O=NUMM-204664.
Spicker, P. (1991) 'Solidarity', in G. Room (ed.), *Towards a European Welfare State?* Bristol: SAUS.
Zoll, R. (1998) 'Le défi de la solidarité organique', *Sociologie et sociétés* 30/2: 2.

SPEENHAMLAND SYSTEM

A system of allowances paid in Britain to labourers to supplement their wages, the amount of such allowances being related both to the prevailing price of bread and to the size of the labourer's family. It is commonly believed that the 'Speenhamland system' was a radical departure from established Poor Law practice. In fact, the principle of temporary wage subsidies was a long-standing one in the Old Poor Law. The Speenhamland system was mainly confined to the southern counties of England, which were experiencing recession; the level of allowances was low and, as far as can be estimated, it had little discernible effect on wages or birth rates. However, the 1834 Poor Law Report argued that it had destroyed the labourers' will to work and had encouraged 'early and improvident' marriages, thus worsening the very poverty problem it sought to alleviate (Neuman 1982).

For the remainder of the nineteenth century, and well into the twentieth century, 'Speenhamland' was held up by classical economists as a symbol of the disastrous effects of indiscriminate, 'overgenerous' welfare, especially when used to subsidize wages. It appeared to be a perfect vindication of the warnings of the Rev. T.R. Malthus in his *Essay on the Principle of Population* (1798). The issue of whether a social security system should subsidise low wages remained, in theory, a highly sensitive one. For example, in Britain, the 1944 White Paper on Family Allowances felt it necessary to make specific reference to the Speenhamland system of child allowances, and, in 1971, the Nixon administration in the USA cast apprehensive eyes back to it when contemplating the introduction of a Family Assistance Plan. In practice, much nineteenth-century outdoor relief subsidized low wages, as did the 1908 old-age pension scheme in Britain and Family Income Supplement (introduced in 1971 and now replaced by tax credits). Supporters of a BASIC INCOME or citizen's income argue that there is a good case for social security subsidizing earnings from paid employment by providing a guaranteed minimum income for all.

REFERENCES

Neuman, M. (1982) *The Speenhamland County: Poverty and the Poor Laws in Berkshire, 1782–1834*, New York: Garland.

SQUATTING

Squatting consists of the possession of land and/or dwellings to which the squatter has no legal entitlement. Squatter settlements – variously termed *barrios, bidonvilles, bustees, favelas, kampongs* and *ranchos* – are characteristic of most Third World cities, in some of which they may form as much as three-quarters of the total residential area. They have grown especially rapidly in the past four decades in cities where the conventional housing markets are unable to cope with the demands produced by rapid urbanization in the Third World. They are created when squatters illegally occupy land, either on the edge of a built-up area or in the interstices of existing development (as in deep gullies in Caracas and alongside railway lines in Mexico City). Such an occupation may be entirely unplanned and piecemeal, but squatter settlements are also the results of planned invasions of land, which neither private owners nor the state are likely to resist. The myth of marginality describes squatting as a normal rather than a marginal pattern of tenure, as squatters move from initial 'bridgeheads' through to 'consolidation' of property and eventual establishment of entitlement (Perlman 1976).

Many squatter settlements lack a basic infrastructure – public utilities such as electricity, running water and sewerage, and garbage removal – and much of the housing is of a poor quality. However, Stokes (1962) distinguished between those which were what he termed 'slums of despair' and those which were 'slums of hope'. The latter are characterized by strong self-help movements, which promote both improvements to individual dwellings and collective investment in the needed infrastructure so as to improve the residents' quality of life.

For many governments, squatter settlements were for long seen as major irritants, creating not only substantial blots on the landscape and potential health hazards for the wider population but also possibly containing radical social movements. From the 1960s on, however, some housing specialists argued that squatter settlements provide a sensible resolution of the housing problem in rapidly growing, relatively poor countries. The conventional housing market cannot cope with the explosion of demand, and scarce capital is better invested elsewhere in the economy. Thus, squatter settlements provide a solution which works, allowing people to invest in housing and its improvement as their circumstances allow.

In some countries, the squatter settlement movement has been encouraged both by assisting groups in the search for land on which to establish their communities and by providing a basic infrastructure – a piped water system, a basic drainage network, and an electricity grid, for example. In some cases, basic dwellings (core rooms – a kitchen and one bedroom, perhaps) are provided, which the occupants can extend when money is available. However, such policies are condemned by others as ways of ideologically sustaining class differentials within divided societies (Burgess 1981).

In countries where the pattern of land tenure is more firmly set, squatting refers primarily to use of existing vacant housing. 'Licensed squatting' is the use of vacant housing which is subsequently sanctioned by the property owner.

REFERENCES

Burgess, R. (1981) 'Ideology and Urban Residential Theory in Latin America', in D.T. Herbert and R.J. Johnston (eds), *Geography and the Urban Environment*, vol. 4, Chichester: John Wiley.

Johnson, R.J. (1994) in R.J. Johnson, D. Gregory and D.M. Smith (eds), *The Dictionary of Human Geography*, Oxford: Blackwell.

Hardoy, J. (1989) *Squatter Citizen: Life in the Urban Third World*, London: Earthscan.

Lloyd, P.C. (1979) *Slums of Hope: Shanty Towns in the Third World*, Harmondsworth: Penguin.

Perlman, J. (1976) *The Myth of Marginality*, Berkeley: University of California Press.

Stokes, C.J. (1962) 'A Theory of Slums', *Land Economics* 38: 127–37.

Ward, P. (1990) *Mexico City: The Production and Reproduction of an Urban Environment*, Ale World Cities Series, London: Belhaven Press.

STANDARD FOOD BASKET

The calculated price of a set of basic foodstuffs (sometimes including basic commodities), and standardized, for example according to percentage of expenditure on food and size of household. In the ECLAC–UNDP (Economic Commission for Latin America and the Caribbean–United Nations Development Programme) study the standard food basket (SFB) variant consists of the following steps:

• In each country an SFB is defined for the average individual (or for the average individual in each household), based on diets observed in surveys of household income and expenditure and on recommended nutritional requirements in terms of age, weight and height, sex and type of activity. This provides a list of quantities of foodstuffs which satisfy the predefined nutritional requirements of the 'individual' (in general terms of proteins and calories). The quantities of foodstuffs are then multiplied by the prices which in principle each household must pay, although in practice there is usually a single range of prices (or one rural and one urban). The total cost of the per capita food basket is thus obtained (it should be noted that fuel and all other costs associated with the preparation and consumption of food have been excluded). The cost is interpreted as the *per capita extreme poverty or indigence line.*

• This line is then divided by the Engel coefficient (proportion of household expenditure devoted to food) to obtain what is called the *per capita poverty line.*

The two per capita poverty lines are compared with household income, also on a per capita basis. Households with per capita incomes below the POVERTY LINE are considered to be poor. Those with incomes below the extreme poverty or indigence line are classified as extremely poor. Individuals are classified on the basis of the households to which they belong.

REFERENCES

Boltvinik, J. (1991) 'La medición de la pobreza en América Latina', *Comercio Exterior* 41/5.
Boltvinik, J. (1992) 'El método de medición integrada de la pobreza. Una propuesta para su desarrollo', *Comercio Exterior* 42/4.

STIGMA

Stigma is variously understood as:

• a sense of shame, which makes people reluctant to claim benefits or services (Titmuss 1968);
• a loss of status (Pinker 1971);
• an attribute or characteristic which is discrediting (Goffman 1963);
• a pattern of social rejection (Scott 1972), analogous to EXCLUSION.

Stigmatization is part of the condition of poor people, because poverty itself is seen as a negative attribute, as it is associated with other negative attributes (like dependency), and as many conditions which lead people to be poor (like disability, unemployment, or single parenthood) are also socially rejected.

The term 'stigma' is also used to refer to the reluctance of people to claim entitlements and use the services that are available for them. The term was extensively used in relation to social assistance, where it was deliberately fostered as a means of discouraging dependency, and the removal of stigma has been a primary objective of many social policies subsequently. In recent years its use has been eclipsed by the idea of 'exclusion'.

REFERENCES

Goffman, E. (1963) *Stigma*, Harmondsworth: Penguin.
Pinker, R. (1971) *Social Theory and Social Policy*, London: Heinemann.
Scott, R.A. (1972) 'A Proposed Framework for Analysing Deviance as a Property of Social Order', in R.A. Scott and J.D. Douglas, *Theoretical Perspectives on Deviance*, New York: Basic Books.
Titmuss, R.M. (1968) *Commitment to Welfare*, London: Allen & Unwin.

STREET CHILDREN

There is no commonly agreed concept or definition of street children. However, the Study Group on street children of the Council of Europe (1994) has adopted a description of the phenomenon:

> Street children are children under 18 who, for shorter or longer periods, live in a street milieu. They are children who live wandering from place to place and who have their peer groups and contacts in the street. Officially these children may have as their address their parents' home or an institution of social welfare. Most significantly they have very few or no contacts with those adults, parents, school, child welfare institutions, social services, with a duty towards them.

The definition was not intended to be exclusive, but rather to be used as an instrument for determining the scope of the phenomenon.

The widespread media images of young Brazilians protesting in the streets of Rio de Janeiro symbolize street children to many people in Europe. Street children are understood to be children without any shelter. Although in most of Europe such street children are the exception, in the megacities of the developing world large numbers of children live and work on the streets. The World Health Organization (WHO 1995) estimates that there may be 100 million street children worldwide, with 40 million in Latin America, 25 million in Asia, 10 million in Africa and another 25 million in the rest of the world, including developed countries. Many of these children are at high risk of malnutrition, disease and violence. Research by WHO in 1993 showed that although poverty and rapid urbanization are major contributing factors to the problem of street children, many claim that physical and sexual abuse were the reasons for their leaving home.

REFERENCES

Council of Europe (1994) *Street Children*, Strasbourg: Council of Europe Press.
WHO (1995) *The World Health Report 1995: Bridging the Gaps*, Geneva: World Health Organization.

STRUCTURAL ADJUSTMENT

The World Bank introduced structural adjustment lending in 1979, initially as a temporary measure for developing countries with balance-of-payments problems and/or large debt burdens. Influential country subscribers to the World Bank, notably the USA, Germany and the UK, were from the early 1980s encouraging a focus on economic restructuring as a prerequisite to social welfare improvements. In part as a response to these pressures, structural adjustment became, and continues to be, a prominent feature of World Bank lending. Heavily indebted developing countries, of which there were many after the 'debt crisis' broke in 1982, had little alternative but to accept the offer of structural adjustment programmes (SAPs), a form of lending with stringent economic (and, later, political) conditions attached. These were designed, claimed the World Bank, to restructure 'maladjusted' developing-country economies in order to lay the foundations for subsequent social welfare improvements.

The most important of these conditions in the early years of adjustment was undoubtedly the prior acceptance by the recipient country of International Monetary Fund (IMF) 'stabilization' measures before SAPs could be approved. Stabilisation conditionality typically included targets for export-led growth (often agricultural exports, at the expense of subsistence farming), cuts in public expenditure and borrowing, devaluation of the currency, privatization of parastatal organizations, liberalization of the economy and other measures. The direct and indirect effects of many of these policies had seriously debilitating effects on the poor, but it was not until a crescendo of criticism in the mid-1980s, culminating in a UNICEF study *Adjustment with a Human Face* (Cornia et al. 1988) that the World Bank began to take these criticisms more seriously.

The World Bank's renewed interest in poverty was reflected in its 1990 *World Development Report*. Recognizing the harsh consequences of adjustment for the poor, the *Report* focused on the provision of targeted anti-poverty projects to protect the poorest in the short term, coupled with a policy thrust that encourages increased production through lowering labour costs even further. Critics lamented the lack of progress towards poverty reduction in the 1990s (see, e.g., Woodward 1992) and, for a number of countries (in sub-Saharan Africa particularly), the lack of any significant economic upturn or a significant reduction of their debt burden. A statement by the All Africa Conference of Churches reflect this continuing concern, declaring that the

> disastrous effects of the payment of the African debt be compared to a low intensity war which brings death, hunger, malnutrition, sickness, unemployment, homelessness and loss of dignity and personal worth to millions of children, women and men, young and old.

REFERENCES

Cornia, A., Jolly, R., and Stewart, F. (eds) (1988) *Adjustment with a Human Face*, Oxford: Clarendon Press.

Mihevic, J. (1995) *The Market Tells Them So: The World Bank and Economic Fundamentalism in Africa*, London, Zed Books.

Mosley, P., Harrigan, J., and Toye, J. (1995) *Aid and Power*, vol. I: *Analysis and Policy Proposals*, London: Routledge.

Woodward, D. (1992) *Debt, Adjustment and Poverty in Developing Countries*, London: Save the Children.

STRUCTURAL DEPENDENCY

In the sociological literature, structural dependency is DEPENDENCY conditioned by people's economic position and relationship to society, rather than by their intrinsic capacities. The term might be used in relation to elderly people or people with physical disabilities (Walker 1980; Phillipson et al. 1986).

In the literature of development studies, dependency refers generally to the structural economic dependency that poor countries have in relation to the developed world, and in particular to the financial indebtedness that has arisen (Packenham 1992).

REFERENCES

Packenham, R. (1992) *The Dependency Movement: Scholarship and Politics in Development Studies*, Cambridge MA: Harvard University Press.

Phillipson, C., Bernard, M., and Strang, P. (eds) (1986) *Dependency and Interdependency in Old Age*, London: Croom Helm.

Walker, A. (1980) 'The Social Creation of Poverty and Dependency in Old Age', *Journal of Social Policy* 9/1.

STRUCTURAL POVERTY

Structural explanations for poverty attribute poverty to the social or economic structure. Typically these explanations attribute poverty to patterns of inequality (including class, race, gender and geographical inequalities), or to the structure of power, including economic, political and elite structures. Within the global economy, equally, developing countries may be considered to have a position of structured disadvantage or STRUCTURAL DEPENDENCY. Structural poverty accordingly refers to poverty that is patterned by the social or economic structure. It refers principally to long-term situations or conditions, but in circumstances where the structure leads to marginal and precarious situations it may also account for transitory or dynamic understandings of poverty.

There are two main perspectives. The first, close to Anglo-Saxon development studies, econometric approaches and 'livelihood' analyses and focused on chronic poverty, defines structural poverty in terms of lack of access to income and basic assets. The chronic poor are those who experience poverty for extended periods of time, whose children are also likely to remain poor, and who have benefited least from economic growth, and national and international development initiatives. This perspective, being influential on Africa and Latin America poverty research, has intended to go beyond the limitations of static studies on poverty by building a sequential picture of longitudinal surveys of increases or decreases in welfare, (Øyen et al. 1996).

The second perspective views poverty as a multidimensional and structural phenomenon. Structural poverty results from long-term processes of inequality, persistent exclusion, concentration of economic power, lack of access to political resources, and systematic violation of basic social, political and human rights. A group of researchers from Thailand have related structural poverty with deprivation of the right to resources – access to land, water, mass media, political decision-making, and of the right to everyday cultural self-expression (Hassarungsee and SAWG 2001). Two factors contribute to this lack of access: (1) the centralized management of resources by the state, whose main objectives are making profit and land speculation; and (2) the loss by the poor of their bargaining power and access to political decision-making in areas affecting their life. If structural poverty reflects an oppressive political structure, the lifting of oppression by means of equal distribution of resources to all people and sectors is expected to redress the balance (Sachs 1993). Moreover, to understand structural poverty, from this point of view, is to fight an outdated learning culture and build up a new study on the poverty issue.

In this connection, two alternative understandings of structural poverty are found in Africa. The first sees it as the product of a power politics that maintains a grip on resources (political, natural or otherwise) at the expenses of citizens' rights through ruthless exploitation, seemingly harmless cronyism, and patron–client relationships. This point of view advocates the adoption of a depoliticized focus on poverty, since the apolitical 'needs' of 'victims' obliterate the real issues of rights and justice. This means also advocating policies that go beyond addressing only the immediate needs of the poor. 'Eradicating poverty requires more than simply providing food, digging wells, donating seeds and farm tools, and offering technical assistance. Indeed to tackle the root causes of poverty, issues of politics, justice, and rights must be addressed' (Dixon 2002).

The second view addresses the reason why poor people stay poor for long periods of time. This is not only a matter of asset deprivation and lack of access to jobs. Structural poverty, in this view, has 'an engagement with the meaningful complexities of social and power relations'. This argues for a 'close look at the underlying structural dimension that may undermine people's attempt to escape poverty, by the interactions between asset poverty, cash hunger, job insecurity and unemployment … their subjection to exploitative power relations', and also at the deeply racialized and authoritarian history of some countries in Africa (Du Toit 2005).

REFERENCES

Dixon, L.G. (2002) 'The Antidote to Patronage, Power Politics, and Structural Poverty?', *Praxis* 17: 1–11.

Du Toit, A. (2005) *Chronic and Structural Poverty in South Africa: Challenges for Action and Research*, Centre for Social Science Research (CSSR) Working Paper No. 121, University of Cape Town, www.cssr.uct.ac.za/index.html.

Hassarungsee, R., and SAWG (2001) *Thailand and Structural Poverty*, Social Agenda Working Group, www.cusri.chula.ac.th/network/social/eng2001.pdf.

Øyen, E., Miller, S., and Samad, S. (1996) *Poverty: A Global Review. Handbook on International Poverty Research*, Oslo: Scandinavian University Press.

Sachs, W. (1993) '"Poverty" in Need of a Few Distinctions, You Can't Measure Wealth by Cash Alone?', *Exploring Our Interconnectedness* 6.

SUB-EMPLOYMENT

Matza and Miller (1976: 661–2) use the term 'sub-employment' to describe the situation of people who have a marginal position in relation to the labour market. Marginal groups include migrant workers, single parents, some disabled people, and many people with low employment status or skills, who may find themselves employed only casually, intermittently or for limited periods of time. Their work is of low status and earning power; when work is scarce, they are likely to be unemployed. The position of sub-employed people is related to the concept of a 'dual labour market' but distinguished from that by its irregular, unstable circumstances. Sub-employed people are likely to move through various types of ephemeral labour, including temporary employment, casual labour, and work in which they are unable to maintain any tenure, as well as experiencing periodic spells of unemployment.

The concept of sub-employment is an attempt to describe a class position, or relationship to economic structures, rather than a consistent form of UNDEREMPLOYMENT or low-paid work. The complexity of changing patterns of employment, makes it difficult to identify patterns of sub-employment clearly in empirical terms. However, work by Morris and Irwin identifies a distinct set of patterns of marginal employment. (Morris and Irwin 1992) In France, these kinds of conditions are generally referred to in terms of PRECARIOUSNESS.

REFERENCES

Matza, D., and Miller, H. (1976) 'Poverty and Proletariat', in R.K. Merton and R. Nisbet (eds), *Contemporary Social Problems*, New York: Harcourt Brace Jovanovich.
Morris, L., and Irwin, S. (1992) 'Employment Histories and the Concept of the Underclass', *Sociology* 26/3: 401–40.

SUB-PROLETARIAT

Marxist class analysis describes the 'proletariat' as those who sell their labour to those who own and control the means of production. The 'lumpenproletariat' is a term coined by Marx in his analysis on the surplus population: 'every labourer belongs to it during the time when he is only partially employed or wholly unemployed' (1974: 600). He uses the concept to make reference to those left outside the relative population such as vagrants, criminals and prostitutes. Marx was dismissive of the lumpenproletariat, which he referred to as 'social scum'; the derogatory usage is reflected in current views about the UNDERCLASS. By contrast, contemporary Marxists in French-speaking countries have preferred the term 'sub-proletariat' to signify those who are marginalized within the economic system (e.g. Vercauteren 1970). The purpose of the term is to indicate that there is a class of people, identifiable in terms of their relationship to the means of production, who fall below the proletariat in the social structure.

REFERENCES

Marx, K. (1974) *Capital*, Volume I, London: Lawrence & Wishart.
Vercauteren, P. (1970) *Les sous-proletaires*, Bruxelles: Éditions Vie Ouvrière.

SUBJECTIVE POVERTY LINES

Subjective poverty lines are also known as the income proxy method (Veit-Wilson 1987) or consensual poverty lines (see Walker

1987; Halleröd 1995a for discussion). Subjective poverty lines are estimations by populations (obtained in surveys) about the minimum income level at which it is still possible to live 'decently'. The most important advantage of the subjective method is that the level of the poverty line is not fixed by experts but defined by society itself. The term 'subjective' here is potentially misleading: the line seeks to identify a consensual level of the adequacy of resources, which is based in a social norm rather than individual opinions.

In most cases, the subjective method produces poverty lines at a relatively high level. Deleeck et al. (1988) have argued that, in many cases, the poverty line is at such a level that it would be very difficult to maintain that all households below it are poor in the sense of being socially excluded (see EXCLUSION). The term 'insecurity of subsistence' meaning a situation in which households encounter some (financial) difficulty in participating in the average or most widely shared life-style, would be more appropriate. All methods of estimating a subjective poverty line make use of a minimum income question designed to measure the smallest income required to live 'decently' or 'adequately' or to 'get along'. However, the exact wording of the minimum income question varies considerably in different studies. Empirical studies have shown that estimates of the subjective poverty line usually rise systematically with the actual income of the household/individual (Citro and Michael 1995). Therefore, subjective poverty lines tend to fluctuate over time depending on changes in the social reference group (e.g. due to an increase in the overall living standard of the elderly, they respond with a higher necessary minimum income) and on the period of reference (e.g. in a period of crisis aspirations might decline). Given the wide variations in economic and social circumstances between regions and countries, the subjective poverty lines are less suitable for comparative purposes across time and space.

The subjective method has been developed independently by Kapteyn, Van Praag and others (the SPL method) (Van Praag et al. 1980) and Deleeck (CSP line) (Deleeck et al. 1988). The basic ideas are the same, but the operationalization is different.

To derive the income standard, it is assumed that only households that are just able to balance their budget (i.e. that are on the brink of insecurity of the means of subsistence) are able to give a correct estimate of what level of income is necessary to participate in the normal standard of living. The views of households whose incomes are either above or below the minimum level are biased because of the differences in style of living. However, it is not self-evident which households are in a state of budgetary balance. The difference between the two subjective methods lies in the way they identify those households. In the CSP method a second question is asked for this purpose, namely:

With your current monthly income, everything included, can you get by: with great difficulty / with difficulty / with some difficulty / fairly easily / easily / very easily / for your household?

Households that answer 'with some difficulty' are supposed to be just able to balance their budgets. On the basis of their declarations on the minimum level of income, the CSP standard is calculated.

The SPL method assumes that households with an actual income equal to their estimate of the minimum income required to live decently are in budgetary balance (Muffels and de Vries 1989). Subjective poverty lines have been used to measure poverty in the Netherlands (Hagennaars and de Vos 1988), the United States (Colasanto et al. 1984), Ireland (Nolan and Whelan 1996), Australia (Saunders and Matheson 1992) and Sweden (Halleröd 1995a). A number of multi-country comparative studies have also used subjective poverty line methods (see Halleröd 1995a for discussion). Halleröd (1995b) has combined the SPL subjective poverty line method with the consensual poverty approach of Mack and Lansley (1985) to produce a scientific measurement of poverty in Sweden. Nolan and Whelan (1996) have discussed the merits of this new approach.

REFERENCES

Citro, C.F., and Michael, R.T. (eds.) (1995) *Measuring Poverty: A New Approach*, Washington DC: National Academy Press.

Colasanto, D., Kapteyn, A., and van der Gaag, J. (1984) 'Two Subjective Definitions of Poverty Results from the Wisconsin Basic Needs Study', *Journal of Human Resources* 19/1: 127–38.

Deleeck, H., de Lathouwer, L. and van den Bosch, K. (1988) *Social Indicators of Social Security. A Comparative Analysis of Five Countries*, Antwerp: Centre for Social Policy.

Hagenaars, A.J.M., and de Vos, K. (1988) 'The Definition and Measurement of Poverty', *Journal of Human Resources* 23/2: 211–21.

Halleröd, B. (1995a) 'Perceptions of Poverty in Sweden', *Scandinavian Journal of Social Welfare* 4/3: 174–89.

Halleröd, B. (1995b) 'The Truly Poor. Indirect and Direct Measurement of Consensual Poverty in Sweden', *Journal of European Social Policy* 5/2: 111–29.

Mack, J., and Lansley, S. (1985) *Poor Britain*, London: Allen & Unwin.

Muffels, R., and de Vries, A. (1989) *Poverty in the Netherlands: First Report of an International Comparative Study*, Tilburg: Tilburg University Work and Organization Research Centre.

Nolan, B., and Whelan, C. (1996) 'Measuring Poverty, Using Income and Deprivation Indicators Alternative Approaches', *Journal of European Social Policy* 6/3: 225–40.

Saunders, P., and Matheson, G. (1992) 'Perceptions of Poverty: Income Adequacy and Living Standards in Australia', *Reports and Proceedings* 99, Social Policy Research Centre, University of New South Wales, Sydney.

Van Praag, B., Hagenaars, A., and van Weeren, J. (1980) *Poverty in Europe, Report to the Commission of the EC*, University of Leiden.

Veit-Wilson, J.H. (1987) 'Consensual Approaches to Poverty Lines and Social Security', *Journal of Social Policy* 16/2: 183–211.

Walker, R. (1987) 'Consensual Approaches to the Definition of Poverty: Towards an Alternative Methodology', *Journal of Social Policy* 16/2: 213–26.

SUBSISTENCE

The maintenance of a basic level of living, below which needs are not met. This is associated with the 'biological' approach, though not confined to it as subsistence may be viewed in terms of a broader view of needs.

Beveridge (1942) argued that a subsistence standard should include 'food, clothing, fuel, light and household sundries, and rent, though some margin must be allowed for inefficiency in spending'. Atkinson (1990: 10) defines a subsistence standard of poverty by the formula:

$$(1 + h) \, p.x^*$$

where:

x^* is a vector denoting a basket of goods,
p is the price of the basket, and
h is a provision for inefficient expenditure or waste.

This allows for 'secondary' poverty within the definition of subsistence: PRIMARY AND SECONDARY POVERTY.

REFERENCES

Atkinson, A.B. (1990) *Comparing Poverty Rates Internationally*, London: London School of Economics Welfare State Programme.

Beveridge, W. (1942) Cmd 6404, Social Insurance and Allied Services, London: HMSO.

SURVIVAL STRATEGIES

The idea of 'survival strategies' was developed to explain how families manage on inadequate incomes. In the 1960s, the idea of the CULTURE OF POVERTY represented poor people as apathetic, passive and unwilling to participate; the assumption was based on an opposite view, putting special emphasis on the creativity, ability and resourcefulness of the poor. Like studies of the culture of poverty, these studies were ethnographical in nature. Some studies focus on the behaviour of family units. Others are concerned with the relationship to wider groups and to society at large. The study *How Do Marginalized People Survive?* by Larissa Adler de Lomnitz (1975) is pioneering in this line and starts a more active representation of poverty, emphasizing the abilities and creativity of the poor in facing the problems. According to Adler de Lomnitz, the poor show a very significant ability to survive. These abilities are called survival mechanisms.

The related idea of 'survival strategies' was developed Duque and Pastrana (1973: 177) from work done in poor neighbourhoods in Santiago de Chile. They found that families developed 'objective livelihood strategies ... the central aspect of which consists of a rearrangement of functions in the family units, emphasizing the participation of all their members, if not most of them'. Studies of survival strategies explained the importance of reciprocity in families and communities, and of other means of generating alternative resources.

The PISPAL and the Comisión de Población y Desarrollo de FLACSO (FLACSO Population and Development Committee) (PISPAL 1978, cited in Rodríguez 1981; Torrado 1981, 1982) reframed the concept, calling it *family strategies*, since the family, focused on as the basic unit of social, economical and political *life*, belonging to different class and social categories on the basis of their living conditions, develops behaviour aimed at guaranteeing the social and biological reproduction of the group (PISPAL 1978, cited in Rodríguez 1981: 239). According to Torrado (1981, 1982), family strategies represent social processes directly related to the reproduction of the labour force. In this case, the analysis is not limited to the strategies of individuals, families and groups themselves, but is concerned with the ways in which society reproduces itself through political and economic processes.

REFERENCES

Adler de Lomnitz, L. (1975) *Como sobreviven los marginados*, Madrid: Siglo XXI.

Duque, J., and Pastrana, E. (1973) *Las estrategias de supervivencia familiar económica de las unidades familiares del sector popular urbano: una investigación exploratoria*, Santiago de Chile: Programa ELAS/CELADE.

Rodríguez, D. (1981) 'Discusiones en torno al concepto de estrategias de supervivencia. Relatoria del taller sobre estrategias de supervivencia', in *Demografía y Economía* 15/2.

Torrado, S. (1981) 'Sobre los conceptos de estrategias familiares de vida y proceso de reproducción de la fuerza de trabajo', *Demografía y Economía* 15/2.

Torrado, S. (1982) 'El enfoque de las estrategias familiares de vida en América Latina, orientaciones teórico metodológicas', *Cuadernos del CEUR* 2, Buenos Aires.

T

TARGETING

Targeting is the process by which policies are focused on certain individuals or groups within a population. This is sometimes identified with SELECTIVITY, but targeting may be based on factors other than need – for example, age, gender, race or locality.

There is no intrinsic reason why the target should be the needs of particular individuals, let alone poor individuals; it may be possible, for example, to target broader categories of people, like single parents, or residents of particular neighbourhoods (Gilbert et al. 1993: 84–5). Cornia and Stewart, considering the effectiveness of food subsidies in helping poorer people in developing countries, are not concerned with precise measurement, but with the way the benefits relate to the circumstances of poorer groups (Cornia and Stewart 1995). Food subsidies are considered to be targeted not because they are confined to poor people, but because they can be chosen in order to benefit poor people.

The World Bank has advocated 'indicator targeting' – directing resources to the correlates of poverty, rather than to the problem itself – on the pragmatic basis that it is less costly administratively than directing resources to individuals (World Bank 1990: 92). Coady et al. (2003) suggest that some methods, including means-testing, geographical targeting and work-based programmes are more effective at redistributing resources to people on low incomes. By contrast, programmes which target elderly people, and those requiring communities to bid, are less effective, and may be regressive.

REFERENCES

Coady, D., Grosh, M., and Hoddinot, J. (2003) *Targeting Outcomes Redux*, Washington DC: World Bank.
Cornia, G., and Stewart, F. (1995) 'Food Subsidies: Two Errors of Targeting', in F. Stewart, *Adjustment and Poverty*, London: Routledge.

Gilbert, N., Specht, H., and Terrell. P, (1993) *Dimensions of Social Welfare Policy*, Engle-wood Cliffs NJ: Prentice Hall.

World Bank (1990) *World Development Report 1990*, Oxford: Oxford University Press.

TIP-CURVES

TIP stands for 'The Three Is of Poverty' (TIP): incidence, intensity and inequality, being the three dimensions of aggregate poverty.

The TIP curve is obtained by ranking people from poorest to richest, accumulating their poverty gaps, and plotting them. The x-axis indicates the cumulative population share; the y-axis indicates the cumulative POVERTY GAP index PGI.

The TIP curve is a concave curve with slope at a given percentage equal to the poverty gap for that percentile. The curve is horizontal for all income above the poverty line. The figure is an example of a TIP curve for a country with a head-count index H of 25 per cent and an average poverty gap I of 37.5 per cent so that the poverty gap index is PGI = H.I = 0.095.

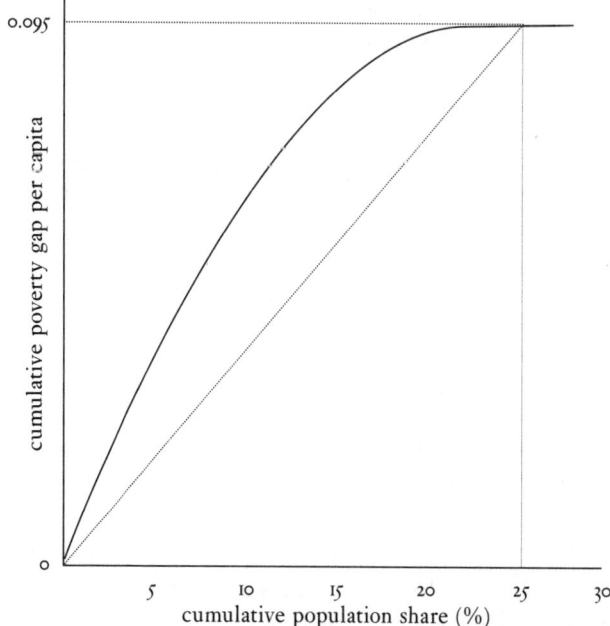

The curve includes all three dimensions of poverty. Jenkins and Lambert (1996):

> The Incidence aspect of poverty is summarized by the length of the TIP-curve's non-horizontal section [25 per cent in this case]. The head-count ratio H is that p at which the curve becomes horizontal. The Intensity dimension of poverty is summarized by the height of the TIP-curve: the vertical intercept at p=1 is the aggregate poverty gap averaged across all income-receiving units. The Inequality aspect is summarized by the degree of concavity of the non-horizontal section of the TIP. If there were equality of incomes amongst the poor – if poverty gaps were equal – this section would be a straight line with slope equal to $(z - \mu_q)$ where μ_q is the average income of the poor.

Consider two countries A and B and a common poverty line z. Jenkins and Lambert mathematically prove that there is more poverty in B than in A if the TIP curve of B is everywhere higher or in any case nowhere lower than that of A. This is valid for all poverty lines $z' < z$ and for all poverty indicators that belong to the FGT family, including H, PGI and FGT. They prove that TIP dominance of B over A is necessary and sufficient to ensure that there is more poverty in B than in A for all poverty lines $z < z_{max}$ and for all poverty measures of the FGT family.

REFERENCES

Jenkins, S.P., and Lambert, P.J. (1996) 'Three 'I's of Poverty Curves: TIPs for Poverty Analysis', mimeo, University of Essex and University of York, May.

Sen, A.K. (1976) 'Poverty: An Ordinal Approach to Measurement', *Econometrica* 44: 219–31.

TOTALLY FUZZY AND RELATIVE (TFR) POVERTY MEASURES

Cheli and Lemmi (1995) try to overcome the drawbacks of econometric POVERTY LINES by defining poverty as a completely relative concept. According to that concept, everybody is poor except the richest of the rich. All living standards are compared with the highest living standard. They do not need the arbitrary choice of the location of poverty lines any more. In fact, the poverty line corresponds with the highest living standard. Cheli and Lemmi (1995) call this approach

Totally Fuzzy and Relative (TFR). They use a membership function that corresponds with the population share above a certain living standard level:

$$p_n = 0$$
$$p_i = p_{i+1} + \frac{pop_i}{1 - pop_n}$$

where:

p_i is the degree of poverty of the ith person with respect to the richest person n, such that only the richest person is not poor:
$$p_n = 0$$
pop_i is the population share of group i
pop_n is the population share of the richest group n.

According to this membership function, the degree of poverty p_i corresponds with the cumulative population share counting backwards from the richest to the poorest group.

Assessing poverty as a completely relative concept with the implication that everyone is considered poor except the richest of the rich is an extreme point of view. Besides, the empirical outcomes of the above membership function are not very satisfactory. According to the above membership function, the degree of poverty of a person with the median living standard is 50 per cent and the degree of poverty of the poorest of the poor is 100 per cent. This result would imply that two persons with the median living standard contribute equally to total poverty as one very poor person.

Therefore, both on conceptual and empirical grounds, the search for other, more acceptable, membership functions continues.

REFERENCES

Cheli, B., and Lemni, A. (1995) 'A "Totally" Fuzzy and Relative Approach to the Multidimensional Analysis of Poverty', *Economic Notes* 24: 115–33.

U

UBN–PL METHOD

Following a line of analysis introduced by Beccaria and Minujin (1985) and by Katzman (1989), and a conceptual approach first suggested by Boltvinik (1989, 1990), whereby a new method was constituted through the use of the UBN (Unsatisfied Basic Needs) and PL (Poverty Line) procedures, the UNDP Regional Project for Overcoming Poverty promoted and implemented a method for measuring poverty in various Latin American countries.

The UBN–PL method is the simultaneous use of two methods: the STANDARD FOOD BASKET and the procedure known as UBN, the prototype which was used for the 'Poverty in Argentina' project (1986).

The poverty criterion adopted in the UBN–PL method considers as poor those households (and their occupants) whose per capita income is below the poverty line and/or who have one or more unsatisfied basic needs. In other words, the head-count ratio is obtained by a combination of criteria. This increases the incidence of poverty in a country, sometimes considerably, compared with findings of whichever of the two different methods were used previously. Four categories can be defined by this combination of both methods: (a) people who are poor according to both methods (the intersection of both sets); (b) people who are poor if PL is applied; (c) people who are poor if UBN is applied but not if PL is applied; and (d) those who are not poor using either method.

Analysis of the empirical evidence in the first empirical applications of this procedure led to the following conclusions: (a) the incidence of poverty under UBN shows a systematic trend downward; (b) the incidence under PL fluctuates in accordance with the ups and downs of the economy; (c) in general, as regard households defined as poor under both methods the correlation is very low; (d) people who are poor according to UBN have a greater tendency to be poor also according to PL than vice versa.

REFERENCES

Beccaria, L., Boltvinik, J., Fresneda, O., Sen, A.K., et. al. (1992) *América Latina: El reto de la pobreza*, Regional Project to Overcome Poverty, Bogota: UNDP.
Beccaria, L., and Minujin, A. (1985) *Alternative Methods for Measuring the Evolution of Poverty*, Amsterdam: Proceedings of the International Statistical Institute.
Boltvinik, J. (1989) 'Hacia una estrategia para la superación de la pobreza', in *Necesidades básicas y desarrollo*, ILPES–ILDIS, La Paz: Instituto de Estudios Sociales de La Haya.
Boltvinik, J. (1990) *Pobreza y Necesidades Básicas. Conceptos y Métodos de Medición*, Regional Project to Overcome Poverty, Caracas: UNDP.
Boltvinik, J. (1992) 'El método de medición interada de la pobreza. Una propuesta para su desarrollo', *Comercio Exterior* 42/4.
Katzman, R. (1989) 'La heterogeneidad de la pobreza. El caso de Montevideo', *Revista de la CEPAL* 37 (April).

UNDERCLASS

The 'urban underclass' and the 'ghetto underclass' are two similar concepts which have emerged from research on poverty in the United States. Better-off African Americans have moved from the inner city to suburbia to join the white middle class. Poor African Americans, together with other ethnic minorities and disadvantaged groups, remain in spatial ghettos which create and reinforce an urban underclass. This process is exacerbated by industrial and social transformations (Wilson 1987, 1993).

The term may have been introduced by the Swedish economist Gunnar Myrdal (1963), who described those long-term marginalized or unemployable by the labour market as an underclass. Gans (1995) criticizes the concept as a labelling phenomenon which stresses the negative aspects of poverty and is too imprecise as a tool for renewed analytical understanding.

REFERENCES

Gans, H. (1995) *The War against the Poor*, New York: Basic Books.
Myrdal, G. (1963) *Challenge to Affluence*, London: Gollancz.
Wilson, W.J. (1987) *The Truly Disadvantaged*, Chicago: University of Chicago Press.
Wilson, W.J. (1993) *The Ghetto Underclass*, Newbury Park CA: Sage.

UNDEREMPLOYMENT

Underemployment occurs when the terms of employment offered to people are inadequate for their training, their needs or their demand for work. The concept of underemployment, like that of unemployment, presupposes a structure of employment in a formal economy. There are two main types of underemployment: time-related underemployment and inadequate employment (ILO 1998).

According to the ILO, 'time-related under-employment exists when the hours of work of an employed person are insufficient in relation to an alternative employment situation in which the person is willing and available to engage.' This includes people who are willing or available to work additional hours, or those who worked for less than an agreed national 'threshold' or norm. This may include both part-time workers and people working less than their usual hours.

'Inadequate' employment refers to the situation of people in employment who wanted to change their current work situation, activities or environment. The ILO resolution distinguishes three types of inadequate employment situations:

- *skill-related inadequate employment*, characterized by inadequate utilization and mismatch of occupational skills, thus signifying poor utilization of human capital;
- *income-related inadequate employment*, resulting from low levels of organization of work or productivity, insufficient tools and equipment and training or deficient infrastructure;
- *inadequate employment related to excessive hours*, specifically the situation where persons in employment suffered a reduction in income because they want or seek to work for less time.

REFERENCES

ILO (1998) 'Resolution Concerning the Measurement of Under-employment and Inadequate Employment Situations', Sixteenth International Conference of Labour Statisticians, www.ilo.org/public/english/bureau/stat/res/underemp.htm.

UNEMPLOYMENT

The definition of 'work' adopted by the international agencies tends to assume the model of central capitalist economies (Wainerman and Giusti 1994), and unemployment is generally identified with a lack of salaried work. An unemployed person is someone who has no work, in the sense of selling his or her wage labour. The concept of unemployment presumes a structure of employment, and so of

integration into a formal economy. It is primarily applied in consequence to developed economies.

The resolution of the XII International Conference of Labour
Statisticians (ILO 1982) on economically active population, employment and unemployment was intended to address this bias. Their
definition is as follows:

> 'The 'unemployed' comprise all persons above a specified age who
> during the reference period were:
> (a) 'without work', i.e. were not in paid employment or self-
>   employment,
> (b) 'currently available for work', i.e. were available for paid employ-
>   ment or self-employment during the reference period; and
> (c) 'seeking work', i.e. had taken specific steps in a specified recent
>   period to seek paid employment or self-employment.

The direct reference to self-employment in this definition makes it
possible to record people whose work is in the INFORMAL SECTOR
as being 'unemployed'. However, in virtually every country keeping a record, statistics are more reliable for activities linked to the
formal sector. The 'specified age' differs between countries, being for
example 10 years in Ecuador and 16 in Scotland.

Colledge (2000) identifies three reference periods used in the
definition of unemployment:

• a specified brief period, either one day or one week, during which
  a person is without work, i.e. not in paid employment or self
  employment;
• a period during which the person is available for work, i.e. the
  'availability' period; and
• a period during which the person takes active steps to find employment, i.e. the 'job search' period.

The type of unemployment usually recorded by labour market
statistics is known as open unemployment. Some authorities take
account of another category: hidden unemployment, so-called. Re-
cording hidden unemployment is complex. It has been accepted that
the concept should be related to a loss of expectations while job
searching. For the ILO (1997), hidden unemployment is the position
of discouraged people who have given up looking for an occupation
(Monza 2002).

REFERENCES

Colledge, M. (2000) *Labour Force Indicators Review of Standards and Practices*, www. unescap.org/stat/meet/keyindic/oecd_labourforce.pdf.

Monza, A. (2002) *Los dilemas de la política de empleo en la coyuntura argentina actual*, OSDE-CIEPP, www.fundacionosde.com.ar/Fundacion_OSDE/pdf/biblioteca/monza.

ILO (1982) 'Resolution Concerning Statistics of the Economically Active Population, Employment, Unemployment and Underemployment', adopted by the Thirteenth International Conference of Labour Statisticians, www.ilo.org/public/english/bureau/stat/res/ecacpop.htm.

ILO (1997) *Youth, Older Workers and Social Exclusion: Some Aspects of the Problem in G7 Countries*, G7/1997/1, Geneva: International Labour Organization, www.ilo.org/public/english/bureau/inf/pr/1997/31.htm.

ILO (2002) *Medición del desempleo*, Equipo Técnico Multidisciplinario para los Países Andinos Desempleo, www.oitandina.or.pe/datoslab/medesem.html.

Teulon, F. (1996) *Le Chomage el les politiques de'emploi*, Paris: Seuil.

Wainerman, C., and Giusti, A. (1994) '¿Crecimiento real o aparente? La fuerza de trabajo en la Argentina en la última década', *Desarrollo Económico* 34/135.

UNITED STATES OF AMERICA POVERTY LINE

The governmental MINIMUM INCOME STANDARD in the USA is known as the poverty thresholds. The USA was one of the first nations to adopt an official poverty line (Will 1986). It has a decades-long tradition (e.g. US Bureau of the Census 1969) of using the poverty thresholds to produce official annual statistics on the number of persons in (officially defined) poverty.

The thresholds are not a complete BUDGET STANDARD, but were developed by applying an ENGEL COEFFICIENT – the 'multiplier' – to a partial budget standard for food only. They were developed in the mid-1960s by Mollie Orshansky (1965, 1969) in connection with the War on Poverty. Orshansky used food plans – partial budget standards for food – developed by the US Department of Agriculture (USDA). There were four such food plans providing nutritionally adequate diets at different cost levels. Orshansky initially used the two cheapest food plans. War on Poverty policymakers decided to use the lower thresholds based on the 'economy food plan', which USDA described as 'designed for temporary or emergency use when funds are low' (Fisher 1992a).

For families of three or more, the poverty threshold for a family of a given size and composition was calculated by multiplying the cost of the relevant 'economy food plan' by 3. (Somewhat different procedures were used for smaller families.) The multiplier of 3 was derived from the USDA's 1955 Household Food Consumption Survey, which showed that the average share of after-tax money income going for food was one-third for families of three or more. Thus, for the base year 1963, the poverty threshold for a non-farming family of four was $3,128.

No major changes have been made in the poverty threshold methodology since the 1960s. The thresholds are adjusted each year for changes in consumer prices, but not for changes in the general standard of living (INCOME ELASTICITY OF THE POVERTY LINE). Since the real standard of living is higher than it was in the 1960s, living conditions among the officially poor are further below the average American lifestyle in the 1990s and 2000s than in the 1960s. As real incomes have increased, the average American family's share of income going for food has decreased, from one-third in 1955 to less than one-sixth in the 1990s, suggesting that the use of 3 as the multiplier of the food budget is inadequate (Harrington 1984; Citro and Michael 1995; Nolan and Whelan 1996). Many other criticisms have been raised about aspects of both the poverty thresholds and the US Census Bureau definition of money income used with them.

The poverty guidelines – a simplified version of the poverty thresholds – are also produced each year. These are used for determining eligibility for certain federal programmes, such as Food Stamps, the Head Start Program, and parts of Medicaid (Fisher 1992b). However, the guidelines are not used either to determine eligibility or to set benefit levels for cash assistance programmes. In 1995, a Panel on Poverty and Family Assistance appointed by the National Research Council proposed a new approach for developing an official US poverty measure (Citro and Michael 1995). For its reference threshold, the Panel proposed not a specific dollar figure but a dollar range. While expressing this range as a percentage (range) of median expenditures for food, clothing, shelter, and utilities (FCSU), increased by a small multiplier to allow for other needs, the Panel actually determined the dollar range based in part on consideration of expert family budgets and relative and subjective poverty thresholds. The threshold would be updated annually based on changes in median actual consumption expenditures for FCSU – a 'quasi-relative' updating procedure. The threshold would be adjusted for different family sizes using an explicit equivalence scale. The Panel would redefine family resources (income) to be consistent with its threshold concept, including money income and certain near-money benefits but excluding taxes and certain expenses. Research (e.g., Short et al. 1999) is continuing on the Panel's proposals, but they have not been adopted as a new official poverty measure.

REFERENCES

Citro, C.F., and Michael, R.T. (eds) (1995) *Measuring Poverty: A New Approach*, Washington, National Academy Press.

Fisher, G.M. (1992a) 'The Development and History of the Poverty Thresholds', *Social Security Bulletin* 55/4: 3–14.

Fisher, G.M. (1992b) 'Poverty Guidelines for 1992', *Social Security Bulletin* 55/1: 43–6.

Harrington, M. (1984) *The New American Poverty*, New York: Holt, Rinehart & Winston.

Nolan, B., and Whelan, C.T. (1996) *Resources, Deprivation and Poverty*, Oxford: Clarendon Press.

Orshansky, M. (1965) 'Counting the Poor: Another Look at the Poverty Profile', *Social Security Bulletin* 28/1: 3–29.

Orshansky, M. (1969) 'How Poverty is Measured', *Monthly Labor Review* 92/2: 37–41.

Short, K., Garner, T., Johnson, D., and Doyle, P. (1999) *Experimental Poverty Measures: 1990 to 1997*, US Census Bureau, Current Population Reports, P60–205, Washington DC: US Government Printing Office.

US Bureau of the Census (1969) *Current Population Reports*, Series P-60, No. 68, Poverty in the United States: 1959 to 1968, Washington DC: US Government Printing Office.

Will, B.P. (1986) 'Poverty: That Intangible which Evades Definition or Measurement', internal working document, Ottawa: Statistics Canada, Social and Economic Studies Division.

URBAN SEGREGATION

Urban segregation is the process in cities by which classes or groups of people become spatially concentrated in different areas. These areas differ in terms of wealth, status and hierarchy (Castells 1984).

In the 1970s, Latin American urban segregation followed a common pattern: the occupation of space through so-called 'irregular' settlements on previously unsettled plots of land where precariousness of tenure was generally combined with poor living conditions, in areas which were often run-down, marginally located or at environmental risk. These forms of occupation took on a wide array of names: *callampas* (Chile), *cantegriles* (Uruguay), *favelas* (Brazil), *tugurios*

(Costa Rica), *villas miserias* and *villas de emergencia* (Argentina), *chabolas* (Ecuador).

The process of urban segregation has been described by the theories of peripheral urbanization and urban super-exploitation. The former accounted for growing urban segregation stemming from the development of a local economy which reflected the interests of global capital and external demands (e.g. an export-focused economy, growing centralization of economic activities, expansion of the informal economy and minimum-income jobs) (Walton 1984). Urban super-exploitation describes the infrastructure, service and housing exclusion of urban workers which results in domestic overwork, unpaid self-construction of housing and community-developed urban services, with the municipality playing little or no role in service provision.

In the 1980s, the processes of urban segregation were associated with economic, social and cultural developments which affected the distribution of poverty and urban protest. Queiroz Riveiro (2005) argues that a growing segmentation of the labour market occurred, which resulted in the creation of jobs that were either core or peripheral to the main economy, and also in the emergence of a survival economy oriented towards the needs of the poor. The spatial expression of these changes in global capitalism was increased urban segregation, which activated certain areas of the urban periphery as sites for export production or as markets, while it deactivated others considered too poor or unstable for profitable use. Wacquant (2001) discusses 'advanced marginality' in cities as the process of spatial isolation of the poor through increased physical (fenced rich communities), economic (high housing costs) and social barriers, which results in reduced contact and interactions between social classes.

In some countries, urban segregation is compounded by ethnic and cultural discrimination. The segregation found in ghettos is a result of more than just economic changes and poverty (Wacquant 2004), discriminatory processes such as restrictive covenants, racial zoning, policy instruments, and threats of violence also contribute to the formation of ghettos (Massey and Denton 1993). These processes often also result in poverty, inadequate housing, unemployment, lack of professional opportunities and high levels of crime (Borja and Castells 1977).

REFERENCES

Borja, J., and Castells, M. (1997) 'La Ciudad Multicultural', *La Factoría* 2 (February), www.lafactoriaweb.com/articulos/borjcas2.htm.

Castells, M. (1984) *La cuestión urbana*, Mexico: Siglo XXI.

Massey, D., and Denton, N. (1993) *American Apartheid*, Cambridge MA: Harvard University Press.

Queiroz Riveiro, L.C. (2005) 'Segregación residencial y segmentación social: el "efecto vecindario" en la reproducción de la pobreza en las metrópolis brasileñas', in S. Alvarez Leguizamón (ed.), *Trabajo y producción d e la pobreza en Latinoamérica y el Caribe, estructuras, discursos y actores*, Buenos Aires: CLACSO/CROP.

Wacquant, J.L. (2001) *Os condenados das ciudades*, Rio da Janeiro: Revan/Observatorio das Metrópolis.

Wacquant, J.L. (2004) 'Ghetto', in N.J. Smelser and P.B. Baltes (eds), *International Encyclopedia of the Social and Behavioral Sciences*, London: Pergamon Press.

Walton, J. (1984) 'La economía internacional y la urbanización periférica', in *Ciudades y Sistemas Urbanos*, Buenos Aires: CLACSO.

V

VAGRANCY

Controlling the wanderer with no settled abode or regular work has been a long-standing feature of social policy:

> The great object of our early pauper legislation seems to have been the restraint of vagrancy. (Poor Law Report 1834)

More recently, vagrant men and women were seen in terms of DESTITUTION. The response to destitution has changed from that stressing personal inadequacy of one kind or another to the more operational notion of sleeping rough or regularly using night shelters or resettlement units.

REFERENCES

Timms, N., and Timms, R. (1982) *Dictionary of Social Welfare*, London: Routledge & Kegan Paul.

VOICE

The idea of 'voice' is used to refer to perceptions, opinions or representations of people who are personally affected by issues. It is closely linked to PARTICIPATORY RESEARCH models.

The idea has developed through three main routes. The term 'voice' itself was introduced by Hirschman to consider non-financial elements in the relationship of consumers and citizens to service providers (Hirschman 1970). Hirschman referred to the importance of 'voice', 'loyalty', and 'exit' (the power to choose alternative providers). This model had considerable influence in the development of public services in the 1980s and 1990s, and 'voice' was emphasized as an alternative to the power of consumers in an economic market.

The second element has been 'deliberative democracy'. Joshua Cohen describes a model which emphasizes democracy's character of discussion, cooperation and social inclusion. Deliberative democracy bases governance in negotiation and discussion, the representation of interests or the legitimization of dissent (Cohen 1997). The idea of 'voice' has come to refer to the process of participation in democratic deliberation.

Third, voice has come to be identified with the principle of EMPOWERMENT. Voice is a means of enabling people with relatively little power to express views, and to communicate views to those in authority in their own words.

These different elements come together in the development of the Participatory Poverty Assessments (PPAs) sponsored by the World Bank, reported in *Voices of the Poor* (Narayan et al. 2000a, 2000b, 2002). *Voices of the Poor* reports diverse views from more than 20,000 respondents in twenty-three countries. The emphasis in their responses falls primarily on economic and social relationships rather than on specific forms of material deprivation.

REFERENCES

Cohen, J. (1997) 'Deliberation and Democratic Legitimacy', in R. Goodin and P. Pettit (eds), *Contemporary Political Philosophy*, Oxford: Blackwell.

Hirschman, A. (1970) *Exit, Voice and Loyalty*, Cambridge MA: Harvard University Press.

Narayan, D., with Patel, R., Schafft, K., Rademacher, A., and Koch-Schulte, S. (2000a) *Voices of the Poor: Can Anyone Hear Us?*, New York: Oxford University Press for the World Bank.

Narayan, D., Chambers, R., Kaul Shah, M., and Petesch, P. (2000b) *Voices of the Poor: Crying Out for Change*, New York: Oxford University Press for the World Bank.

Narayan, D., and Petesch, P. (2002) *Voices of the Poor: From Many Lands*, New York: Oxford University Press for the World Bank.

VULNERABILITY

Vulnerability is closely related to risk, although there are important distinctions between them. People are at risk if something negative is likely to happen. People are vulnerable when, if something negative happens, it will damage them; vulnerability is defined by the damage, not the risk. People who are at risk are often vulnerable, but many more people are vulnerable than those who are at risk. A person who is in a high-paid, low-security occupation (like executive management) is at risk, but not vulnerable; a person who is in secure, low-paid employment, but is not covered for housing costs in the event of unemployment, is vulnerable but not at risk.

Poor people are, notoriously, more vulnerable than many others. But vulnerability is not equivalent to poverty, and it is possible to construct circumstances in which richer people are more vulnerable than poor ones. This is particularly important in developing countries, where the effect of increasing resources may also be to increase vulnerability (Streeten, 1995). A parallel process is visible in developed countries, where the high level of specialization has made particular groups of workers – such as workers in heavy industry, like miners, steel workers or shipbuilders – especially vulnerable to changes in the structure of the economy.

Chambers (1989) argues that, in general, policies aimed at mitigating poverty have not considered the vulnerability undergone by the poor. Instead of analysing the specific factors that aggravate poverty or expose individuals, households and communities to the risk of impoverishment, these policies have focused on income or consumption levels. Chambers argues that vulnerability relates to 'defencelessness, insecurities and susceptibility to risks, traumas and stress'. Consistent with Chambers's view, the World Bank (Narayan et al. 2000: 61) suggests that vulnerability lies in the lack of assets which expose individuals, households and communities to a greater risk of poverty. Reductions in assets increase the risk of impoverishment. Thus policies are developed with a view to strengthening intangible assets such as social capital and self-help community networks, rather than improving consumption and income (ASSET VULNERABILITY FRAMEWORK).

REFERENCES

Chambers, R. (ed.) (1989) *Special Issue on Vulnerability: How the Poor Cope, IDS Bulletin* 20/2.

Streeten, P. (1995) 'Comments on "The Framework of ILO Action Against Poverty"', in G. Rodgers (ed.), *The Poverty Agenda and the ILO*, Geneva: International Labour Organization.

Narayan, D., with Patel, R., Schafft, K., Rademacher, A., and Koch-Schulte, S. (2000) *Voices of the Poor: Can Anyone Hear Us?*, New York: Oxford University Press for the World Bank.

WEB OF DEPRIVATION

Poverty is often identified in terms of a set of needs or problems, like low income, deprivation and a lack of facilities. The idea of the web of deprivation suggests, by contrast, that there is no simple core set of issues. There is, rather, a constellation of problems, which can be found in different combinations according to circumstances. Research on the pattern of VULNERABILITY to poverty has argued that poverty consists not of a single, unvarying problem or set of problems, but rather of a fluctuating set of conditions characterized by the systematic relationship of the deprivations experienced (Coffield and Sarsby, 1980; Kolvin et al., 1990). By this argument, poverty is like a web, because people who try to pull themselves out of one part of it often stick to another part of the web; they think they have solved one problem, but find they have only exchanged it for another one. The link between these fluctuating, shifting problems rests in the systematic relationship between different forms of deprivation.

The concept has most recently been advanced in the World Bank's study of *Voices of the Poor* (Narayan et al. 2000).

REFERENCES

Coffield, F., and Sarsby, J. (1980) *A Cycle of Deprivation?*, London: Heinemann.
Kolvin, I., Miller, F., Scott, D., Gatzanis, S., and Fleeting, M. (1990) *Continuities of Deprivation?* Aldershot: Avebury.
Narayan, D., Chambers, R., Kaul Shah, M., and Petesch, P. (2000) *Voices of the Poor: Crying Out for Change*, New York: Oxford University Press for the World Bank.

WELFARE

Welfare refers

1. to a state of 'well-being';
2. in the study of the economics of welfare, to the utility (or optimal choices) of individuals or groups;

3. to the provision of benefits, goods and services to ensure well-being;

4. in the United States, to the provision of social assistance.

Welfare is used to describe certain services or institutions and also the ideas of individual and social well-being by which those services or institutions are informed. In this context, it is also important to consider the complementing notion of DISWELFARE: for many, social service provision represents not an increment in welfare but a partial compensation for diswelfares incurred as a result of social change. While ideas of welfare and compensation for diswelfare may be said to inform the social services, it should be acknowledged that 'welfare is only to a very limited extent the product of social services or of social policy. Its roots lie deep in the social and economic system as a whole. Its realisation and enjoyment depend, therefore, on a number of other rights ... including those to property and personal freedom, to work and to justice' (Marshall 1981: 93). It has become increasingly common to identify different models of welfare; Pinker (1979: 245) for example, discusses the models derived from classical political economy, from Marxism and from the effort to make: 'a welfare society in which the terms of exchange and the understandings of obligation and entitlement were decently conditional, neither vulgarly egoistical nor impossibly altruistic'.

REFERENCES

Honderich, T. (1981) 'The Question of Well–being and the Principle of Equality', *Mind* 90: 481–504.
Marshall, T. (1981) *The Right to Welfare and Other Essays*, London: Heinemann.
Pinker, R. (1979) 'Three Models of Social Welfare', ch. 12 of *The Idea of Welfare*, London: Heinemann.
Timms, N., and Timms, R. (1982) *Dictionary of Social Welfare*, London: Routledge & Kegan Paul.

WELFARE HOUSING

Welfare housing is HOUSING provided on a non-profit basis aimed primarily at low-income households. Forms of subsidy, allocation and ownership vary. Welfare housing may refer to dwellings directly provided and managed by local or central government, or to state-subsidized housing managed and owned by a diverse range of housing associations and co-operatives. The diversity of forms of housing intervention and institutional arrangement complicates definitions. Two criteria are important, however, in differentiating welfare housing from any housing provided with state assistance. The key institutions should operate on a non-profit basis and allocation should be on the basis of some assessment of NEED rather than ability to pay (Marloe 1996).

Welfare housing is, as the name implies, associated with WELFARE STATE capitalism. It is to be differentiated, therefore, from direct housing provision in former state socialist societies and is linked with a particular period of development in particular countries. In general terms we can refer to a period extending from around 1920 to 1980 and to the core capitalist countries of Europe, North America and Australasia.

A key issue in welfare housing, and what could be seen as a defining feature, is the extent to which it is the exclusive domain of low-income households. Such issues are often referred to in terms of social mix, meaning the degree to which different social classes or income groups are represented in the public housing sector. Public housing sectors which are targeted on lower income households could be seen as the purest versions of welfare housing – as housing for those households unable to gain accommodation through the market.

REFERENCES

Marloe, M. (1996) *The Peoples' Home*, Oxford: Blackwell.

WELFARE RIGHTS

The idea of 'welfare rights' is used in two different senses: in a general sense to refer to rights to welfare, and specifically to refer to support for people pursuing specific legal entitlements to social security benefits. In the general sense, welfare rights include both moral and positive rights. Moral rights are moral claims or justifications for a course of action towards the person who holds the right. Rights to welfare are based partly in moral statements, such as the

UN Declaration of Human Rights, which guarantees 'the economic, social and cultural rights indispensable for (the person's) dignity and the free development of his personality' (UN 1948: Article 22), and 'a standard of living adequate for himself and his family, including food, clothing, housing and medical care and necessary social services' (Art 25(1)). Positive rights are legally enforceable. They depend on legal sanctions, and so on the legal structures of citizenship. Examples include rights to income support or medical insurance, which are generally subject to frameworks established by law and so capable of redress in case of default. Welfare rights in this general sense are closely related to human rights (see HUMAN RIGHTS AND POVERTY).

In the specific sense, the term 'welfare rights' is used to refer to a range of activities intended to use existing legal rights to promote the principle of a minimum basic income. There are four main types of activity (Spicker 1995):

- *Advice and support* given to individuals who have problems with specific benefits and social services.
- Agencies dedicated to *advocacy* and specialised advice. This is intended not only to help people in particular circumstances, but to challenge and test the work of agencies in the welfare field. Test cases are used to establish precedents and general principles.
- *Publicity*, extending awareness of legal entitlements.
- *Political campaigning*. This draws on information gained from practice to argue for legal and administrative changes in the treatment of service users.

REFERENCES

Spicker, P. (1995) *Social Policy*, Hemel Hempstead: Harvester Wheatsheaf.
UN (1948) *Universal Declaration of Human Rights*, United Nations, www.un.org/Overview/rights.html.

WELFARE STATE

The idea of the 'welfare state' is widely used but often ill defined (Veit-Wilson 2000). It was 'invented' by William Temple, the Archbishop of Canterbury (Briggs 2000) – possibly based on a translation of the German term *Wohlfahrtsstaat* – and defined as the embodiment of European values by the historian E.H. Carr in an editorial entitled 'The New Europe' in the *The Times* newspaper on 1 July 1940:

> Over the greater part of Western Europe the common values for which we stand are known and prized. We must indeed beware of defining these values in purely nineteenth-century terms. If we speak of democracy, we do not mean a democracy which maintains the right to vote but forgets the right to work and the right to live. If we speak of freedom, we do not mean a rugged individualism which excludes social organization and economic planning. If we speak of equality, we do not mean a political equality nullified by social and economic privilege.

In the 1950s Richard Titmuss argued that the welfare state was a manifestation, 'first, of society's will to survive as an organic whole, and secondly of the expressed will of all the people to assist the survival of some people' (Titmuss 1958). In the 1960s, the British sociologist Dorothy Wedderburn defined the purpose of the 'welfare state' in more narrow 'poverty alleviation' terms

> There is, though, a central core of agreement that the welfare state implies a state commitment of some degree which modifies the play of market forces in order to ensure a minimum real income for all. (Wedderburn 1965: 127)

The idea of the 'welfare state' is used in three main senses. It refers, first, to an idealized model of the provision of welfare, characterized by the reform of welfare in the period following World War II. Asa Briggs identifies the main elements of this model as including

- a guarantee of minimum standards, including a minimum income;
- social protection for circumstances in which people were likely to be in need;
- the provision of welfare at the best level possible (Briggs 2000).

This model is sometimes described in terms of 'institutional' welfare. Institutional welfare is based on a view of need and dependency as a normal or institutionalized aspect of social relationships. Provision is made as of right in 'a state in which organized power is deliberately used (through politics and administration) in an effort to modify the play of market forces' (Briggs 2000).

Second, the idea of the 'welfare state' is also associated with the
provision of an extensive system of social protection, provided not by
the state, but by a combination of voluntary, independent, mutualist
and government-based services. The European 'welfare states' rely
on plural provision. The role of government is to plan services and
supplement provision as necessary. This is sometimes described in
terms of 'corporatism', a system of government in which autonomous
non-governmental organizations are coopted into activities which
might otherwise be done by government. The primary purpose of
this 'type' of 'welfare state' is seen not as poverty alleviation but as
social integration. Van Kersbergen (1995) has argued that this 'corporatist' conception of the 'welfare' state, and in particular the ideology
and role of Christian Democratic agendas in Europe, has been largely
ignored by many welfare state theorists; 'Christian democracy and
its impact on social policy performance are conspicuously under-
studied and often misunderstood phenomena' (Van Kersbergen 1995:
26–7). Christian Democrats have pursued a specific political project
aimed at social integration, class compromise, and political mediation
between conflicting interest groups. The central goal for Christian
Democracy (particularly in Germany) has been class reconciliation
and class cooperation to restore the 'natural and organic harmony of
society' (Van Kersbergen and Bekker 2002). Similarly, in France the
primary purpose of the welfare state is often seen as to prevent social
exclusion (*les exclus*) rather than the prevention of poverty.

Third, the 'welfare state' is used to refer to the provision of welfare
by the state. Any provision of welfare by government, including
partial and residual provision, might be described in these terms.
This usage is particularly prevalent in the United States.

Esping-Andersen classifies three principal forms of welfare regime
(Esping-Andersen 1990). The 'liberal' model is characterized by reli-
ance on the free market and an emphasis on 'residual' welfare, where
welfare is confined to a safety net for people unable to manage by other
means. The 'corporatist' models are characterized by welfare pluralism, methods of working where the state acts in partnership with non-
governmental agencies, and an emphasis on the relationship between
welfare provision and economic development. The 'social democratic'
regime emphasises social rights, equality and 'decommodification' or
removal of provision from the market. Liberal regimes tend to offer

less support to the poor, while social-democratic regimes offer more. This kind of modelling has been criticized, however, because few regimes in practice hold consistently to any single pattern of service delivery, and most countries refer to varied principles both between services and within them (Mabbett and Bolderson 1999).

REFERENCES

Briggs, A. (2000) 'The Welfare State in a Historical Perspective', in C. Pierson and F.G. Castles (eds), *The Welfare State Reader*, Cambridge: Polity Press.

Esping-Andersen, G. (1990) *The Three Worlds of Welfare Capitalism*, Cambridge: Polity Press.

Mabbett, D., and Bolderson, H. (1999) 'Theories and Methods in Comparative Social Policy', in J. Clasen (ed.), *Comparative Social Policy: Concepts, Theories and Methods*, Oxford: Blackwell.

Titmuss, R.M. (1958) *Essays on the Welfare State*, London: Allen & Unwin.

Wedderburn, D. (1965) *The Aged in the Welfare State*, London: Bell.

Van Kersbergen, K. (1995) *Social Capitalism: A Study of Christian Democracy and the Welfare State*, New York: Routledge.

Van Kersbergen, K., and Becker, U. (2002) 'Comparative Politics and the Welfare State', in H. Keman (ed.), *Comparative Democratic Politics*, London: Sage.

Veit-Wilson, J. (2000) 'States of Welfare', *Social Policy and Administration* 34/1: 1–25.

WORKFARE

Workfare is a condition attached in the United States to the receipt of Temporary Aid to Needy Families, the federal social assistance scheme, requiring recipients of benefit to work for a period as a condition of benefit receipt (Ogborn 1988).

REFERENCES

Ogborn, K. (1988) 'Workfare in America: An Initial Guide to the Debate', *Social Security Review* 6, Canberra: Australian Government Publishing Service.

WORKHOUSE; WORKHOUSE TEST

The British POOR LAW workhouses were intended to be deterrent institutions, designed to enforce less eligibility by making the claiming of relief as unpleasant as possible. Under the 1834 Poor Law reform, the 'offer of the house' was to be an infallible method of filtering out the deserving from the undeserving. Only if truly destitute would applicants submit themselves to the workhouse regime as a condition of receiving relief. As the 1834 Poor Law Report argued:

> If the claimant does not comply with the terms on which relief is given to the destitute, he gets nothing; and if he does comply, the compliance proves the truth of the claim – namely, his destitution. (Checkland and Checkland 1974: 378)

Inmates of workhouses received institutional care as 'indoor relief'. The workhouse regime was designed to be harsh. For example, the able-bodied would be given arduous tasks to perform (e.g. stone-breaking); and for other inmates (such as the aged) monotonous work (e.g. oakum picking) would be prescribed. By the end of the nineteenth century, proposals for alternatives to the workhouse were increasingly being made, notably state old-age pensions for the aged and 'boarding out' for orphans.

REFERENCES

Checkland, S., and Checkland, O. (eds) (1974) *The Poor Law Report of 1834*, Harmondsworth: Penguin.

WORLD BANK POVERTY LINES

One of several definitions produced by the World Bank is a 'universal poverty line [which] is needed to permit cross-country comparison and aggregation'. Poverty is defined as 'the inability to attain a minimal standard of living' (World Bank 1990: 27, 26). Despite its acknowledgement of the difficulties in including, in any measure of poverty, the contribution to living standards of public goods and common-property resources, the World Bank settles for a standard which is 'consumption-based' and which comprises two elements:

> the expenditure necessary to buy a minimum standard of nutrition and other basic necessities and a further amount that varies from country to country, reflecting the cost of participating in the everyday life of society. (World Bank 1990: 26)

The first of these elements is stated to be 'relatively straightforward' because it could be calculated by 'looking at the prices of the foods that make up the diets of the poor'. However, the second element is 'far more subjective; in some countries indoor plumbing is a luxury, but in others it is a "necessity"' (World Bank 1990: 26–7). For operational purposes, the second element was set aside and the first assessed as PPP (purchasing power parity) – $370 per person per year for all the poorest developing countries. Those with incomes per capita of less than $370 were deemed 'poor', while those with less than $275 per year were 'extremely poor'.

The standard is simple to comprehend and apply. It does not depend on the arduous and continuous collection and compilation of data about types as well as amounts of resources, changing patterns of necessities and changing construction of standards of living. At the same time, it is not truly 'global' and is not assumed to be applicable to countries other than the poorest. The Bank has acknowledged the need for an international poverty line which is more than 'consumption-based'. No cost is estimated for the second 'participatory' element of the definition.

In the same report is found also a definition of poverty as a low GNP per capita, supplemented by other criteria such as consumption per capita, under-5 infant mortality, life expectancy and primary-school enrolment.

The World Bank has initiated a set of country-specific *Poverty Assessments* which bring together quantitative and qualitative data accessed through household surveys, poverty profiles, participatory studies, beneficiary assessments, public expenditure reviews, country-economic memoranda and sector reviews. Poverty assessments are important for identifying key poverty issues for each country, and bring together different definitions of poverty.

However, the best known and most widely used poverty line produced by the World Bank is 'a-dollar-a-day' adjusted measurement for extreme poverty.

REFERENCES

World Bank (1990) *World Development Report 1990: Poverty*, Washington DC: World Bank.
World Bank (1996) *Poverty Assessments: A Progress Review*, Washington DC: World Bank.

Definitions of poverty: twelve clusters of meaning

PAUL SPICKER

Words acquire meaning from their use, and words that are used extensively are liable to acquire not a single meaning, but a range of meanings. Wittgenstein analysed, as an example, the word 'game' (Wittgenstein 1958). The different meanings of 'game', he argued – for example, a form of play, a sporting event, fighting spirit and the target in hunting – arose not simply as distinct uses, but as part of an interrelated network of meanings, a 'family'. Each member of the family could bear a resemblance to any of the others, but there is no reason to suppose that because A is like B, and B like C, that A is like C. Terms which are linked by family resemblance do not, then, necessarily have any single element in common; there is no 'essential core' of meaning. Rather, there are clusters of meaning. Terms are used if they are judged to be appropriate and like other usages, not because they fit a set of agreed criteria. This tends, over time, to lead to new layers of meaning being added onto other uses.

Debates on poverty have been bedevilled by an artificial academic formalism, which has insisted that there must be an agreed core of meaning, that contradictory examples showed that certain uses were 'right' while others were 'wrong', and that disagreement was based not in a difference of interpretation or the focus of concern, but in a failure to understand the true nature of the problem. Poverty does not, however, have a single meaning. It has a series of meanings, linked through a series of resemblances.

TWELVE DEFINITIONS

In the social sciences poverty is commonly understood in at least twelve discrete senses. The senses overlap; many of the main protagonists in the debate take two or three positions simultaneously. They are discrete because they can be logically separated, so that circumstances which apply in one sense do not necessarily apply in others.

POVERTY AS A MATERIAL CONCEPT

The first group of definitions concern poverty as a material concept. People are poor because they do not have something they need, or because they lack the resources to get the things they need.

NEED   The first set of definitions understands poverty as a lack of material goods or services. People 'need' things like such as food, clothing, fuel or shelter. Vic George writes:

> poverty consists of a core of basic necessities as well as a list of other necessities that change over time and place. (George 1988: 208)

Baratz and Grigsby refer to poverty as

> a severe lack of physical and mental well-being, closely associated with inadequate economic resources and consumption. (Baratz and Grigsby 1971: 120)

The factors which go to make up well-being include 'welfare' values, including self-esteem, aspirations, and stigma and 'deference' values, including aspects of status and power. These views stem from apparently opposed positions: George is advocating an 'absolute' view of poverty, Baratz and Grigsby a 'relative' view. But these are interpretations of the social construction of need, not different definitions of poverty. Both agree that poverty is a lack of something, and they are largely agreed on what is lacking. The main disagreement is about the source and foundation of the needs.

A PATTERN OF DEPRIVATION   Not every need can be said to be equivalent to poverty, and there are several interpretations of what makes up poverty. Some interpretations emphasize certain kinds of need, like hunger and homelessness, as particularly important. Some emphasize the seriousness of the deprivations that are experienced: food and shelter are often seen as more important than entertainments and transport (though there may still be grounds to consider people who are deprived of entertainments and transport as 'poor'). The duration of circumstances is potentially important: a person can be homeless because of a natural disaster, but still be able to command sufficient resources to ensure that needs are met, and met rapidly. Poverty generally refers not just to deprivation, but to deprivation experienced over a period of time (Spicker 1993). Deleeck et al. write:

> Poverty is not restricted to one dimension, e.g. income, but it manifests itself in all domains of life, such as housing, education, health. (Deleeck et al. 1992: 3)

People may experience particular needs (like homelessness or cold) without this being sufficient to constitute 'poverty' – though needs are still clearly important as primary indicators of poverty (Whelan and Whelan 1995). Duration is important, because temporary deprivations (like those experienced by the victims of catastrophes) are not enough to constitute 'poverty'. Poverty is defined, then, on the existence of a pattern of deprivation, rather than by the deprivation itself. Following the argument about lack of basic security, it would be possible for a poor person to be subject to multiple deprivation even though that person was not experiencing a specific deprivation at a particular point of time. The definition of poverty would depend, rather, on cumulative experience over time. *Voices of the Poor*, a series of studies for the World Bank, refers to the idea of the 'web' of deprivation (Narayan et al. 2000) – an expressive metaphor, referring to a constellation of issues where people might suffer from shifting combinations of problems over time (Coffield and Sarsby 1980; Kolvin et al. 1990).

LIMITED RESOURCES Needs are closely linked to resources; every need is a need for something. Poverty can be taken to refer to circumstances in which people lack the income, wealth or resources to acquire or consume the things which they need. Booth wrote that

> The 'poor' are those whose means may be sufficient, but are barely sufficient, for decent independent life; the 'very poor' those whose means are insufficient for this according to the usual standard of life in this country. (Booth 1971: 55)

Ashton writes:

> Deprivation is surely about 'essential' needs that are unmet. This
> may be due to a lack of money resources – but it need not be (since
> adequate resources may be misspent). Poverty, on the other hand,
> must refer to a lack of the money necessary to meet those needs.
> (Ashton 1984: 97)

Limited resources, or more precisely a limited command over resources, does tend to imply low consumption, but the terms are not
equivalent; some feminists argue that women with limited resources
in the household may be poor if they do not have an income in their
own right (e.g. those cited in Millar 1996: 56–7). This would apply
even though their consumption and standard of living are high.

It is possible to hold to a definition of poverty as limited resources
while accepting the preceding definitions; poverty can be a form of
need caused by limited resources. The UN has defined poverty as:

> a condition characterized by severe deprivation of basic human needs,
> including food, safe drinking water, sanitation facilities, health,
> shelter, education and information. It depends not only on income but
> also on access to services. (UN 1995: 57)

If poverty is defined primarily in terms of need, a need which was
not caused by limited resources would be sufficient to make someone
poor; if poverty is only a result of limited resources, it would not.

POVERTY AS ECONOMIC CIRCUMSTANCES

If poverty is related to a lack of resources, it can also be understood in economic terms. One of the most widely used approaches
to the measurement of poverty is in terms of income, to the point
where some social scientists have started to think that poverty is
low income.

STANDARD OF LIVING   The idea of 'need' supposes that some items
or issues are particularly important or necessary. Although the idea of
a standard of living is intimately linked with need, it is in its nature
a general concept, referring not to specific forms of deprivation but
to the general experience of living with less than others. The International Labour Organization suggests that

> At the simplest level, individuals or families are considered poor
> when their level of living, measured in terms of income or consump-
> tion, is below a particular standard. (ILO 1995: 6)

Rowntree's *Poverty* did not define poverty precisely, but the chapter in
which he begins the discussion of the topic is called 'The Standard
of Life' (Rowntree 1902). Ringen argues that poverty is 'a standard
of consumption which is below what is generally considered to be a
decent minimum' (Ringen 1988: 354). The World Bank defines poverty
as 'the inability to attain a minimal standard of living' (World Bank
1990: 26). Their poverty line, probably the most widely used standard
of poverty internationally, is based on an arbitrary figure (one or two
dollars a day) and used to identify poverty by reference to the overall
standard of living which such an income must command.

The distinction between this and what people 'need' should be
clear. We might not 'need' tea, newspapers or concerts – three examples used by Rowntree in his definition of the conditions of primary
poverty – but people who cannot afford what they do not need might
still be considered poor. The standard which can be set might, like
the World Bank's level, be set rather below what people need; it
might be set above it, at a level appropriate to maintain decency, or
at a level relative to wages, or whatever else is thought appropriate.
In *The Poor and the Poorest*, Abel-Smith and Townsend argue that

> Whatever may be said about the adequacy of the National Assist-
> ance Board level of living as a just or publicly approved measure of
> 'poverty', it has at least the advantage of being in a sense the 'official'
> operational definition of the minimum level of living at any particu-
> lar time. (Abel-Smith and Townsend 1965)

INEQUALITY   People may be held to be poor because they are disadvantaged by comparison with others in society. O'Higgins and
Jenkins write:

> Virtually all definitions of the poverty threshold used in developed
> economies in the last half-century or so have been concerned with
> establishing the level of income necessary to allow access to the
> minimum standards of living considered acceptable in that society
> at that time. In consequence, there is an inescapable connection
> between poverty and inequality: certain degrees or dimensions of
> inequality ... will lead to people being below the minimum standards
> acceptable in that society. It is this 'economic distance' aspect of

inequality that is poverty. This does not mean that there will always be poverty when there is inequality: only if the inequality implies an economic distance beyond the critical level. (O'Higgins and Jenkins 1990)

This approach has important defects: the effect of defining poverty in these terms is that reduction in the resources of the better-off is equivalent to a reduction in poverty, and it becomes impossible to talk of a society in which the majority of people are poor. But that is not to say that the use is necessarily illegitimate, or that it is not widespread.

ECONOMIC POSITION   A 'class' of people is a group identified by virtue of their economic position in society. Class is an aspect of inequality, but the inequality it represents is a matter of the social structure, not of the inequality of resources or consumption; resources and consumption are at best an indicator of social position. Miller and Roby argue:

> Casting the issue of poverty in terms of stratification leads to regarding poverty as an issue of inequality. In this approach, we move away from efforts to measure poverty lines with pseudo-scientific accuracy. Instead, we look at the nature and size of the differences between the bottom 20 or 10 per cent and the rest of society. (Miller and Roby 1967)

The argument that poor people should be understood as a class is based in a range of different arguments. In Marxian analyses, classes are defined in terms of their relationship to the means of production, and in developed countries poor people are primarily those who are marginalized in relation to the economic system. Miliband argues:

> The basic fact is that the poor are an integral part of the working class – its poorest and most disadvantaged stratum.... Poverty is a class thing, closely linked to a general situation of class inequality. (Miliband 1974: 184–5)

In the Weberian sense, classes refer to people in distinct economic categories: poverty constitutes a class either when it establishes distinct categories of social relationship (like exclusion or dependency), or when the situation of poor people is identifiably distinguishable from others. Charles Booth explicitly identified poor people in terms of classes; the famous 'poverty line' was not based on a measurement of income, but on the lowest wage rates available for a man in full-time work, and so in the distinction between those who were working and those who were not (Booth 1902, vol. 1: 33; vol. 5: 266).

SOCIAL CIRCUMSTANCES

SOCIAL CLASS   The consideration of class shades into the social circumstances of poor people. The idea of 'social class' identifies economic position with socio-economic status, a concept based on the linkage of class with social and occupational roles. The concept of class is used both as a means of conceptualizing the position of the poor in structural terms, and as the basis for empirical research on the distributive implications of policy (for example, relating to education or health care) (Edgell 1993). The main description of poor people as a 'class' in recent years has been in terms of the 'underclass', and in that sense it has been roundly criticized by many observers who see the term as a condemnation of the poor. At the same time, many of those who have used the term academically have been leading writers in the study of poverty, including Myrdal, Titmuss and Townsend (cited in Macnicol 1987).

DEPENDENCY   Poor people are sometimes taken to be those who receive social benefits in consequence of their lack of means. The sociologist Georg Simmel argued that 'poverty', in sociological terms, referred not to all people on low incomes, but to those who were dependent:

> The poor person, sociologically speaking, is the individual who receives assistance because of the lack of means. (Simmel 1908: 140)

Engbersen has described poverty as

> the structural exclusion of citizens from all social participation, along with a situation of dependence in relation to the state. (cited Cantillon et al. 1998: 19)

This usage may seem initially unfamiliar, because it has featured very little in the social-science literature. There is, rather, a tendency simply to elide any distinction between poverty and the receipt of social assistance – an elision apparent, for example, in *The Poor and the Poorest*, or in Buhr and Leibfried's study of social assistance recipients (Abel-Smith and Townsend 1965; Buhr and Leibfried 1995).

By contrast, dependency is a major element in the discussion of poverty in the media and popular culture, particularly in discussions in the USA (see, e.g., Critchlow and Hawley 1989 or Schram 1995, for measured analyses). In this discourse, 'the poor ... are increasingly with us, breeding future generations of uneducated bastards dependent on welfare, mugging and drug dealing' (Steizer 1995). As such, the reference to poverty as dependency is still appropriate as a description of how the term is used, and so of its meaning.

LACK OF BASIC SECURITY   Although a lack of basic security has been defined in terms directly equivalent to need (Duffy 1995: 36), it may also be seen in terms of vulnerability to social risks. Charles Booth referred to poor people as 'living under a struggle to obtain the necessaries of life and make both ends meet; while the 'very poor' live in a state of chronic want' (Booth 1902, vol. 1: 33). Wresinski identified poverty with a 'lack of basic security', understood as

> the absence of one of more factors that enable individuals and families to assume basic responsibilities and to enjoy fundamental rights ... chronic poverty results when the lack of basic security simultaneously affects several aspects of people's lives, when it is prolonged, and when it seriously compromises people's chances of regaining their rights and of resuming their responsibilities in the foreseeable future. (Wresinski Report of the Economic and Social Council of France 1987, cited in Duffy 1995: 36)

By this argument, it would be possible for someone to be poor who is not in need; the distinction between this definition and the first is strong. Although lack of basic security and limited resources are linked, the link is not direct. There are cases, in particular in developing countries, where the effect of increasing resources is also to increase vulnerability.

> Diversified subsistence farmers may be poor but are not vulnerable. When they enter the market by selling specialised cash crops, or raising their earnings by incurring debts, or investing in risky ventures, their incomes rise, but they become vulnerable. There are trade-offs between poverty and vulnerability (or between security and income). (Streeten 1995)

LACK OF ENTITLEMENT   Wresinski, above, defines lack of security in terms of a lack of rights. Drèze and Sen argue that both deprivation and lack of resources reflect lack of entitlements, rather than the absence of essential items in themselves (Drèze and Sen, 1989) Homelessness results from lack of access to housing or land, not from lack of housing; famines, Drèze and Sen argue, result not from lack of food, but from people's inability to buy the food that exists. The lack of entitlement is fundamental to the condition of poverty; people who have the necessary entitlements are not poor.

EXCLUSION   The idea of exclusion has become the dominant paradigm in the discussion of poverty in the European Union, where the idea was seen as a means of avoiding some of the political controversy that had attended the concept of poverty itself.

> Social exclusion affects individuals, groups of people and geographical areas. Social exclusion can be seen, not just in levels of income, but also matters such as health, education, access to services, housing and debt. Phenomena which result from social exclusion therefore include:
> - the resurgence of homelessness
> - urban crises
> - ethnic tension
> - rising long term unemployment
> - persistent high levels of poverty. (Tiemann 1993)

The arguments about exclusion stress the multidimensional nature of the problems. The same case has, of course, been made in relation to poverty.

Poverty can be seen as a set of social relationships in which people are excluded from participation in the normal pattern of social life. The European Community has defined poverty as exclusion resulting from limited resources:

> The poor shall be taken as to mean persons, families and groups of persons whose resources (material, cultural and social) are so limited as to exclude them from the minimum acceptable way of life in the Member State in which they live. (European Community 1985)

This extends beyond the experience of deprivation to include problems which result from stigmatization and social rejection, though there is a tendency to use 'exclusion' more specifically in relation to material needs. Clerc sees this as the distinction between exclusion and marginality:

Exclusion results from penury, while marginalisation comes from distance – voluntary or not – from social norms. (Clerc 1989: 625)

POVERTY AS A MORAL JUDGEMENT

Poverty consists of serious deprivation, and people are held to be poor when their material circumstances are deemed to be morally unacceptable. Piachaud argues that poverty consists not just of hardship, but of UNACCEPTABLE HARDSHIP. The term 'poverty', he writes, 'carries with it an implication and moral imperative that something should be done about it. Its definition is a value judgment and should be clearly seen to be so' (Piachaud 1981). To describe people as poor contains the implication that something or other should be done about it. One of the reasons why the existence of poverty in Britain has been challenged is that in accepting that poverty exists people also accept the moral imperatives relating to poverty. It is also why so many critics on the political right discount poverty in moral terms; often the only effective way to argue against a moral position is to adopt a different moral position.

The moral elements of the definition of poverty make it difficult to establish agreement about the elements of the concept, though the consensual approach to poverty pioneered in the Breadline Britain survey identifies a method by which it can be done; the views expressed about minimum standards represent not simply a jumble of opinions, but an indicator of the norms that define what is and what is not acceptable in a society (Mack and Lansley 1985; Gordon et al. 2000).

CLUSTERS OF MEANING

There is some arbitrariness in any classification of this type. This presentation is concerned with the senses in which the term 'poverty' is used, rather than with the elements of definitions; it would be possible to introduce a wide range of subcategories. For example, 'need' includes measures of subsistence, 'basic needs' in the sense used by the UN, and socially constructed needs; exclusion covers social exclusion, economic exclusion, and marginality; class includes Marxist, Weberian and sociological definitions. Looking at different operational measurements of, for example, resources, income, needs or deprivation, it would be possible to present more 'definitions' if a 'definition' is taken to refer to every particular of the description of poverty.

The omission which may surprise many people in the field is that of absolute and relative poverty. Both are composites, but the core of the distinction between them is a debate on the origin of social need, not on the meaning of poverty itself. The classification also does not consider as distinct categories some synthetic definitions of poverty which have been proposed, such as Paugam's 'social disqualification', which covers class, exclusion, dependency and lack of basic security (Paugam 1993), or Townsend's concept of 'relative deprivation' (Townsend 1979), which incorporates elements of the standard of living, limited resources, exclusion, class and inequality. There is no problem, in principle, with a model that cuts across a range of definitions – though there may be some risk of arbitrariness in determining which factors to include and which not.

The definitional clusters focused on here are conceptually different meanings of poverty; need is not lack of resources, lack of resources is not dependency, and so on. These definitions are discrete, in the sense that they are logically separable and can refer to distinct circumstances. They also overlap; in certain cases, all these interpretations could be applied simultaneously to the same set of circumstances – whether that refers to a homeless person in Calcutta or a single parent claiming benefit in Britain. And the definitions are linked by family resemblance; need is closely related to standard of living, standard of living is closely related to resources, and so on. None of the concepts considered falls so far away from the others for a relationship to be impossible, though there is a gap between, for example, the view of poverty as inequality and of poverty as lack of basic security, or poverty as standard of living and poverty as dependency.

The figure shows the definitions in a ring; each is closely related to the adjacent definitions. The definitions have been classified, for heuristic purposes, as relating to economic position, social position and material circumstances, but the boundaries of each category are fuzzy, and permeable. There are also links across the circle: exclusion and lack of entitlements can both be identified with low resources, and multiple deprivation is sometimes linked with class position. The view that poverty is a moral term can be applied to any of the other concepts of poverty. Alcock argues:

FAMILY RESEMBLANCES BETWEEN DIFFERENT CONCEPTS OF POVERTY

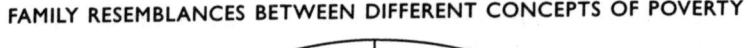

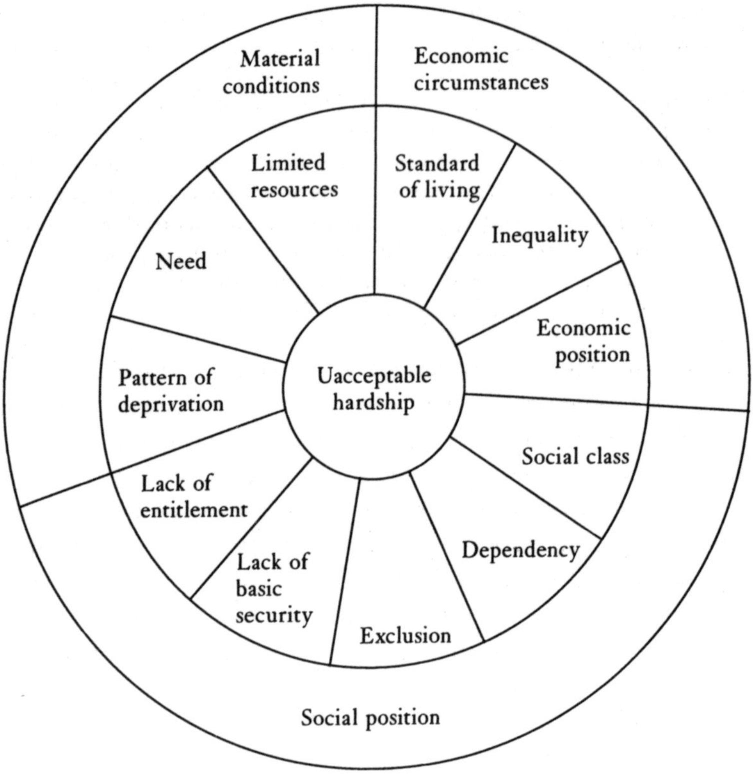

The diagram shows concentric circles with labels. Outer ring: Material conditions, Economic circumstances, Social position. Middle ring: Limited resources, Standard of living, Inequality, Economic position, Social class, Dependency, Exclusion, Lack of basic security, Lack of entitlement, Pattern of deprivation, Need. Centre: Uacceptable hardship.

in understanding poverty, the task is to understand how these different visions and perceptions overlap, how they interrelate and what the implications of different approaches and definitions are. (Alcock 1997: 4)

Poverty needs, then, to be seen as a composite concept, embracing the range of meanings.

UNDERSTANDING POVERTY

The process of understanding poverty has been characterized by two very different approaches. On one hand, many academics have sought to give authoritative definition of the concept. This approach is exemplified by 'An International Approach to the Measurement of Poverty', signed by Peter Townsend and seventy-nine of the leading academics in the field. This declaration states:

European social scientists are critical of the unwillingness at international level to introduce a cross-country and therefore more
scientific operational definition of poverty.... Poverty is primarily
an income- or resource-driven concept. It is more than having a
relatively low income.... If criteria independent of income can be
further developed and agreed, measures of the severity and extent of
the phenomenon of poverty can be properly grounded. That will lead
to better investigation of cause and more reliable choice of priorities
in policy.... All countries should introduce international measures
of these basic concepts and take immediate steps to improve the
accepted meanings, measurement and explanation of poverty, paving
the way for more effective policies. (Townsend et al. 1997)

This represents an influential school of thought. The central argument for a unified approach is that policies have to be judged by their
practical effects, and it should be possible to develop unified criteria
by which the effects of policy can be judged.

The main alternative is represented by the World Bank's participative study, *Voices of the Poor*. The Participatory Poverty Assessments
sponsored by the World Bank have approached poverty in a different
way altogether: examining, not a defined problem, but the terms in
which poor people themselves identify and understand the problem.
The reports bring together more than 20,000 subjects in twenty-three
countries. Irresistibly, with such a large number of participants, this
gives a diverse, complex set of understandings of the idea of poverty.
Poverty is treated as a multidimensional issue. The researchers focus
on ten interlocking dimensions of poverty: precarious livelihoods,
excluded locations, physical problems, gender relations, problems in
social relationships, lack of security, abuse by those in power, disem-
powering institutions, weak community organizations and limitations
on the capabilities of the poor. Statements from different people in
different cultures are classified and brought together in a complex
structure. The inclusion of diverse views of poverty at the same time
is, to some extent, a product of the method, but it represents a view
of poverty: poverty is not a single, easily identifiable condition, but
a fluctuating set of circumstances. It may be that the issues which
poor people point to are not the issues that other people think of as
being part of 'poverty', but the issues still matter to the people they
affect. This approach to understanding poverty is strongly linked,
then, with a commitment to working from the perspective of the

poor. It is, Lister comments, 'less a method than a philosophy' (Lister 2004: 47).

The alternative approaches have significantly different implications for policy. A unified understanding of poverty implies a definable set of problems and clear criteria. This should make it possible to demonstrate the relative effectiveness of alternative responses. A multidimensional approach, by contrast, implies a flexible response to a wide range of problems, judged by several criteria rather than by a single standard. Perhaps more significantly, the multidimensional understanding of poverty is linked to participative methods and responses to poverty. This is not just about concepts and definitions; it is also about empowering the poor.

REFERENCES

Abel-Smith, B., and Townsend, P. (1965) *The Poor and the Poorest*, London: Bell.

Alcock, P. (1997) *Understanding Poverty*, London: Macmillan.

Ashton, P. (1984) 'Poverty and Its Beholders', *New Society*, 18 October: 95–8.

Baratz, M.S., and Grigsby, W.G. (1971) 'Thoughts on Poverty and Its Elimination', *Journal of Social Policy* 1/2: 119–34.

Booth, C. (1971) *Charles Booth's London*, ed. A. Fried and R. Elman, Harmondsworth: Penguin.

Booth, C. (1902) *Life and Labour of the People in London*, first series: *Poverty*, vol. 1; second series: *Industry*, vol. 5, London: Macmillan.

Buhr, P., and Leibfried, S. (1995) 'What a Difference a Day Makes', in G. Room (ed.), *Beyond the Threshold*, Bristol: Policy Press.

Cantillon, B., Marx, I., and van den Bosch, K. (1998) 'Le défi de la pauvreté et de l'exclusion sociale', paper presented to the International Social Security Association conference on Targeting and Incentives, Jerusalem, January.

Clerc, D. (1989) 'La dynamique économique de l'exclusion et de l'insertion', *Revue de droit sanitaire et sociale* 25/4: 623–44.

Coffield, F., and Sarsby, J. (1980) *A Cycle of Deprivation?*, London: Heinemann.

Critchlow, E.T., and Hawley, E.W. (1989) *Poverty and Public Policy in Modern America*, Chicago: Dorsey.

Deleeck, H., van den Bosch, K., and de Lathouwer, L. (1992) *Poverty and the Adequacy of Social Security in the EC*, Aldershot: Avebury.

Drèze, J., and Sen, A. (1989) *Hunger and Public Action*, Oxford: Clarendon Press.

Duffy, K. (1995) *Social Exclusion and Human Dignity in Europe*, Council of Europe CDPS(95) 1 Rev.

Edgell, S. (1993) *Class*, London: Routledge.

European Community (1985) 'On Specific Community Action to Combat Poverty (Council Decision of 19.2.84)', 85/8/EEC, *Official Journal of the EEC* 2/24.

George, V. (1988) *Wealth, Poverty and Starvation*, Hemel Hempstead: Wheatsheaf.

Gordon, D., et al. (2000) *Poverty and Social Exclusion in Britain*, York: Joseph Rowntree Foundation, www.jrf.org.uk/bookshop/eBooks/185935128X.pdf.

ILO (1995) 'The Framework of ILO Action Against Poverty', in G. Rodgers (ed.), *The Poverty Agenda and the ILO*, Geneva: ILO International Institute for Labour Studies.

Kolvin, I., Miller, F., Scott, D., Gatzanis, S., and Fleeting, M. (1990) *Continuities of Deprivation?*, Aldershot: Avebury.

Lister, R. (2004) *Poverty*, Cambridge: Polity Press.

Mack, J., and Lansley, S. (1985) *Poor Britain*, London: Allen & Unwin.

MacNicol, J. (1987) 'In Pursuit of the Underclass', *Journal of Social Policy* 16/3: 300.

Miliband, R. (1974) 'Politics and Poverty', in D. Wedderburn (ed.), *Poverty, Inequality and Class Structure*, Cambridge: Cambridge University Press.

Millar, J. (1996) 'Women, Poverty and Social Security', in C. Hallett (ed.), *Women and Social Policy*, Hemel Hempstead: Harvester Wheatsheaf.

Miller, S., and Roby, P. (1967) 'Poverty: Changing Social Stratification', in P. Townsend (ed.), *The Concept of Poverty*, London: Heinemann.

Narayan, D., Chambers, R., Shah, M., and Petesch, P. (2000) *Voices of the Poor: Crying Out for Change*, New York: Oxford University Press for the World Bank.

O'Higgins, M., and Jenkins, S. (1990) 'Poverty in the EC: 1975, 1980, 1985', in R. Teekens and B. van Praag (eds), *Analysing Poverty in the European Community*, Eurostat News Special Edition 1–1990, Luxembourg: European Communities.

Paugam, S. (1993) *La disqualification sociale: essai sur la nouvelle pauvreté*, Paris: Presses Universitaires de France.

Piachaud, D. (1981) 'Peter Townsend and the Holy Grail', *New Society*, 10 September: 421.

Ringen, S. (1988) 'Direct and Indirect Measures of Poverty', *Journal of Social Policy* 17/3: 351–65.

Rowntree, S. (1902) *Poverty: A Study of Town Life*, London: Longman, Green.

Ryan, A. (1986) 'Poor Relatives', *New Society*, 18 April: 25.

Sen, A. (1983) 'Poor, Relatively Speaking', *Oxford Economic Papers* 35: 153–69.

Schram, S. (1995) 'Words of Welfare', Minneapolis: University of Minnesota Press.

Simmel, G. (1908) 'The Poor', *Social Problems* 1965/13: 118–39.

Spicker, P. (1993) *Poverty and Social Security*, London: Routledge.

Steizer, I. (1995) 'American Dream Lives On', *Sunday Times*, 15 October: 2/11.

Streeten, P. (1995) 'Comments on "The Framework of ILO Action Against Poverty"', in G. Rodgers (ed.), *The Poverty Agenda and the ILO*, Geneva: International Labour Organization.

Tiemann, S. (1993) *Opinion on Social Exclusion*, OJ 93/C 352/13.

Townsend, P. (1979) *Poverty in the United Kingdom*, Harmondsworth: Penguin.

Townsend, P. (1985) 'A Sociological Approach to the Measurement of Poverty – A Rejoinder to Professor Amartya Sen', *Oxford Economic Papers* 37: 659–68.

Townsend, P. (1993) *The International Analysis of Poverty*, Hemel Hempstead: Harvester Wheatsheaf.

Townsend, P., and others (1997) 'An International Approach to the Measurement and Explanation of Poverty: Statement by European Social Scientists', circulated on social-policy@mailbase.ac.uk.

United Nations (1995) *The Copenhagen Declaration and Programme of Action*, New York: United Nations.

Whelan, B., and Whelan, C (1995) 'In What Sense Is Poverty Multidimensional?', in G. Room (ed.), *Beyond the Threshold*, Bristol: Policy Press.

Wittgenstein, L. (1958) *The Blue and Brown Books*, Oxford: Blackwell.

World Bank (1990) *World Development Report 1990: Poverty*, Washington DC: World Bank.

Index